THIS HOUSE OF GRIEF

HELEN GARNER

THE STORY OF A MURDER TRIAL

THIS HOUSE OF GRIEF

TEXT PUBLISHING
MELBOURNE AUSTRALIA

ALSO BY HELEN GARNER

FICTION

Monkey Grip (1977)

Honour and Other People's Children (1980)

The Children's Bach (1984)

Postcards from Surfers (1985)

Cosmo Cosmolino (1992)

The Spare Room (2008)

NON-FICTION

The First Stone (1995)

True Stories (1996)

The Feel of Steel (2001)

Joe Cinque's Consolation (2004)

FILM SCRIPTS

The Last Days of Chez Nous (1992)

Two Friends (1992)

Helen Garner was born in Geelong in 1942. Her award-winning books include novels, stories, screenplays and works of non-fiction.

The Text Publishing Company
Swann House
22 William Street
Melbourne Victoria 3000
Australia
textpublishing.com.au

First published in Australia by The Text Publishing Company, 2014

Cover and page design by W. H. Chong, typeset by J&M Typesetters
Printed in Australia by Griffin Press, an Accredited ISO AS/NZS 14001:2004 Environmental Management System printer

National Library of Australia Cataloguing-in-Publication entry

Author: Garner, Helen, 1942- author.

Title: This house of grief / by Helen Garner.

ISBN: 9781922079206 (paperback)
ISBN: 9781921961434 (ebook)

Subjects: Farquharson, Robert, 1969-
            Gambino, Cindy.
            Filicide—Australia.
            Children—Crimes against—Australia.
            Custody of children—Australia.
            Mothers of murder victims—Australia.
            Murder—Australia.

Dewey Number: 364.15230994

This book is printed on paper certified against the Forest Stewardship Council® Standards. Griffin Press holds FSC chain-of-custody certification SGS-COC-005088. FSC promotes environmentally responsible, socially beneficial and economically viable management of the world's forests.

This project has been assisted by the Commonwealth Government through the Australia Council, its arts funding and advisory body.

Australian Government

Australia Council
for the Arts

MIX
Paper from
responsible sources
FSC
www.fsc.org   FSC® C009448

To the Victorian Supreme Court:
'this treasury of pain, this house of power and grief'
DEZSÖ KOSZTOLÁNYI: *KORNÉL ESTI*

'Are you going to the Farquharson hearing? I've got two reactions to this. He can't possibly have done it. But there's no other explanation.'

LAWYER WALKING PAST THE SUPREME COURT OF VICTORIA, 16 NOVEMBER 2007

...

'There is no explanation of the death of children that is acceptable.'

LEON WIESELTIER: *KADDISH*

...

'…life is lived on two levels of thought and act: one in our awareness and the other only inferable, from dreams, slips of the tongue, and inexplicable behaviour.'

JANET MALCOLM: *THE PURLOINED CLINIC*

Once there was a hard-working bloke who lived in a small Victorian country town with his wife and their three young sons. They battled along on his cleaner's wage, slowly building themselves a bigger house. One day, out of the blue, his wife told him that she was no longer in love with him. She did not want to go on with the marriage. She asked him to move out. The kids would live with her, she said, and he could see them whenever he liked. She urged him to take anything he wanted from the house. The only thing she asked for, and got, was the newer of their two cars.

The sad husband picked up his pillow and went to live with his widowed father, several streets away. Before long his wife was seen keeping company with the concreter they had hired to pour the slab for the new house. The tradesman was a born-again Christian with several kids and his own broken marriage. Soon the separated wife began to accompany him to his church. Next, the husband spotted the concreter driving around town in the car that he had slaved to buy.

Up to this point you could tell the story as a country-and-western song, a rueful tale of love betrayed, a little bit whiny, a little bit sweet.

But ten months later, just after dark on a September evening in 2005, while the discarded husband was driving his sons back to their mother from a Father's Day outing, his old white Commodore swerved off the highway, barely five minutes from home, and plunged into a dam. He freed himself from the car and swam to the bank. The car sank to the bottom, and all the children drowned.

…

I saw it on the TV news. Night. Low foliage. Water, misty and black. Blurred lights, a chopper. Men in hi-vis and helmets. Something very bad here. Something frightful.

Oh Lord, let this be an accident.

…

Anyone can see the place where the children died. You drive south-west out of Melbourne on the Princes Highway, the road that encircles the continent. You bypass Geelong, resist the call of the Surf Coast turn-off, and keep going inland in the direction of Colac, on the great volcanic plain that stretches across south-western Victoria.

In August 2006, after a magistrate at a Geelong hearing had committed Robert Farquharson to stand trial on three charges of murder, I headed out that way one Sunday morning, with an old friend to keep me company. Her husband had recently left her. Her hair was dyed a defiant red, but she had that racked look, hollow with sadness. We were women in our sixties. Each of us had found it in herself to endure—but also to inflict—the pain and humiliation of divorce.

It was a spring day. We passed Geelong and were soon flying along between paddocks yellow with capeweed, their fence lines marked by the occasional windbreak of dark cypresses. Across the huge sky sailed flat-bottomed clouds of brilliant white. My companion and I had spent years of our childhoods in this region. We were familiar with its melancholy beauty, the grand, smooth sweeps of its terrain. Rolling west along the two-lane highway, we opened the windows and let the air stream through.

Four or five kilometres short of Winchelsea we spotted ahead of us the long, leisurely rise of a railway overpass. Was this the place? Talk ceased. We cruised up the man-made hill. From the top we looked down and saw, ahead and to the right of the road, a body of tan water in a paddock—not the business-like square of a farm dam but oval-shaped, feminine, like an elongated tear drop, thinly fringed with small trees. Its southern bank lay parallel with the northern edge of the highway, twenty or thirty metres from the bitumen. I had imagined the trajectory of Farquharson's car as a simple drift off the left side of the highway; but to plunge into this body of water on the wrong side of the road, the car would have had to veer over the centre white line and cut across the east-bound lane with its oncoming traffic. As we sped down the Winchelsea side of the overpass, forcing ourselves to keep glancing to the right, we saw little white crosses, three of them, knee-deep in grass between the road and the fence. We flew past, as if we did not have the right to stop.

We had a vague idea that six thousand people lived in Winchelsea, but a sign at the entrance to the township gave its population as 1180, and by the time we had rolled down the dip to the bluestone bridge that spanned the Winchelsea River, then up the other side and past a row of shops and a primary school, the outer limits of the town were already in view. In a place this size, everyone would know your business.

A mile or so beyond the township, we turned down a side road and found a grassy spot where we could eat our sandwiches. We felt awkward, almost guilty. Why had we come? We spoke in low voices, avoiding each other's eye, staring out over the sunny paddocks.

Do you think the story he told the police could be true—that he had a coughing fit and blacked out at the wheel? There is such a thing. It's called cough syncope. The ex-wife swore at the committal hearing that he loved his boys. So? Since when has loving someone meant you would never want to kill them? She said it was a tragic accident—that he wouldn't have hurt a hair on their heads. His whole family is backing him. In court he had a sister on either side and an ironed hanky in his hand. Even the ex-wife's family said they didn't blame him. But wasn't there weird police evidence? The tracks his car had left? And didn't he bolt? Yes. He left the kids in the sinking car, and hitched a ride to his ex-wife's place. He looked massive in the photos—is he a big bloke? No, he was small and stumpy. With puffy eyes. Did you see him close up at the committal? Yes, he held the door open for me. Did he smile at you? He tried to. Maybe he's a psychopath—isn't that how they get to you? By being charming? He didn't look charming. He looked terrible. Wretched. What—you felt sorry for him? Well…I don't know about sorry. I don't know what I was expecting, but he was ordinary. A man.

The cemetery, on the outskirts of Winchelsea, was a couple

of acres of wide, sloping ground, open to the sky. Nobody else was around. We wandered up and down the rows. No Farquharsons. Perhaps the family came from another town? But as we plodded up the path to the car, I glanced past a clump of shrubbery and saw a tall headstone of polished granite that bore a long surname and three medallion-shaped photos. We approached with reluctant steps.

Some AFL fan had poked into the dirt beside the grave an Essendon pinwheel on a wand. Its curly plastic blades whizzed merrily. In the upper corners of the headstone were etched the Essendon Football Club insignia and a golden Bob the Builder. The little boys faced the world with frank good cheer, their fair hair neatly clipped, their eyes bright. Jai, Tyler, Bailey. *Much loved and cherished children of Robert and Cindy... In God's hands till we meet again.* I studied it with a sort of dread. Often, in the seven years to come, I would regret that I had not simply blessed them that day and walked away. In the mown grass sprouted hundreds of tiny pink flowers. We picked handfuls and laid them on the grave, but the breeze kept blowing them away. Every twig, every pebble we tried to weight them with was too light to resist the steady rushing of the spring wind.

...

A year passed between the committal hearing and the trial. When Farquharson's name came up in conversation, people shuddered. Tears would spring to women's eyes. Everyone had a view. The coughing fit story provoked incredulity and scorn. The general feeling was that a man like Farquharson could not tolerate the loss of control he experienced when his wife ended the marriage. Again and again people came up with this explanation. Yes, that must have been it—he couldn't stand to lose control of his family. Either that, or he was evil. Pure evil. I don't get these guys, said a feminist lawyer. Okay, so the wife dumps them. Men don't have biological clocks. Why can't they just find a new girlfriend and have more kids? Why do they have to kill everyone? Whether he did it on purpose or not, said an older woman, a Christian, how is he going to atone? Countless men declared in anger and distress that it couldn't possibly have been an accident; that a loving father would never leave the car and swim away. He would fight to save his kids, and, if he failed, he would go to the bottom with them. Rare were the ones who, after making such a declaration, paused and added in a lower voice, 'At least, that's what I hope I'd do.'

When I said I wanted to write about the trial, people looked at me in silence, with an expression I could not read.

…

On 20 August 2007, two years after his car went into the dam, Robert Farquharson's trial opened in the Supreme Court of Victoria. As a freelance journalist and curious citizen, I had spent many days, solitary and absorbed, in the courtrooms of that nineteenth-century pile in central Melbourne, with its dome and its paved inner yards and its handsome facade along William and Lonsdale Streets. I knew my way around it and how to conduct myself inside its formal spaces, but I could never approach its street entrance without a surge of adrenalin and a secret feeling of awe.

This time I had brought with me a close friend's daughter, a pale, quiet sixteen-year-old with white-blonde hair and braces on her teeth, dressed in jeans and a sky-blue hoodie. Her name was Louise. She was in her gap year. I would come to be grateful for her company, and for her precocious intelligence. We squeezed into the press seats of Court Three with a gang of cheerful journalists. From the tone of their gossip, Farquharson was already hung, drawn and quartered.

The court was beautiful. It had a soaring ceiling, pale plaster walls, and fittings of dark, ponderous timber; but, like all the court-rooms in that grand old building, it was cramped, and awkward to move around in. The dock ran along the rear wall, and in it, behind a red velvet rope, sat Robert Farquharson in a glaring white shirt with a stiff collar and tie. He had entered a free man, but now his bail had ended and he was in custody. Though the room was packed with his supporters, he looked scared, and small, and terribly lonely.

Jeremy Rapke QC, Acting Chief Crown Prosecutor and soon to be appointed Director of Public Prosecutions, had appeared for the Crown at Farquharson's committal hearing. He was a lean, contained-looking man, with a clipped grey beard and a mouth that cut across his face on a severe slant, like that of someone who spent his days listening to bullshit.

'Wow,' hissed Louise. 'He looks like a falcon.'

Lawyers I knew said he was formidable in trials, and at the committal he had been enthralling to watch: he did not seem to exert himself, and he spoke sparingly, in a low, courteous voice, as if his words were only the upper layer of some more crucial process that was going on inside his head. But his final submission that day, delivered in the same conversational tone, had flowed out of him in a scorching stream, elegant and devastating. Now, beside his shiny-faced, brown-haired young junior, Amanda Forrester, who had clattered into court in ankle-strap stilettos, Rapke sat with curved spine low in his swivel chair, his wig tilted forward, his cheek resting on the palm of one narrow, dry-looking hand.

The narrow, glass-paned timber doors at the back burst open and Peter Morrissey SC came barging in, with his black gown hanging off one shoulder and his wig pushed back from a shiny forehead. He was big, fair and bluff, Irish-style, with the bulk and the presence of a footballer: as he strode towards the defence end of the bar table, dwarfing his junior, Con Mylonas, he whistled through exaggeratedly pursed lips the provocative anthem 'Good Old Collingwood Forever'. He veered close to the dock and called out in a hearty, man-to-man voice, 'G'day, Rob!' If Farquharson replied, I did not hear him. Morrissey, people said, was just back from the International Criminal Court in The Hague, where he had won his case. His stocks were high. He looked a spontaneous, likeable man. Farquharson's family seemed to share this view. Out in the lobby they would crowd around his massive, robed figure, looking up at him with trusting smiles that filled me with anxiety.

Justice Philip Cummins entered, a silver-haired man in his sixties with an open, good-humoured face. He wore a scarlet robe, but no wig. A tiny diamond stud flashed a point of light from the lobe of his left ear. Cummins was well known in the city. I did not need the journalists to tell me that his nickname was Fabulous Phil. But he was reassuring to look at, not lofty or threatening; behind his high bench he would lean forward on his elbows and address the court with genial warmth.

A jury was empanelled, ten women and five men, the requisite dozen plus three spares: this trial would not be short. By the next morning one of the women had already been excused. The jurors filed into the box and sat with hands folded, looking about nervously. Their shoulders were bowed, as if their new duties were pressing them into their chairs. From now until the end of the trial, every time they entered the court, Farquharson would spring to his feet in the dock and remain standing until they were seated—a protocol that seemed to say *my fate is in your hands*.

...

On the evening of Sunday 4 September 2005, Father's Day, two young Winchelsea men, Shane Atkinson and Tony McClelland, left their dogs to be minded overnight by a lady they knew, and set out in Atkinson's Commodore for a barbecue in Geelong, to celebrate the birth of a baby that Atkinson's fiancée had, that day, brought home from hospital.

As Atkinson, the Crown's first witness, negotiated the narrow aisle past the family seats, two women who, from the shape of their eye sockets, could only be Farquharson's sisters raked him with cold stares. Dark-haired, tall and thin, he was dressed from head to toe in black. He stood in the box, facing the Crown's Ms Forrester with the stooped, appeasing posture of a kid expecting to be told off. Speech was labour for him. He drawled and fumbled, writhed and bowed his head. Whenever a coarse word escaped him he would drop his face and grin with an embarrassed, goofy sweetness.

It was about 7.30, he said, and already dark, when he and his mate Tony approached the railway overpass, four or five kilometres east of Winchelsea. They saw several cars ahead of them suddenly swerve and keep going, as if dodging something. Then a bloke stepped out into their headlights, vigorously waving his arms. Shane's nerves were raw: his brother had taken his own life only a few months earlier. He slammed on the brakes and jumped out. The man ran towards him.

'I said to him, "What the fuck are you doing, standing on the side of the road? Are you trying to kill yourself, mate?" We couldn't get no sense out of him. He was swearing, like, "Oh no, fuck, what have I done? What's happened?"'

The man jabbered that he had put his car into the dam—that he had killed his kids, that he had done a wheel bearing, or had a coughing fit. He had come to and found himself in water up to his chest. All he wanted, he said over and over, was to be taken back to his missus' house, so he could tell her he'd killed his kids.

The bloke was short and chunky, panting and wringing wet, covered in slime and mud. What was this crazy story? Was he all there? Shane thought he might have Down syndrome or something: they got some weird cunts out that way. Tony was a relative newcomer to the township. Until this moment he had barely registered that there was a dam at the foot of the overpass. Shane was a Winch boy, and had driven past the dam countless times, yet even he had no idea it was deep enough for a car to vanish into it without leaving so much as a bubble. He stood up in the doorframe of his Commodore and strained for a better view of the water. He and Tony walked off the road as far as the fence. The night was very dark, but dry and clear. Every time a truck roared down the overpass, they followed the sweep of its headlights to scan the dam's surface. The water looked like glass. Surely nothing had happened here.

Shane had credit on his mobile. He tried to give it to the man so he could ring the ambulance, the police. The man refused. Again and again he begged them to take him to Cindy's.

'I'm not going anywhere,' said Shane, 'if you've just killed your kids! We're two skinny little cunts—we can get in the water and try to swim down!'

But the man kept saying, 'probably a hundred times, "No, don't go down there. It's too late. They're already gone. I'll just have to go back and tell Cindy."'

Farquharson, who had wept helplessly right through the terrible accusations of the prosecutor's opening address—'a shockingly wicked and callous act'—listened to all this in the dock with his head tilted and his small eyes narrowed in a sceptical expression.

'And,' said Ms Forrester gently, 'did you take him back to Cindy?'

In the front row of the public seats, accompanied by their quiet husbands, Farquharson's sisters sat still, their mouths stiffly downturned.

Shane Atkinson hung his head. 'Yes,' he said, in a low, miserable voice. 'I done the stupidest thing of my whole life, and I did.'

Shane made the sodden man sit beside him in the front, with Tony in the back 'so he could punch him in the head if he went nuts'. He spun the car round and headed back to Winchelsea. Just as they reached the outskirts of the town, Shane flicked on the interior light and took a proper look at their passenger. The penny dropped. It was Robbie Farquharson. Since Shane was a little fellow, he had seen Robbie mowing people's grass and driving the same sort of Commodore as Shane had now, except that Shane's had mag wheels. And suddenly he twigged which Cindy he was raving about, this wife he was so keen to see—Cindy Farquharson, his ex, who everyone in Winch knew was on with another bloke, Stephen Moules.

They pulled into Cindy's drive, all three men panicking and yelling. Farquharson and Shane ran to the back doorstep and shouted for Cindy. One of Stephen Moules' kids came to the screen door. Cindy followed him. Where was Rob's car? Where were the kids?

Farquharson gave it to her straight. There'd been an accident. He'd killed the kids. Drowned them. He'd tried to get them out, but he couldn't. Cindy started to scream. She called him 'a fucking cunt'. She went to hit him. Shane stepped between her and Farquharson and tried to take her in his arms. Then he leapt back into his car and drove so fast to the police station that when he pulled up outside he did a doughnut.

The station was locked. He ran to the sergeant's house next door. Nobody home.

By now every man and his dog was out on the street. Somebody dialled 000 and Shane told the ambulance where the car had gone into the water. A bloke called Speedy from the State Emergency Service rushed off to get his truck. Shane got into his car with Tony and a couple of strangers who had jumped in. He drove back to Cindy's but her car was gone, and so was she, with Farquharson and the kid from the kitchen door. Shane roared out on to the highway.

He pulled up near the overpass. Farquharson was standing against the fence, nodding, lurching, wheezing. He was 'smoking cigarette after cigarette', and begged the new arrivals for another.

Tony McClelland threw a whole packet at him, climbed through the fence and ran stumbling across the dark paddock. Shane hung back. 'I didn't wanna go near the dam,' he told the court, hanging his head as if ashamed of his dread.

Cindy had got through to 000 on her mobile and was rushing back and forth on the bank in the dark, sobbing and shrieking directions to the operator, but she kept calling it the Calder Highway instead of the Princes. She must have rung Stephen Moules earlier. He was already there, stripping off to wade into the dam. The water was black and terribly cold. Moules took a few steps in from the edge and the bottom dropped away under his feet. Tony had to grab his arm to save him. This was the moment they all realised how deep the dam was.

But not until the police gave their evidence in court would its true dimensions become clear. It was not an ordinary farm dam with sloping sides. It was the pit left behind when the road-makers dug out the soil to build the overpass, and it went straight down for seven metres.

...

Tony McClelland stalked past the Farquharson family to the witness stand with a self-possession that looked like anger. He too had dressed in black. He was thin and tousled, with sharp cheekbones and high eyes, a face of striking beauty. He had no memory of Shane offering his mobile to Farquharson, but he recalled that, on the wild drive back to Winch, Farquharson had mumbled, 'My wife will kill me.' When Farquharson announced to Cindy that the boys were in the water, she cried, 'Why didn't you stay there?' Farquharson replied, 'They've already died.'

At this, Farquharson lurched forward in the dock and covered his whole face with his handkerchief.

At the dam it was McClelland who enfolded the shrieking Cindy in a bear hug and grabbed the phone from her hand. He gave the 000 operator coherent directions. It seemed only moments then until the emergency services arrived. Shane moved his car to make way for the ambulance. He and Tony gave the police their details.

Then they sat in the car for a little while, Tony McClelland, twenty-three, apprentice carpenter, and Shane Atkinson, twenty-two, new father, currently unemployed. They had a smoke, and tried to talk. They told each other that they should have looked for the car. They were distraught because the kids had died, and because they were the ones who had taken Farquharson away.

...

A big plasma screen had been set up facing the jury, in the narrow space between the press seats and the pews where the families were sitting. Displayed on this Smart Board were digital photographs of the road, the paddock and the dam. Mr Morrissey, cross-examining, asked Atkinson and McClelland to make marks on the images with a special pen, to show the relative positions of various vehicles on that night of the crash. Farquharson's family continued to gaze faithfully at Mr Morrissey, but the purpose of his complex manoeuvre was a mystery to me.

The young men too looked baffled, but strove to cooperate. To sketch cars and trucks and ambulances with their little markers, they had to leave the witness stand, edge along the aisle, and reach up past the journalists' heads to the screen. We could see the gel that messed up their hair, the fineness of their skin, the tremors of their facial muscles, the details of McClelland's piercings. On the stand, inarticulate and awkward, they could have been misread as off-hand. Up close, they radiated a troubled solemnity, a jaw-grinding guilt and sorrow. When Atkinson was finally excused, when he trudged out of the court followed by the glares of Farquharson's sisters, Louise, the gap-year girl, said to me in a shaky whisper, 'You feel you should at least be able to give him a hug.'

Next morning I opened the *Herald Sun* and saw a photo of the young men crossing the road outside the Supreme Court. Tony leads the way, scowling, gripping a bottle of water in one hand, his knees flexed, his torso bending forward as if he is about to break into a run. Behind him strides the taller Shane, with a wool beanie pulled down to his brow, shoulders back, arms along his sides, his face broad and sombre. They are thin, dark-clad figures with haunted eyes: two souls fleeing before the blast.

...

Farquharson may not have plunged into the water to search for his boys, but other men did.

One of the Winchelsea SES members who headed for the dam as soon as Shane Atkinson raised the alarm had rushed out the door barefoot in track pants and a singlet. His level-headed wife gathered up an armload of dry clothes and towels, and drove out the highway after him. She told the court that she pulled up beside the dam and saw Farquharson standing on his own, soaking wet, with a blanket round him. 'Robbie!' she said. 'It's not you?' She threw her arms around him and he began to sob. Then he stepped back and looked her in the eye. He said, 'I've had this flu. I had a coughing fit and blacked out. Next thing I knew, the car was filling up with water.' He told her he had tried and failed to get the kids out. Then he said, 'How can I live with this? It should have been me.'

Two volunteer fire-fighters from the Country Fire Authority, one of them a high-school student of sixteen, took the stand. They had arrived at the dam towards 8 p.m. and heard a woman sobbing somewhere in the dark, crying out that she would not be able to bury her children. They stumbled round with their torches, following tyre marks in the grass, looking for the spot where the car had gone in. Was it here, where a piece of a tree had been snapped off and broken glass was scattered on the ground? By then a police chopper was hovering over the dam, shining a spotlight on to its surface. There was no sign of the car. Someone would have to get into the water.

Tethered by ropes to other firemen, the two CFA volunteers and the owner of the property waded into the dam. Not far from the edge, the bottom drastically dropped away. They began to swim. The water was shockingly cold. They put their heads under and were blinded by murk. They could not feel the bottom with their feet. Had the car floated before it sank? Had it drifted sideways? Without equipment, shallow diving was the best they could do. They floundered about in the water for fifteen minutes, gasping and shivering, until the paramedics shouted at them to get out. Of the car they found no trace.

When the paramedics had pulled up on the shoulder of the road, they found Farquharson standing near the fence, wet through, with a blanket round his shoulders. His skin was cold and he was shivering. His pulse rate was up, his blood pressure normal. Neither of his lungs was wheezing or crackling. They asked him to cough. He brought up no phlegm. Breathalysed, he blew zero. He had no history of blackouts, he said, but had had a dry cough for the past few days.

He told the paramedics that his oldest son had opened the door, causing the car to fill up with water and sink; that he himself had got out, flagged down a vehicle, and gone to Winch to tell the police and his ex-wife what had happened.

On the drive to Geelong Hospital the paramedics considered that their patient was more stunned than in shock. They heard him give vent to several more unproductive coughs. As the ambulance sped along the dark road, Farquharson, from his stretcher in the back, asked one of the paramedics, 'Did I do the right thing? How am I going to live with myself after all this has happened?' Perhaps these questions were merely philosophical. Perhaps Farquharson was murmuring to himself. Either way, the paramedic in the witness box, badged and epauletted in his dark blue uniform, did not say whether he had replied or tried to offer comfort. He told the court only that Farquharson then fell silent, and lay in the ambulance shaking his head.

...

Just across Lonsdale Street from the Supreme Court, outside the glass façade of the County Court, stands a shiny metal caravan that houses an espresso machine and a pair of gun baristas. Everyone from the world of the law seems to patronise it: the loftiest silk in wig and rosette; Homicide detectives with their sinister black folders; road police in bomber jackets; constables in caps and tunics; irritable tipstaffs smoking over the turf guide; all the way down to the lowly drifters from the Magistrates' Court in William Street with spider webs tattooed on their necks and hinges in their elbow crooks. Even the occasional judge has been seen to throw back a short black at that democratic counter.

On the Monday morning of the trial's second week, a couple in the coffee queue struck up a conversation with the gap-year student and me. Hadn't they seen us in court, with our notebooks? They introduced themselves: Bob and Bev Gambino, the parents of Cindy, Farquharson's former wife—the drowned boys' grandparents. We looked at them in awe, but they chatted on in their unguarded country way, drinking the good coffee, watching the lawyers come and go. Bob was short and round-faced and solid, Bev slender with fine-rimmed glasses and straight, greying hair. They told us they lived near Winchelsea, in the town of Birregurra. Since Bob was a CFA volunteer and one of their three sons a full-time firey, the firefighters' union had offered them free use of a flat above the Fire Services Museum for the duration of the trial. Everything about the city seemed to please them: the hospitals, the trams, the fresh food you could buy at the Victoria Market. Bob rambled on unprompted, in his drawling voice.

'The court people kept asking us "Which side are *you* on?" First

I didn't know what they meant. Then I realised they didn't want to make us sit with Rob's family if we didn't want to. So I said to the bloke, "Listen, mate, there aren't two sides."

'Rob and I used to work together on the shire,' he went on, jerking his head in the direction of the Supreme Court. 'He was a lazy little bugger. If he didn't want to do something, well, he didn't. Not motivated. He was—you know—a sook.'

These unflattering estimations he delivered with an indulgent grin, as if teasing someone he was fond of or had at least learnt to put up with. His wife made little contribution, apart from her friendly attention.

It was nearly 10 a.m. On the other side of the road I spotted Farquharson's sisters and their husbands heading for the Supreme Court entrance in a phalanx: ordinary, reputable working people, self-effacing in their comportment. The woman I picked as the elder sister, identified by the Gambinos as Carmen Ross, had a soft, intelligent face and a serious demeanour. Kerri Huntington, the younger, more flamboyant one, wore her hair in a big bleached perm that flowed back over her shoulders. On my fridge door at home I had a newspaper photo of Farquharson leaving the court with the curly-headed blonde on the summer day he got bail after his arrest. What made me clip the photo and keep it was the way she is hauling Farquharson across the pavement. He trots beside her. She has an impatient, double-fisted hold on his left wrist that yanks his hand like a toddler's across the front of her hips. As the eldest of six children I recognised that hold: it was a bossy big-sister grip. Now I watched her charge up the steps into the court, her hair bright as a banner in the grey street.

'Today,' said Bob, draining his paper cup and chucking it into the bin, 'it'll be the cops.'

. . .

Victoria Police contains a highly respected outfit called the Major Collision Investigation Unit. Its officers drive out at all hours from their bases in Brunswick and Glen Waverley to attend traffic accidents in which people have been killed or suffered life-threatening injuries. These are the cops we see on the TV news, standing pensively on the freeway edge around a pile of gashed and smoking metal.

Sergeant Geoffrey Exton was the MCIU officer who had first taken command of the chaos on the night of the crash. He was a tough-looking fellow in his late fifties, with a thick moustache and a cannon ball of a skull that bristled with short grey hair. 'Another perfect buzz cut,' whispered Louise. 'They must have a barber in there 24/7.' He took the oath in a hoarse, smoker's voice, holding the Bible away from him with a rigid arm.

When Exton got to the dam towards 10 p.m., and found that a Search and Rescue Squad diver was already preparing to enter the water and that the coroner was on his way, he and Senior Constable Jason Kok set off to do a walk-through of the scene.

Stooping and crouching to shine their torch beams along the ground, the two police officers worked their way down the right-hand verge of the sealed carriageway on the Winchelsea side of the overpass. Part way down the slope they found marks in the roadside gravel that they thought must have been made by the tyres of a vehicle leaving the bitumen in the direction of the dam, at an angle of about thirty degrees. Then, in the grass beside the road, they spotted some rolling tyre prints that seemed the natural extension of the marks in the gravel, angled in a general westerly direction and curving slightly to the right. With no sign of braking or skidding, the rolling prints continued across the longer grass, through a broken post-and-wire farm fence, and all the way to the dam's edge, where debris from a side-mirror housing suggested that the vehicle had clipped a small tree on the bank before it plunged into the water. From the bitumen edge to the bank of the dam the car appeared to have travelled about forty-four metres.

From there, the men turned and retraced their steps, following in reverse the same long, linear indentations in the grass back to the point where they had first seen the tyre marks in the roadside gravel.

These marks Sergeant Exton outlined with stripes of yellow paint from a spray can.

...

On the face of it, this was a brutally simple account of the car's trajectory. Now it would be Mr Morrissey's job to complicate it. In fact, to defend Farquharson against the Crown's claim that, in order to get into the dam on that arc, he must have made 'three steering inputs' and thus could not possibly have been unconscious at the wheel, Morrissey would have to blast the police evidence full of holes. He would have to make the jury doubt the accuracy and even the integrity of the Major Collision investigation. He set about his onerous task with a will, aided by certain errors and miscommunications the police had made on the night and later.

Of these there were quite a few.

For example, Sergeant Exton's yellow paint marks in the aggregate turned out, even before the sun rose on the Monday morning and the investigation continued, to be not quite parallel with each other. Nor were they correctly aligned with the rolling tyre prints in the grass; and the reconstruction team from Major Collision, when they arrived at the dam, had apparently based their entire mapping of the crash on one of these imperfectly angled paint marks. Furthermore, twenty-nine photos that Sergeant Bradford Peters, one of the police investigators, took at the dam on the Monday and Tuesday—some from a helicopter, some at ground level—had been brought back to Major Collision HQ on a memory stick, downloaded into a job file, and forgotten for two years. It was only now, a fortnight into the trial, that the Crown, let alone the defence, had been made aware of their existence.

Morrissey brought these errors to light with glee. For the next few days, he challenged police witnesses to defend their methods and to pronounce upon a bewildering array of photographs, both terrestrial and aerial. On the Smart Board he put up images sprinkled with dots and lines and arrows that purported to show the relative whereabouts of cars and emergency vehicles, of scuff marks on gravel and pale marks in lush grass. Police were confronted with booklets of photos, with their own diagrams and scale plans, with 3D mock-ups of the scene. They were tackled on road cambers, on steering-wheel turns, on terrain, on tussocks. And always, always, Morrissey dragged their attention back to the burden of his song: the mistakenly angled yellow paint marks that Exton had sprayed that night on the verge of the road.

Morrissey's labour was tremendous. Soon, though, I began to suspect that it was also counter-productive. No matter how earnestly I strove to grasp it, his cross-examination felt cloudy and insubstantial. The material itself was intractable. It was fiddly, maniacally detailed, and catastrophically lacking in narrative. It made me—and, by the looks of them, also the jury—feel panicky and stupid. By the end of the week Justice Cummins would refer, with a desperate sympathy, to 'three days talking about tufts of grass'. Worst of all, Morrissey's style of cross-examination on this technical evidence was jerky and parenthetical. He was forever rephrasing things, backing and filling, apologising, changing tack. He could not make the torrent of measurements run clear. With the best will in the world, I could not follow it or see what he was trying to do. To add to his troubles, he had developed a dry, barking cough that rivalled the one he argued had sent his client's car into the dam.

As the hours and days ground on, the air in the court became a jelly of confusion and boredom. The judge took off his spectacles and violently rubbed his eyes. Journalists sucked lollies to stay awake. Jurors' mouths went square with the effort to control their gaping yawns. Their heads swayed, or dropped forward on to their chests. But Morrissey, oblivious to the fact that he had lost his audience, fought doggedly on, his forehead gleaming, his gown trailing floorwards off his shoulders. Once, when he suggested to a witness that some vehicle other than Farquharson's might have left the disputed tyre track in the roadside gravel, when he seemed about to return for the hundredth time to the torture of what he called 'the Exton marks', I saw Rapke's junior, Amanda Forrester, close her eyes, twist her long legs round each other, and beat, beat, beat the knuckles of her fist against her forehead.

Was it some sort of barrister's technique, to fill the courtroom with a soporific gas? One lunchtime I consulted an old friend of mine, long retired from the bar. His wife had died, and he spent his lonely days at home in a bayside suburb: I imagined him standing at his lounge room window with a pair of binoculars, critically inspecting passing vessels. His sole concession to the modern world was a mobile phone. He loved to be asked for advice.

'Farquharson's counsel,' I texted, 'is killing us with boredom.'

He replied at once: 'A time-honoured approach, when no feather to fly with. Still, one has heard it said that the fear of boring oneself or one's listeners is a great enemy of truth.'

...

The only thing that woke the jury from its stupor was the Homeric clash between Morrissey and Sergeant Exton. Under his brow Exton fixed the barrister with a level, burning gaze. The two men lowered their big heads and went at each other like heavyweights. Exton seemed galvanised by a rage that only his elaborate sarcasm could control. He spoke with a droll punctilio, decorating every sentence with the word 'Sir'. When a pretty woman in a tightly belted white coat tiptoed out of the court, he paused mid-sentence to appreciate her all the way to the door. His demeanour was so powerfully wrought and outrageously complex, so glowering with dark energy, that I kept wanting to break into anxious laughter. Louise, the teenager, contemplated him with alarm. She passed me a note: 'Imagine having *him* for a father.' I did not reply; but I thought, 'A bloke like that would take a bullet for his daughter.'

When Morrissey took it right up to him about the faults in the yellow paint marks, suggesting sloppiness, wilful interference, or even conspiracy—when the lawyer seemed for a few moments to have the old cop on the ropes—Exton's face blackened with fury. He was prepared to acknowledge that he had sprayed the yellow paint marks on the wrong angle, but maintained, with a tenacity Morrissey could not make a dent in, that the mistakes were irrelevant; that the purpose of the paint was not to indicate angles but simply to show the reconstructionists the spot where it was believed the vehicle had left the bitumen surface. Challenged about the mysterious losing and finding of Major Collision's twenty-nine extra photos of the scene, Exton went out on a limb and complimented his fellow investigator on the quality of his shots.

Wearily Mr Morrissey rocked back on his heels. 'So,' he said, folding his arms high on his chest, 'you think Sergeant Peters is a pretty good photographer, do you?'

'Going by these photos, excellent!' declared the officer. His fist of a face split open into a big white grin. The whole court went up in a shout of laughter: not just the jury and the journalists, but Morrissey, Rapke, the judge, the two families, even Farquharson himself.

After Mr Morrissey's *Sturm und Drang*, Mr Rapke rose and shone a steady light on the matter. Over the uneven terrain between the road and the dam, Sergeant Exton would have expected a car that was not being steered to have deviated quite abruptly from a smooth arc: certainly at the drain, definitely at the fence, and then more moderately between the fence and the dam. But there were no marks on the bitumen, on the gravel shoulder, or on the grass leading to the dam, to show that Farquharson's car was ever out of control.

...

Sergeant Bradford Peters, a serene-looking man in his mid-forties, was on the stand for a long time. Against the ramparts of his cheerful persona Morrissey's artillery thundered in vain. Peters made it seem absurd to suggest that the police might have scuffed out the disputed tyre track between the yellow paint marks. Why on earth would they do that, he asked, when they had already photographed it? At one stage in his tracing of the rolling tyre prints, the yellow paint in his spray-can had run out. Chivvied by Morrissey as to why he had planted a plastic marker on a certain section of the track instead of walking back to the car for a fresh can of paint, Peters said with a good-humoured shrug, 'I don't remember. I must have just been too lazy to go back and get one.' A gentle ripple of liking flowed across the court towards him. The battered jury smiled and shifted in their seats, released by his insouciant air from some constraint.

One day, late in that week, Louise and I came back from lunch a few minutes early and found the court empty. One of Sergeant Peters' aerial photos was still displayed on the high screen, which from the press seats we had been able to see only at a frustratingly acute angle. We sneaked along the deserted bar table and stood right in front of the photo. Daylight. Thick grass. Wheel tracks, a single set, outlined by police markers in a flat arc between road and dam. We gazed up in silence. Then, in her dry, thoughtful voice, the girl said, 'Coughing fit my arse.'

On the Monday of the trial's third week, waiting and gossiping with the media people outside the court in weak spring sunlight, we calculated that the following day would be the second anniversary of the children's deaths. Imagining Farquharson's dread as the date approached, I allowed myself the luxury of the word *pitiful*. One of the print journalists, a court veteran whose work I had long respected, spun round and bit my head off.

'Pity?' she cried. 'How can you say he's pitiful when he's done the worst, the most terrible thing? Murdered his own children, who trusted and loved him? Three of them! Premeditated! And to get back at his wife! The utmost betrayal! Why is *that* pitiful?'

I flushed and fell silent. But that morning, when Farquharson was brought up from the cells and stuck out his hands at the door to have his cuffs removed, he looked even more blighted and rigid than usual. The next Crown witness would be his former wife.

Cindy Gambino slid in without fanfare, past the seats where her family and Farquharson's sat tightly wedged. How small she was, this woman whose loss was beyond imagining, yet who would not lay blame. Her hair hung past her shoulders in silky falls. Her smooth face with its large, heavy-lidded eyes showed no expression, but her skin was the pale greyish-brown of a walnut shell, as if grief had soaked her to the bone, and she walked so carefully that she appeared to be limping. The raised witness box, near the front of the court, and the dock at the back were only fifteen metres apart. Down the length of the court, above the lawyers' heads, Gambino and Farquharson would have to look straight at each other.

Mr Rapke leaned forward over the bar table and narrowed his eyes at Gambino like a man gazing into too bright a light. When he named the dead boys and gave their birth dates, when he asked her if she was their natural mother, Farquharson pulled his handkerchief out of his pocket, held it to his face with both hands, and began to weep.

For several years, said Gambino, she had known Farquharson merely as a friend. Then, in 1993, a year after the man she was involved with was killed in a road accident, she took up with Rob, who, at twenty-four, was still living at home with his parents. Even after they set up house together, Gambino was haunted by her grief for the man who had died. Soon Farquharson told her that, if they were going to get serious, she would have to put away her mementoes of him, take down his photos, and stop wearing his ring.

In 1994 their first child, Jai, was born. Postnatal depression joined forces with her unresolved grief, and she and Farquharson needed help from a counsellor.

He was not happy working for the shire. In 1996 he arranged a redundancy payout, and they bought a Jim's Mowing franchise. Farquharson lugged his mower through the surrounding countryside, along the Surf Coast and down the Great Ocean Road, but the work was too much for him on his own. They lost money and had to surrender the franchise, which dropped them into $40,000 worth of debt.

'I had a lot of resentment against Rob,' said Gambino. 'He wanted to work for himself. I didn't want him to.'

Their second son, Tyler, was born in 1998. They had to move in with Gambino's parents in Birregurra for six months, with the two little boys. Eventually Farquharson found a steady job as a cleaner at the Cumberland Resort in the upmarket seaside town of Lorne, where Gambino's mother was in charge of hospitality. They managed to pull their finances into better order.

In 2000 they married. They built a house, but the work was not done to the standard they wanted. They sold it and moved into a rented place. In 2004 they bought a block of land in a Winchelsea street called Daintree Drive, and started to build another house.

All this moving, these houses. It seemed that Gambino's will had been the driving force in the relationship, that she had had to drag her man through life. She had ambitions and restless hopes that his energy could not match. Their needs were at cross-purposes.

'Rob didn't want to build. He wanted to buy an established house. But I wanted to build again. We agonised over that. I usually got my own way.' She gave a small, wretched laugh. 'I wanted another child. Rob was unsure. He didn't know if he could cope with three children. But he was pretty much a softie. He always gave in to what I wanted.'

Tears began to slide down her cheeks. Farquharson wept on, behind his red velvet rope. Except when he scrubbed at his face with his handkerchief, he did not take his eyes off her.

Rob's mother, whom he loved and was very close to, was diagnosed with cancer in 2000, and died in 2002, the year Bailey, their youngest, was born. 'He grieved,' said Gambino. 'He had mood swings. He was always down and out. He felt like he was never happy. I can understand that.'

By now she was speaking in a series of soft, gasping cries. Farquharson leaned forward with his elbows on his thighs and mopped hopelessly at his tears. People in the court had their hands over their mouths. The air was filled with a faint rustling.

Farquharson suffered from foot and back pain, exacerbated no doubt by his slogging physical work. When he got sick, he got really sick. Gambino had never seen him pass out from coughing, but most winters he had a cough that would sometimes take his breath away. If he went to the doctor about it, he would be told, 'You've got what everyone else has got. Deal with it.' Gambino's experience of postnatal depression allowed her to recognise some of her husband's symptoms, particularly mood swings and sleeplessness. She urged him to get help, but he would say, 'No, I'm not depressed. I'm all right.'

By the latter half of 2004, Gambino was coming to the end of her tether. 'I found it throughout my marriage very hard,' she said, 'to give my heart to my husband. You can love someone, but you can also be in love with someone, and I found it hard to be in love with Rob. He was a very secure person, he was a very good provider, but I just found it hard to give myself to him.'

In October 2004, when Bailey was almost two, Farquharson agreed at last to see their family GP about his mood swings. Dr

McDonald put him on anti-depression medication, but for Gambino it was already too late. She levelled with him the following month, and it came at him out of nowhere.

Mr Rapke left her the silence, and she filled it, holding a handful of tissues to her eyes, her voice so high and weak that we had to strain to hear.

'I didn't want the marriage any more. I asked him to leave.'

There it was, the unbearable blow she had dealt him—expulsion from his family and his home. Like so many emotionally numbed, inarticulate and stoical husbands, he had failed to see it coming.

'He went to live with his dad,' she said. 'He was devastated. It was a case of you don't know what you've got till it's gone.'

'Did you consent to see him,' asked Rapke, 'after you separated?'

She gave a harsh gulp. 'I think I had him over to tea once. And that was for the children's sake.'

I did not risk a glance at the journalist who had forbidden pity. But surely mine was not the only heart to ache, at that moment, for the hunched and humiliated figure in the dock.

...

Cindy Gambino was at pains to stress that the concreter, Stephen Moules, had not been the cause of her marriage break-up. They met in the winter of 2004. In September she engaged him to pour the slab for the new house. By November she had sent Farquharson back to his father.

Moules was still extricating himself from a child-custody mess with his former wife. He needed to maintain things with Gambino on a friendly footing, and for quite some time he kept her at arms' length. It was not till after she ended her marriage that their relationship grew more intimate. When they began to sleep at each other's houses that summer, Farquharson took it badly, but he claimed not to care what she and Moules were doing. His jealousy focused on the children. It bugged him that his boys had to associate with Moules' two unruly sons. Jai Farquharson, at ten, became a very different little boy: he believed he would never be happy again. His parents, in turns, took him to see a counsellor for help in managing his anger and sadness. In spite of Gambino's assurances, Farquharson was afraid of being edged out of his children's lives. He feared that Moules was going to take his place as their father.

It took a while for Farquharson to get the hang of being a part-time dad in his own father's house, which Gambino found so cold and child-unfriendly that she called it 'the morgue'. He was not confident with Bailey, the toddler. At first he had the boys to sleep over only rarely. But football was their shared obsession and, once the season started, they stayed with him every second weekend.

Farquharson had agreed, without need of Family Court involvement, to pay maintenance at the monthly rate laid down by the Child Support Agency. Half of it he put straight into the mortgage payments on the house, and the rest he gave to Gambino, who as a supporting mother was receiving her own government cheque. He liked to buy his children gifts of clothes and toys, but financially he was struggling. He could not see how to get his life back on track. In the winter of 2005 his wages went up, and his maintenance payments were about to be raised accordingly. The letter announcing this increase did not arrive until after the boys had died, but he knew it was coming, and he was very angry with the Child Support Agency. He thought they 'didn't give the guy a fair go'. On what would turn out to be the last Wednesday of their children's lives, Gambino suggested to Farquharson that he should stop paying her the non-mortgage part of the maintenance, and put that money towards a house of his own, so that when the boys wanted to see their dad they could hop on their bikes and go. But he said no, because it was not legal.

And then there was the sore point of the two cars. At the time she ended the marriage, Gambino had pressed Farquharson to take from their house whatever he liked. Many a rejected spouse has heard that rush of guilty generosity at the door, 'I'll give you everything!'—with its unspoken rider—'except what you really want: my love'. The only thing she asked for, because she would have the kids full-time, was the newer of their two cars—a 2002 VX Commodore. The dejected Farquharson went along with it, but he did not like it one bit.

...

Father's Day 2005 did not fall on one of Farquharson's scheduled access weekends, but at Jai's football presentation on the Friday evening, Gambino suggested to Farquharson that she should bring the boys to him on Sunday afternoon for a special visit. They arrived just as Farquharson got home from work. They brought gifts they had chosen for him: a framed picture of themselves, and a set of saucepans. Jai, the eldest, was upset because he had forgotten to bring a wooden back-scratcher that he had bought especially. The boys asked if they could stay with their father for tea. He was not expecting them for a meal, and had no food in the house. The children saw the chance for a rare treat: Kentucky Fried Chicken in Geelong. Farquharson agreed to have them back at Gambino's place by 7.30 p.m.

'It was three o'clock,' she told the court. 'Bailey said, "Cuddle, Mum". I gave them a cuddle.' Her voice rose to a register almost beyond audible. 'That was the last time I saw my children.'

...

Gambino and Stephen Moules spent the rest of the day in Geelong, where Moules had to inspect the progress of a job. They got back to his house in Winchelsea by 6.30 p.m. and he started to cook the tea. Just before the appointed hand-over time, Gambino drove to her own house, taking with her Moules' younger son Zach, who was keen to see her boys. Ten minutes later, while she was drawing the curtains against the dark, she saw a white Commodore pull in. 'Here they are now,' she thought.

But on her doorstep she found Farquharson with two men. He was saturated, delirious, and he kept saying, 'The kids are in the car. They're in the water.'

In the witness stand Gambino began to rock on her feet, a rhythmic swaying.

She called Moules on her mobile, then jumped into her car, with Zach beside her and Farquharson in the back seat, and headed out on to the Princes Highway. 'Where? Where?'

'Near the overpass!' Farquharson shouted. 'Keep going. Keep going!'

The boy screamed, 'Slow down! You're frightening me!'

She looked at the speedo. She was doing 145. She pulled up near the guardrail of the overpass.

'We couldn't see the dam. It was so dark, we couldn't see anything.'

Moules and his cousin arrived in another car, and ran into the paddock.

'We were trying to find out where the car had gone in,' said Gambino. She began to sob. 'The wire was down. It was spread across the paddock. Rob asked Stephen for a cigarette. Stephen said, "What? Where are your kids? Get out of my face before I kill you. *Where are your kids?*" Rob didn't know. He kept going like *that*.' She mimicked a flat-handed pointing gesture. 'I said to him, "What happened?" And he said, "I blacked out." He tried to comfort me, but I pushed him away.'

Farquharson between his guards was weeping soundlessly, without shame, his mouth gaping, his eyes locked on hers. A great knotted current of agony surged back and forth between the dock and the witness stand: a flood of terrible compassion. Something was happening to Gambino's voice. It dissolved, it thickened, it throbbed and took on colour; it rose and fell in octaves, like a chant.

'It was dark. It was so *dark*. I was running up and down the paddock, trying to ring 000, but I was so hysterical I couldn't press the numbers properly. Stephen was in the water. I remember sitting in the front seat of his parents' car. Rob was standing in front of the car with his arms crossed. He was soaking wet. He was like a person, but there was no movement. He wasn't doing anything. He was like in a trance.'

There was a helicopter over the dam. A paramedic walked up to her. She asked him, 'How long has it been?' 'Forty minutes.' 'What are their chances?' 'Very slim.'

One of her brothers arrived. He took her away to his house in Winchelsea and called a doctor. It was a very long wait. Her socks were wet. At last the doctor came. He drove them through fog to the Winchelsea hospital. She staggered through the doors and someone came to her with the needle.

...

All Mr Morrissey wanted from Gambino, in cross-examination, was her assurance—which she gave earnestly and without hesitation—that Farquharson had loved his children very deeply. He was such a softie with them that the role of disciplinarian had fallen to her. The football side of things was his forte. After the separation he grew much closer to the boys. She had done everything in her power to foster this closeness. He was proud of them, especially of Jai, who at ten was intelligent, mature, responsible, a good sportsman, a very good big brother.

'Everybody loved my kids,' said Gambino, her voice thinning to a soft wail. 'They were so *popular*.'

In the dreadful days after they died, asked Morrissey, had her family written Farquharson a card? Had she and Rob spoken to each other on the telephone? Had they offered each other words of comfort? Yes, she said, with an anguished gentleness, yes—they had.

Gambino left the stand with a wad of wet tissues held to her cheek. As she stumbled towards the exit, Farquharson's head swung to follow her, and I caught the full blast of his distress. His face was ravaged, beseeching: his teeth bared, his cheeks streaming. The doors thumped shut behind her. Masonry, glass and timber could not muffle the rending sobs and cries that echoed in the cold hall outside.

The sleeve of Louise's hoodie was black with tears. 'Did she look at him on the way out?' she whispered. 'Did she *look* at him?'

'She turned her head a little bit,' I said. 'I think she looked at him.'

Out on the street, seeing me wipe my eyes, the veteran journalist snapped at me, '*I* was at the *funeral*.'

Years later, when we befriended each other, I would see that she had been forcing me back to the point, but now she made me feel like a sentimental amateur. I was afraid of her, and it shocked me that she would not hold her fire, even for a moment, in the face of what we had just witnessed: two broken people grieving together for their lost children, in an abyss of suffering where notions of guilt and innocence have no purchase.

...

No sooner had we steadied ourselves after the spectacle of Cindy Gambino's loyalty to the husband she was no longer in love with, than the prosecution called to the stand her new partner—and father of her eleven-month-old son, Hezekiah—Stephen Moules.

He faced Rapke's junior, Amanda Forrester, in a grey suit, lavender shirt, and white tie. His hair was thick and fair. He had an upright posture, and a smooth, open face with the all-seasons tan of the outdoor worker. I was not the only woman in the court who shot at Farquharson a furtive glance of comparison. He sat with shoulders slumped and eyes downcast.

Moules described himself to the court as a former concreter turned full-time father. The water in the glass he sipped from trembled; but still he gave off that little buzz of glamour peculiar to the Australian tradie. Surely the month of September 2004, when the Farquharsons hired him to pour the slab of their new house, had marked the beginning of a period of exhilaration and fantasy for Gambino, while to Farquharson it must have brought nothing but suspicion, jealousy and pain.

Everything Moules said about himself suggested a figure of resolute virtue. His own family may have collapsed into chaos, but he seemed determined to haul it back to the light, and to establish himself in full view as a decent citizen. When the Farquharsons engaged him, he already knew their eldest, Jai, from the Cub Scout troupe he led. He was an active member of the Bayside Christian Church, an evangelical outfit formerly known as the Assemblies of God, and taught Sunday School there. The name of his concreting company was God's Creations.

His initial dealings with the Farquharsons, he said, were only 'a business relationship'. But, having recently watched a bunch of blokes pour a concrete slab in my own backyard, I was equipped to imagine the effect of this sight on a young woman in Cindy Farquharson's stifling situation. A concrete pour is a dramatic process. It demands skill, speed, strength, and the confident handling of machinery; and it is so intensely, symbolically masculine that every woman and boy in the vicinity is drawn to it in excited respect. Spellbound on the back veranda between my two small grandsons, I remembered Camille

Paglia's coat-trailing remark that if women were running the world, we'd still be living in grass huts. Could it be that Farquharson's days as a husband were numbered before that slab had set?

...

Late in 2004 Gambino offered, in a neighbourly spirit, to pick up Moules' two boys from school in the afternoons and look after them at her place until he finished work. Moules saw no harm in it, and was grateful for the help. It made me flinch to think of Farquharson stumping home sore-footed from his cleaning job, only to find his house thundering with another man's kids and his wife flushed and enlivened by her new friendship with their father.

Across the dying months of the marriage, though, Farquharson naively confided in Moules his anxiety and distress. Even after his wife had called the whole thing off and he had moved back to his father's—which chanced to be only five doors along from the house Moules was renting—Farquharson would often turn up at Moules' place looking for somebody to talk to. He took the break-up very hard. He was distraught when Cindy did not want to reconcile. 'He did not know what to do,' said Moules, 'in any way, shape or form.' Moules ran a Christian line with him. He 'counselled' him on how to get his marriage back together. 'I tried to sort of steer him,' he said, miming the two-handed motion of driving a car. He gave Farquharson advice both spiritual and worldly, and recommended he see a counsellor from Bayside Christian Church. Finally he realised his efforts were falling on deaf ears. He gave up.

But Moules' role as his neighbour's counsellor must have been uncomfortably compromised, for Cindy Farquharson too, over the same period, was a frequent visitor to his house. She used him as an ear, said Moules, to 'vent to'. They would 'just sit there talking'. According to Moules' police statement, she told him that Farquharson had spoken of moving up to Queensland, that he wanted to 'wean himself off his boys, because that was how it would end up anyway'.

Once Farquharson had moved out of their house, Cindy made it apparent to Moules that she had feelings for him. Next, she changed her name back to Gambino. Her signals were unmistakable. Moules had to struggle, he said, to keep their relationship platonic. He declined to be used as a scapegoat. He wanted Gambino to 'have all her business clear-cut' before anything further developed between them. But Farquharson, he said, was beginning to hold him responsible for the failure of the marriage.

'It's got to be your fault,' he said to Moules. 'I can't understand any other reason why the marriage shouldn't be.'

And Moules replied, 'Your wife is your wife, okay? I've got custody of my kids. I'm starting my life again. I don't need any more dramas.'

...

When he spoke about the night of Father's Day, Moules' voice became low and husky. Tremors flickered in the skin around his eyes. To control the trembling of his hands he had to clasp them on the timber rail of the witness stand. He mimed his incredulity at Farquharson's first words to him when he arrived at the dam:

'Where's your smokes?' He described his helpless diving into the bitterly cold water, his repeated requests to Farquharson to tell him where the car had gone in, and Farquharson's answer: 'I don't know. I had a coughing fit and blacked out.' Two young men—they must have been Shane Atkinson and Tony McClelland—shouted guidance to him from the bank: 'I think I see bubbles. Try there. Try there.' Moules tried to dive in the direction of any movement he thought he could sense in the water. But it was too dark and too cold, and he was shuddering too much and swallowing too much water. It got to the point where he said to himself, 'This is ridiculous.' One of the men yelled to him, 'Come on, mate. Get out or you'll be next.'

Moules' teenage cousin, who shared his house, drove him home to get dry clothes. Mistakenly believing Gambino to have been taken to Geelong Hospital, Moules set out with a friend at the wheel to find her there. On the way past the dam he asked the driver to stop so he could let the police know he had been, as he put it in his witness statement two days later, 'first at the scene'. In that statement, Moules said he had been asked whether he had told an officer or anyone else that night that Farquharson had killed his kids. He was very angry on the night, he said, and he might have said something like it, but he did not remember it.

...

Kerri Huntington, the younger of Farquharson's big sisters, took the stand, her flamboyant blonde hair massing on her shoulders. Although at times she wept, she looked like the extrovert of the family, someone who would know how to throw a party, a warm person with laugh-crinkles radiating from her small, deep-set Farquharson eyes.

When Rob's marriage had crashed, Kerri and her husband, Gary, opened their home to him and his sons. The Huntingtons' house was kid-friendly. They had a pool. Their two daughters loved Rob's boys, who would often come to stay with them on his access weekends. The Huntingtons would even have asked Rob to move in with them, but their house lacked an extra bedroom, and anyway they lived at Mount Moriac, halfway to Geelong; what Rob needed was a house in Winchelsea, so the boys could come to him off their own bat.

Kerri, who worked part-time at Kmart in the Geelong suburb of Belmont, kept an eye on real estate. She spotted the perfect house, right across the road from the Winch footy oval. But the Daintree Drive house still wasn't sold; Rob couldn't afford to buy. The Huntingtons offered to lend him what they could, and to help him get a better car. He didn't want to be in debt to them. He said no.

Around six on the evening of Father's Day, Kerri was about to go on her break at Kmart when Rob and his kids wandered in. She was surprised. His normal fortnightly access date had been the previous weekend; she remembered it because he had been so sick, with his lingering chest cold, that he had rung and asked her for help with the boys. When they had got to her place, Rob was lethargic with a nasty cough. It didn't make him pass out, but it took his breath away. She had made him lie on the couch and sleep, while she looked after the boys.

Now, on the wrong weekend, here they were in her store, pestering Rob to buy them a cricket ball and some DVDs. They told her they were going to stop off at her place on their way home to collect a football that Tyler had lost in her garden the weekend before. Kerri and Rob made a plan to get their kids together the following Saturday, and away the four Farquharsons went.

Gary Huntington testified that boys and father did rock through the Mount Moriac house half an hour later. They picked up the footy, and towards seven, all correctly buckled into their seats, they set off for Winchelsea.

...

Outside on Lonsdale Street at lunchtime, while Louise and I were standing in a patch of sun against the Supreme Court's honey-coloured stone wall, Bob Gambino drifted up to us.

'You girls still here?'

'Oh yes. We'll be here till the end.'

He looked pleased, and stuck his hands into his coat pockets. His natural expression seemed to be a small, lopsided smile. 'Some of those jurors,' he said, without apparent animus, 'aren't even there. That dark one. She's just eatin' chewy and lookin' round. She's in a dream.'

I burst out, 'Cindy was incredible. I couldn't believe how she kept going.'

'Nah,' he said, looking into the stream of traffic. 'You never expect to have to sit through this. I'll certainly never forget that night. This arvo it'll be the divers.'

Louise turned a whiter shade of pale.

'They asked us if we wanted not to be here for that,' said Bob.

'But we know it already. We know it all.'

We stood there, keeping him company, in the bent rectangle of sun.

...

Before the jury was called in that afternoon, Mr Morrissey asked the judge for permission to show them two photographs.

The first was of Jai and Tyler jumping into the Huntingtons' swimming pool. This, he said, would demonstrate that the two older boys were so confident and enthusiastic in water, so 'not hopeless', that it would have been 'a risky proposition' to try to drown them.

I was too embarrassed to look at Morrissey. Could he really believe that there was a meaningful connection between a joyful daylight leap and a violent plunge into the dark?

The second photo showed two-year-old Bailey on his father's lap in an armchair, both of them sound asleep. Morrissey particularly wanted the jury to see the poignant shot of the slumbering father and son: it would counter what he said was the Crown's suggestion that Bailey had been, to his father, an unwanted child.

The Crown declared it had made no such suggestion. Justice Cummins jibbed at the sleeping picture. 'Naked sympathy is just as inappropriate as naked prejudice. Are you going to introduce a family album? Why pick this one out?'

'I'm seeking,' said Morrissey doggedly, 'to demonstrate that he loved that child.'

There it was again, the sentimental fantasy of love as a condition of simple benevolence, a tranquil, sunlit region in which we are safe from our own destructive urges. Surely, I thought, Freud was closer to the mark when he said, 'We are never so defenceless against suffering as when we love.'

A pause. Justice Cummins shook his head. He gave Morrissey leave to tender the swimming pool picture, but he would not admit the second photo. So little Bailey was left to dream on, forever unregarded, curled in his sleeping father's lap.

...

It was a woman who finally got deep enough into the dam, that night, to find the car.

Crop-haired and wiry in her dark blue uniform, a huge diver's watch on her wrist, Senior Constable Rebecca Caskey of the Search and Rescue Squad stood in the witness stand with her hands clasped loosely behind her. Something in her easy posture reminded me of nurses I had seen at work: women of few words, unflappable, alert and calm.

Search and Rescue figured out, from the scattered debris their torch beams located near the dam, the car's likely departure point from the bank. By 10.30 p.m. that night, Caskey was fully kitted up, with an attendant on the bank holding her lifeline.

In she went, all the way down. Compared with a farm dam, it was clean: there was no entangling vegetation. But the bottom was pure mud. The water was black and very cold. She could not see at all. A torch would have been useless in water so full of sediment. They used an arc search pattern: the man on the bank let out a length of line, and Caskey, keeping it tight between them, searched the available curve. He let out another arm-length and swept her back the other way.

She started feeling bits of metal and plastic on the bottom. Then she bumped into something with her head, something that moved. She touched it with her hand. It spun freely. A wheel. On the witness stand she squeezed her eyes shut, put her long-fingered hands out in front of her, and mimed blind groping gestures up and down an imaginary wall. 'What was facing me,' she said, 'was the underside of the car. It was vertical.'

She backed away, and surfaced. They calculated the car's position: wedged nose down in the mud, twenty-eight metres from the bank, in seven and a half metres of water. Standard procedure for Search and Rescue is to remove bodies from a submerged vehicle before they haul it out. But they agreed with Major Collision that Farquharson's car should be sealed and brought up intact.

Oh God. This could only get worse. I sneaked a look at Farquharson. His lips were white, his mouth very low on his face. Like a child he ground his knuckles into his eyes.

Caskey dived again. In the mud at the bottom, working blind, she felt her way to what she guessed was the driver's side of the vertical car.

'The first thing I noticed on the driver's side was an open door, just above the level of my head. Its window was closed. I felt around the edge of the door.'

Again, eyes shut and palms exposed, she mimed her fumbling search.

'And then,' she said, 'I felt, slightly protruding from the car, a small person's head.'

On the witness stand she cupped both hands before her face, and delicately moved an imaginary object sideways.

'I pushed it back in. And I shut the door.'

She swam up the driver's side of the car and down the passenger side, checking the windows and doors. All were closed.

Soon after midnight Caskey clambered out of the water for the last time. A police 4WD winched the Commodore to the edge of the dam, and a commercial tow-truck dragged it, still full of water, up on to the bank. Caskey had been in the water for several hours. She was cold. She was keen to get changed and go home.

Before she left, she took a quick look into the car. She saw three children. Two were in the back. Lying in the front was the one whose head she had touched and, for a moment, held in her hands.

...

The men from Major Collision looked into the recovered car before they opened it to drain the water out. Ten-year-old Jai was lying face down across the front seats with his head towards the driver's door. When he was taken out of the car he showed signs of rigor mortis. Seven-year-old Tyler lay on his right side behind the driver's seat. His head was near the door and his legs were between the two front seats. Two-year-old Bailey was lying across the top of the baby seat, facing rearwards and still tangled in his safety harness.

The police took careful note of the positions of the car's controls. The key was in the ignition, off and locked. The automatic gearshift was in drive. The handbrake was off, as were the headlights and parking lights. The heater was off: its knob was at ten o'clock, in the blue part of the dial. All three seatbelts were unbuckled. The windows were all shut. The two rear doors were locked. When Sergeant Exton tried to open the driver's side rear door, the exterior handle snapped off in his hand.

At two in the morning, the children's bodies were formally identified by Stephen Moules.

. . .

Dr Michael Burke, a small, grey-haired, bespectacled forensic pathologist, was taken through his evidence fast and light, as if in mercy, but Farquharson's face as he listened was contorted with anguish. He gasped and sobbed in silence, wiping at his eyes again and again. His sisters' faces were flushed. They too wept without sound.

Apart from the surrounding circumstances, there is no definitive test to show that a person has died of drowning. A particular kind of foam, however, a plume of white matter, is often seen in drowned people, and this was found around the children's mouths and noses. Toxicology tests revealed no evidence of alcohol, carbon monoxide, or other drugs or poisons. All three bodies showed minor abrasions and bruises here and there, marks that could have been caused either by the impact of the crash or by ordinary childhood play. Jai, who had been riding in the front beside his father, was marked above his left eyebrow; the left side of his face was discoloured; the soft tissue at the back of his neck was bruised in a way that suggested whiplash. A tiny flap of skin had been scraped from one of Tyler's fingers. As for Bailey, the pathologist had found only a scratch on his elbow, with a bandaid on it.

···

At the end of the gruelling day the jury looked older, weary and sad. The men's brows were furrowed, the women were stowing sodden handkerchiefs. Out in the courtyard we passed Bev Gambino. She gave us a small, shaky smile. Her face was thin, her eyes hollow behind the pretty spectacles. A puff of wind would have carried her away. Louise and I were beyond speech. We parted in Lonsdale Street. On the long escalator down to Flagstaff station I could not block out of my mind those small bodies, the tender reverse-midwifery of the diver. The only way I could bear it was to picture the boys as water creatures: three silvery, naked little sprites, muscular as fish, who slithered through a crack in the car's rear window and, with a flip of their sinuous feet, sped away together into their new element.

···

At the coffee cart, early next morning, Louise rushed up to me in a fluster.

'One of the jurors was on my train. That tall one with the nerdy fringe. He spoke to me.'

'He *what*?'

'He said "Are you Zach?" I had no idea what he was talking about and I couldn't *believe* he'd spoken to me. I said no, coldly, and walked away. What did he mean?'

'Zach. Isn't that Stephen Moules' son? The one who was in Cindy's car when she drove to the dam—remember? Who begged her to slow down?'

We looked around nervously. No one was in earshot.

'Don't let's tell anyone,' she said. 'I'd hate the trial to be aborted and for it to be my fault.'

It would hardly have been her fault. Surely the juror knew the rules, even if he could not tell the difference between a girl and a boy. But I felt for him. Starved as he was of human facts, restricted to the narrowest version of the evidence, his curiosity must have overwhelmed him. Like his fellow jurors, like us, he was striving to construct for each stranger an identity and a meaningful place in the mysterious web of the story.

Robert Farquharson did not know, when he gave in to his wife's pressure and took his gloom to the family GP on 12 October 2004, that his marriage would be over within a month. But perhaps he sensed its end approaching, for the long list of complaints he produced that day sounded to me like a classic description of what used to be called, before the medicalisation of our sorrows, a broken heart.

Dr Ian Robert McDonald, a slender, faded, gentle-looking man who had been treating Farquharson since he was a child, ran through for the court the symptoms his patient had reported. Farquharson was anxious. He had mood swings and paranoid feelings, emotional ups and downs. He couldn't sleep. He dwelt on things. He was teary. He had no interest or motivation. He was tired, stressed and irritable. And he was finding it hard to cope with his children.

Farquharson did not strike me as the sort of bloke who would spend hours on the internet, but he told the doctor he had been 'looking things up', and that he thought he might 'have depression'. He did not volunteer an explanation of his state, and Dr McDonald showed surprisingly little curiosity about it. He simply accepted the self-diagnosis, and prescribed Farquharson the anti-depressant, Zoloft.

Three weeks later, on 3 November, Farquharson returned and announced that his wife had, that very day, ended the marriage. She could no longer cope with his moods. McDonald referred him to a psychologist in Geelong, a Dr David Sullivan. But Sullivan charged $142 a session. Farquharson came back from Geelong saying he couldn't afford to see him again. Around this time Cindy Gambino and a woman friend got in touch with the receptionist at Dr McDonald's surgery. They were worried that Farquharson might try to overdose on sleeping pills. McDonald arranged for him to be seen 'urgently' by Psychiatric Services in the smaller town of Colac. This body felt that Farquharson was 'not within their scope', and referred him on to Colac Mental Health.

The court did not hear what had happened in Colac, but when Farquharson came back to the GP three weeks later, still angry, still waking at two in the morning, McDonald sat him down for a long counselling session. His patient's state, he thought, was due less to depression than to his marital troubles. He changed his medication from Zoloft to Avanza, an anti-depressant with more sedative qualities.

By mid-December Farquharson told Dr McDonald that his hopes of saving his marriage had been dashed. He was upset, but did not strike the GP as angry. He went away with a fresh script for Avanza and a sample pack of the sleeping pill Stilnox.

Something must have kicked in. Farquharson did not return for five months. In May 2005 he told McDonald that he was regularly seeing a counsellor in Colac who was helping him make sensible plans for his future. The strongest emotion he admitted to was 'annoyance' with his wife: he felt manipulated by her demands that he should get the Daintree Drive house to lock-up stage so they could sell it.

Annoyance. The numbness, the breathtaking shallowness of this word. What deeper rage did it paper over? It is tempting, in retrospect, to think, with Freud, that 'unexpressed emotions will never die. They are buried alive and will come forth later in uglier ways.'

In August 2005 Farquharson turned up at Dr McDonald's clinic several times, first complaining of a bad cold, then later of a chesty cough that came on in the night air and made his ribs ache. The GP listened to his chest. His lung fields were clear. His temperature was normal. He did not cough in McDonald's presence, nor did he mention feeling dizzy or passing out, and it did not occur to McDonald to ask him about such symptoms, for he regarded them as an extremely rare complication of coughing. He changed Farquharson's antibiotic and told him to come back for blood tests if he was not better in a couple of days.

Farquharson never returned for the blood tests.

Twelve days later, his children drowned.

On his way out of the court Dr McDonald glanced at his former patient in the dock. Farquharson kept his eyes down.

...

A large chunk of potential insight—if insight is what courts are after—had fallen between the cracks of Dr McDonald's testimony.

Before the GP took the stand that morning, Justice Cummins delayed calling in the jury so he could have a discussion with counsel. 'It's better to think out loud while the jury's not here,' he said, 'so we can all look ahead.' Apparently a piece of information had just surfaced, something that the judge thought had 'a real bite to it, a real sting'. Was it to be admitted into evidence, or not?

On his sole visit to Dr Sullivan, the Geelong psychologist whose fees he could not afford, Farquharson had said that he had been thinking about and planning suicide.

Hearing this word, Farquharson recoiled extravagantly in the dock. Whenever suicide was mentioned during the rest of the wrangle about this evidence, he would turn to his sisters, knit his brows into an indignant scowl, and furiously shake his head.

It was Dr Sullivan's professional duty to inform Dr McDonald immediately, in writing, of what Farquharson had said; and he did so. Rapke read part of his brief report aloud: 'I explained to Mr Farquharson the importance of his continuing use of anti-depressant medication…and his responsibility to adopt a new role in his inter-action with his wife, Cindy. I am concerned about the potential for Mr Farquharson to behave impulsively, and accordingly I have asked him to consider making a commitment to seek out and speak with someone he trusts when he feels vulnerable.'

The arrival of this report was what had caused Dr McDonald to send Farquharson straight to Colac Psychiatric Services. But the rules of evidence—so bizarrely counterintuitive to the layperson—classed the information in Sullivan's report as hearsay: Farquharson had never spoken directly to the GP about suicide, so Dr McDonald could not be questioned about it in front of the jury. The suicide conversation could be raised in court only if Dr Sullivan himself gave evidence about it.

'I would have thought,' said Justice Cummins, 'that an expression by the accused that he was contemplating suicide would be relevant to the issues?'

Surely the prosecution could clear this up in a simple, direct way? Why did the Crown not call Dr Sullivan? Months after the trial was over, I would learn that Sullivan had declined to make a statement to the police. The Crown considered it too risky to subpoena a witness in those circumstances: what might he have said? But now, Morrissey, before whom lay a battered copy of the *Diagnostic and Statistical Manual of Mental Disorders-IV* that bristled with yellow Post-Its, announced that he intended to question Dr McDonald about the final sentence of his witness statement: '*At no time did Robert express to me any suicidal tendencies or anger to any person that I can recall.*'

Rapke's narrow hands moved restlessly among his papers. He got to his feet.

'I'm putting my friends on notice,' he said, in his light, ominous voice, 'that if this issue is opened up, then Sullivan *will* give evidence, and this will become a much more significant issue in the trial.'

Should Morrissey put his toe in the water at all, about this doctor? 'It seems to me,' said Justice Cummins, 'you would be well-advised not to.'

The judge gave counsel a short break to work this out, and left the bench. We waited in our seats, frustrated, imagining the barristers slugging it out in whatever private chamber they had retired to. I remembered my sister, when she was on a jury, bursting into tears one night at the dinner table: 'We know there's heaps they're not telling us! How can we make up our minds?' Ten minutes later the barristers returned, demure. Morrissey had decided not to put McDonald's final sentence before the jury. By common consent they let the subject rest. It was never mentioned again. The jury was called in, and the trial was back on the rails.

'WTF?' scribbled Louise. 'Is somebody bluffing?'

The last thing Morrissey wanted, I supposed, was for the whole story to swing around into a failed suicide attempt. Forget the coughing fit. A wounded, bitter man decides to obliterate himself and his children in one blow. Driving down the overpass he swings the wheel and plants his foot. But the cold water shocks the death wish out of him. He flounders to the bank and runs away, leaving his boys to drown.

Jurors are not permitted to speculate. This possible scenario was withheld from them. It disturbed me to watch them file out of their room and into their seats unenlightened, with their bowed shoulders and serious, trusting faces.

...

Dr McDonald's witness statement contained another haunting detail that was never raised in court. On the day his wife asked him to move out, Farquharson had asked the GP to refer him for a vasectomy. McDonald did not record his response, and nobody asked him about it. The request, I thought, struck a discordant note: hasty and self-punishing, full of bitterness about the past and despair of the future. On the simplest level, it could be dismissed as the wild notion of a man who at that moment experienced the very idea of children as a source of pain. But perhaps it might be seen, rather, as a fantasy that sent a surge of destruction in both directions: refusal of whatever was to come and, retrospectively, a symbolic cutting-off of the fact that his three sons existed—an urge to amputate his fatherhood, to annihilate everything that he and Gambino as a couple had brought into being.

...

On the night of 4 September, while the police, the emergency service crews and the townspeople of Winchelsea were struggling in the dark at the dam, Farquharson arrived by ambulance at Geelong Hospital. The duty consultant in Emergency that night was Dr Bruce Bartley. A bulging-browed young man with a tiny beard on the tip of his chin, he entered the court briskly, wearing an anachronistic three-piece suit.

When the paramedics brought Farquharson in, Bartley gave him a routine road trauma examination. Temperature, oxygen saturation, chest and neck X-rays, blood and, over the following twenty-four hours, a heart monitor—all the tests came back normal. Bartley made a provisional diagnosis, based on what his patient told him, of cough syncope: Farquharson had coughed to the point of passing out.

Syncope (pronounced *sing*-c'-pee)—a brief loss of consciousness caused by a sudden drop in blood pressure—commonly crops up in emergency departments, but cough syncope is so rare that most doctors have only read about it. No, Bartley had never before diagnosed it, or even come across a patient who had reported an attack of it. No test exists to prove retrospectively that a person has blacked out as a result of a paroxysm of coughing. Like all diagnoses of this elusive and extremely rare medical event, Bartley's was based solely on the assumption that everything Farquharson had told him was true.

Another GP flashed briefly through the court, Dr Christopher Gore, a chunky grey-haired man who worked in a bulk-billing clinic in Belmont. On 30 September 2005, some three weeks after the crash, Farquharson presented himself at Dr Gore's surgery, in the company of a woman 'said to be his sister', complaining of a persistent cough. His companion mentioned a recent accident that had involved a coughing fit, but nothing was said about a blackout, and Dr Gore simply prescribed Farquharson a new antibiotic. He had never seen Farquharson before, and he never saw him again.

One person was able to describe Robert Farquharson in the throes of a coughing fit: she had seen it with her own eyes. Susan Bateson, a trim little sparrow of a woman in a coffee-coloured blouse and silver nail polish, was a supervisor at the Cumberland Resort in Lorne. She had first met Rob through Cindy Gambino's parents, her neighbours. Once she had even babysat Jai and Tyler.

Farquharson had worked under her for five years, as what she called a houseperson. He cleaned the public areas and did the heavier cleaning in guests' apartments. He was a good, hard worker. He didn't take sickies or complain about his wages. After he and Cindy split, he would pass up lucrative weekend shiftwork so he could spend time with his boys. He loved them and was dedicated to them.

In mid-2005, the winter before the boys died, he was off work for ten days with flu. He came back still not a hundred per cent, but worked his normal shifts on the seven days leading up to the crash. On the Friday before Father's Day he came into Bateson's office at lunchtime, opened his mouth to speak, and was overtaken by 'a very dry, grabbing cough' that took his breath away. For ten or fifteen seconds he gasped and wheezed. His face turned an alarming shade of bright red. He did not black out, but Bateson wondered if he was having a stroke. She made him sit down and drink a glass of water, and advised him to get hold of a ventolin inhaler from the chemist. That day, despite the paroxysm, he worked right to the end of his usual 6 a.m.-to-2 p.m. shift.

Outside the court I spread a discarded newspaper on a cold concrete bench and sat on it while Louise queued at the cart. I was familiar with Lorne. As a child I was taken on family drives to the handsome old village on the Southern Ocean, with its famous jetty and huge cypress trees. Wealthy people had holiday houses there. These days it was favoured by barristers and judges. Cindy Gambino had described Farquharson's work at the Cumberland as 'the male side of cleaning: windows'. Waiting for coffee in the noisy street, I remembered a German friend of mine telling me that when he was a student in the sixties he had worked as a window cleaner at a European seaside resort. It was hard work, he said, solitary, and it could make you melancholy. You had too much time to brood on things. You couldn't help looking into the rooms where holiday-makers, richer and luckier and happier than you, were loafing about and having fun. You felt bitterness, and envy. Also, he said, there was the Sisyphus thing. You never got anywhere. No sooner had you finished laboriously polishing a sheet of glass than the wind came in off the sea and sprinkled salt all over it.

…

In October 2004, not long before she called a halt to her marriage, Cindy Farquharson went to see a psychologist called Peter Popko, who practised at the Otway Natural Medicine Centre in the nearby town of Colac. He must have gained her trust, for in January 2005, several months after the split, when ten-year-old Jai became disruptive in his pain and sadness, she brought Farquharson and the three boys to Popko for a special family consultation. The psychologist dealt with the family members in various combinations, then, in February 2005, he started seeing Farquharson on his own.

Like other secondary characters in this story, Popko must have passed many a sleepless night since Father's Day 2005. He took the stand in a dark suit and open-necked shirt, a quiet, slow-talking man with a big fair head.

Farquharson, he said, had struck him as a fairly sensitive, if only moderately articulate man. As a husband he had played a traditional provider's role; when Popko met him, he was grieving for the end of his relationship and the breakdown of his family. Popko had done no formal testing, since Farquharson was plainly not seriously depressed: he took care of himself, dressed appropriately, held down a job, and was actively and keenly engaged with his kids. The depression for which his GP had put him on medication fluctuated, Popko thought, between moderate and mild.

But the psychologist did not hesitate to apply to Farquharson's state the word 'despair'. Certain painful incidents would exacerbate this hopeless feeling. He and Cindy would quarrel on the phone. He would run into her new partner Stephen Moules. Jai would clash with Moules' elder son. Farquharson was furious when Moules came round to his place one evening and ordered him to discipline Jai for having used an offensive word about one of the Moules boys. Farquharson did have a few money worries, but they were not the main things bothering him. What caused him the most agitation was his fear of the influence Moules would have on Jai, Tyler and Bailey.

When Popko asked him if he felt he wanted to harm anyone, Farquharson expressed strong anger towards Moules. He had entertained thoughts of retribution. Retribution? Yes—he thought of getting into an argument and provoking Moules to throw a punch at him, so he could take him to court.

This passive-aggressive fantasy—set up, dob, and stand back to watch the thunderbolt fall—would have been funny if it had not been so pathetic: a manipulative child's way of getting a bigger, stronger, more popular kid into trouble. Farquharson sat frowning in the dock. I remembered his former father-in-law describing him as 'a sook', and the photo of his big sister towing him along the footpath with a two-handed grip on his wrist. Later, Cindy Gambino would remark to the court that as his wife she often used to feel like a single mother with four kids. What had happened to him, or failed to happen, that kept him stuck in childhood?

If the psychologist had broached this territory with his client in private, he did not say so in court, and nor, of course, was he invited to. Perhaps his theoretical focus was elsewhere. Perhaps he did not believe that Farquharson was equipped, by temperament or education, to have any insight into such questions. Farquharson's anger he saw, in the bleakly managerial jargon of cognitive behaviour therapy, as 'a predictable and key phase in the grief and loss process'. Popko's task was to 'offer strategies' that would help Farquharson to live the single life, to care for his kids 'outside the parental dyad', to deal with his 'depressed mood', and to 'establish future goals'. Popko did not say, and was not asked, what these strategies were.

In his witness statement Popko had said that Farquharson had never shown any signs of 'suicidal ideation'. Nor had he mentioned wanting to hurt Cindy and the boys. On the contrary, he was grateful to her for letting him see the children as often as he wanted. Towards the end of the seven or eight solo sessions he had with Popko, which were spaced further and further apart, Farquharson was coming to terms with the fact that he and Cindy would never get back together. Encouraged by his friends, he was even planning to ask another woman out on a date.

Indeed, Popko thought Farquharson was travelling so well, handling his new situation with such integrity and maturity, that he suggested their work together might be done. But Farquharson wanted the sessions to continue. He said he was getting a lot out of his time with Popko and was thankful to have an outlet for his emotions. Is it impertinent to wonder if he might have meant, 'We haven't even scraped the surface yet.'?

On 4 September, exactly a month after his final session with Popko, the car went into the dam.

Here again, before the witness entered the court, startling evidence had been discussed in the absence of the jury, and ruled inadmissible. Several times, after the night the children drowned,

Popko and his former client spoke to each other on the phone. These conversations were picked up by a bug that the Homicide investigators had put on Farquharson's line. He was seized by a panicky fear of an impending lie detector test that he had volunteered to take. But the jury was not to hear this tape, or even to know that there had been phone intercepts, let alone a lie detector test. All they were permitted to hear from Popko on this matter, when he took the stand, was that Farquharson feared the stress of the police investigation—that it might push him over the edge into a nervous breakdown.

Popko was excused from the court with this final remark still hovering in the air.

...

Out in the windy courtyard a bunch of journalists stood yarning.

'What's this about a lie detector test?' asked a shy young man who said he had not covered a murder trial before; his eye whites were as pure as a child's.

'They're not admissible in Australian courts,' said a TV reporter.

'Did he have a brain snap?' said one of the older tabloid blokes. 'Of a thick, childish kind?'

'Cindy's got a bit of style,' said another. 'She's clearly not stupid. People must have thought, shit, she'll make mincemeat out of him. How come she had three kids with a dumb-fuck?'

'Rebound,' said two of the women in chorus.

'If you ask me,' said a thoughtful young woman who usually only listened, 'Cindy's testimony's about the only thing Morrissey's got going for him, so far.'

Towards ten o'clock on the night of the crash, two police officers from Major Collision carried a handheld tape recorder through Emergency at Geelong Hospital and into a cubicle where Farquharson lay under a sheet, taking the occasional suck of oxygen through a mask. They introduced themselves—Senior Sergeant Jeffrey Smith, who was head of Major Collision, and Senior Constable Rohan Courtis—and pressed the record button.

At last we were to hear Farquharson speak.

The voice of the bereaved father is dull and muffled at first, but grows firmer as he begins to answer the bite-sized questions: who he is, where he lives and works. Then, when the officers ask him what happened on the road, his voice fills with energy, gains clarity and strength. He sounds surprisingly young and eager, almost boyish in his speech patterns.

'I think I just went up the overpass, and I started *coughing*… then, I don't remember *anything*, and then all of a sudden I was in this *water*, and me son screamed at me—he opened up the *door*, and we *nose*-dived. I shut the door on him, and I tried to get them out—I tried to get out and get help, thinking I was only just in off the road, not realising I was…I was trying to get up near the road, get people to hear me, to help, and people just drove past, I don't know exactly whereabouts it was, and it's just a big blur, like, you know—it happened so quick.'

'Mate.' Smith, the senior officer, lays it down gently. 'Do you realise that the children didn't—make it? Out of the car?'

Farquharson expels a short breath, and says in a low, flat tone, 'I gathered that.'

His questioners do not pause. What speed was he doing?

'Oh, it was under a hundred.' His voice brightens again and becomes emphatic. He offers his credentials as a father, poignantly still in the present tense: he never drinks with the kids, he never goes over a hundred with them, he's always very cautious, he's never had an accident before.

Once the policemen twig that Farquharson and his wife have parted, and that he was bringing the boys home from an access outing, their antennae begin to quiver. How long has this been going on? Twelve months. What's his ex-wife's full name? He gets it out—Cindy Louise Gambino—but with a heavy sigh. He produces her address and date of birth, then, like a sick person reminding a visitor he has good reason to be horizontal, he emits a muffled grunt of discomfort.

'You realise we have to ask these questions,' says Courtis, the younger officer, politely, in his light, rapid voice. 'Is everything sort of okay with you and your wife? Any dramas?'

'We're building the house,' says Farquharson, in a conversational tone. 'There's a few hassles selling it, but other than that,

I mean, look, how good does a divorce go, so to speak? Of course you have your disagreements and arguments, but the kids have always been put first, and everything like that.'

Pressed for details of the drop-off of the boys that afternoon, Farquharson complains that his arm is sore. Give it a move, mate, says the cop. No, it really is sore, there, just in one spot. He relates the Father's Day arrival and the arrangement to have tea in Geelong and visit Kmart in Belmont. On the road the little one, who was only two and a half, fell asleep in his car seat. So father and sons sat a while in the Kmart car park and listened to the footy on the radio. When the toddler stirred they roused him and went up to Kentucky to eat. Farquharson always had to deliver them back to their mother by 7.30, so, after a look around in Kmart and a quick stop at his sister's place in Mount Moriac, they got back on the road.

He trails off. Courtis nudges him forward. 'Just getting back to the crash. Was there anyone else in the traffic, or…?'

Again Farquharson's voice firms up. 'No. I can't remember nothing.' With growing vehemence, his volume rising and falling with the drama of it, he tells the story a second time: the coughing, the waking up in a lot of water, Jai in the front passenger seat opening the door. He adds that, when he leaned across to slam Jai's door, all the kids were screaming. He tried to unbuckle Jai's seatbelt and to get the other two out of the back, but because Jai had opened the door, the car nosedived. 'Just a nightmare,' he says. 'I'm gettin' distressed.' His voice goes dull again, without expression.

This is the moment the officers choose to caution him. Yeah, he knows he doesn't have to say anything, and that anything he says could be given in evidence.

They surge on. Did he go under the water at all? He falters. 'Yeah, we sort of did, as I—I tried to get up—thinking I was in foot-deep, to try and get round and open the doors and drag 'em out. I'm getting really distressed.' He sounds like a child calling for respite in a game that is getting too much for him. A pause. Then, out of a jumble of hospital white noise, his voice rises again.

'But sir. Can I ask one question?'

'You can ask any question you like.'

'I've never been in trouble before. So what's the likely scenario, for me?' On the word *likely* he gives a tiny, matey breath of a laugh.

Startled, I glanced at the uniformed Courtis sitting behind the bar table. A document dangled from his right hand. The stapled sheets were quivering.

'Well, mate,' says Courtis on the tape, his voice tuneful with surprise, 'at this stage all we know is that you've been in an accident, where you've driven off the road, and your kids have been in the car.'

Farquharson pushes it. 'So what sort of scena—'

Courtis cuts across him. He seems to be controlling himself. 'Mate, it's so early, we're not looking at you for doing *anything* wrong.'

'It's something I've got to live with for the rest of me life,' protests Farquharson. The stress he lays on the word *life*, the complex intonation he gives it, makes him sound plaintive, even petulant—a person with a legitimate grievance that is not being taken seriously. 'What I'm trying to say, you can go through and check that I've got no record—'

Courtis picks up on his anxiety. 'Is there anything you want to tell us?'

'No! That's exactly as it happened. I've got no reason to lie, or anything of that nature.'

His coughing fit, he says, must have been triggered by the car heater, which he had turned on when the kids said they were cold. He has recently been off work for eight days with this cough, one of those colds that linger on. Has he been smoking dope? He gives a gasp of laughter: he doesn't do that sort of thing! He's a normal, average guy, trying to make a living and do the best by his family—and look what he's done now.

'Mate, it's a tragic thing. Your children in the car—what are their names?'

Jai. Tyler. Bailey. Farquharson intones them, spacing them out in a solemn hush.

Courtis breaks it. His voice is soft. 'Did the car just go away from under you? How far under the water did your car go? Did you have to put your head under water? How many times did you have to duck under the water?'

'Oh, several. Several times, probably about three or four or something.' Stammering and chattering, Farquharson tells the story for the third time. Then he lets out a hard panting sound, and puts again his urgent question: 'I mean, I mean, what sort of thing's going to happen to *me*, now?'

'Well,' says one of the cops.

'You don't know, do you.' Again the little nasal out-breath of laughter, the striving for a casual tone, making light of his need to know.

'We haven't even been to the crash site yet. We're on our way down there now.'

Farquharson tries once more. 'What's the scenario? Got no idea?'

Courtis answers vaguely, dreamily. 'We'll go to the scene and have a look, and we'll come back and let you know what's going on.'

...

I took a quick look at Farquharson. He was sitting quite still, staring straight ahead. Were his sisters' hearts in their boots? I remembered Cindy Gambino's account of the way he had stood in front of the car at the dam while would-be rescuers desperately rushed about. 'There was no movement. He wasn't doing anything. He was like in a trance.'

He didn't sound entranced on that tape. He sounded... something else, something not quite right. Too quick to answer? Too eager to please? A nose dive, in foot-deep water? And when they pulled the car out of the dam, wasn't the heater off? My head was full of a very loud clanging. Nothing expert, nothing trained or intellectual. Just a shit-detector going off, that was all. The alarm bells of a woman who had been in the world for more than sixty years, knowing men, sometimes hearing them say true things, sometimes being told lies.

What had passed through Farquharson's mind, that night, on the dark country road where there was nothing to distract a driver from his wild thoughts? Were the boys squabbling? Was there a painful mention of their mother's new man? Or did they just sit quietly in their harnesses as the old car rolled along, making their father's heart ache that once more he had to give them back and say goodbye? Did a casual word, a rush of despair cause everything that he had shored up against his ruins to buckle and give way?

And could it be that, underneath it all, naked on that hospital gurney, he was not yet grieving, but seething instead with incredulous vitality? Was a fresh force surging through this dull, lonely, broken-hearted man, deafening him, obliterating without shame or mercy everything but the astonishing fact that he was still alive?

Wheels leave different traces as they pass over the surface of the earth. A skid mark happens when all four wheels lock and are dragged along the ground by the vehicle's momentum. A yaw mark occurs typically when a car is over-steered, and front and back tyres track separately, leaving four tyre marks instead of two. And a rolling print is simply the impression left by a cleanly rotating wheel: a raised pattern of tyre tread in gravel or dirt; grass pushed down in the direction of the vehicle's travel. In the paddock between the road and the dam, Farquharson's car had left rolling prints. This undisputed fact was something we—and no doubt the jury—had to hang on to grimly, during Mr Morrissey's blistering cross-examinations of the police.

...

Mr Rapke began with Senior Constable Courtis of Major Collision. After the unsettling interview with Farquharson at Geelong Emergency, Courtis drove on to the dam. It was a clear night and the road was dry, but by the time Courtis came down the overpass at about 11 p.m., he noticed the odd patch of drifting fog. The murkily lit rescue attempt was spread out on the right-hand side of the road. He parked, and set about his task: to survey the scene and take photos of it.

The only tyre prints he found in the roadside gravel were the ones that Sergeant Exton, his boss, had already marked with the dashes of yellow paint. With his torch Courtis followed the pair of rolling prints that ran through the long grass down to the edge of the water. Only when he looked back up towards the road did he notice that the angle of Exton's paint marks was not right: it did not match up precisely with the angle of the rolling prints.

Here Courtis struck a snag. While he was trying to set up a new piece of surveying equipment, a Riegl 3D laser scanner, he bent one of the fine prongs on its cable. Because he didn't have a spare cable, he packed up the Riegl and used instead Major Collision's older and more familiar device, the geodimeter, sometimes known as George.

On the stand, the young police officer battled to express in ordinary language the digital and mechanical capabilities of the Riegl scanner and the geodimeter. His testimony was studded with terms like *infrared*, *dot-to-dot*, *prism*, *raw data* and *numerical codes*. The jurors were given small bound books of photos that Rapke referred to by numbers, but in the press seats, lacking a clear view of the visual aids and having to follow by ear, we stumbled behind.

When Morrissey rose to cross-examine, the atmosphere of the court sagged again into a sort of irritable misery. No wonder Courtis's notes had been quivering. He was grilled on why he had not measured the road's camber and crossfall, on whether vehicles necessarily left tyre prints on bitumen or in gravel, on the accuracy of his coding of the marks he claimed to have seen in gravel and through grass. Morrissey suggested that Courtis was ill-trained and incompetent—'You're not a professional surveyor by any means, are you? You're a professional policeman'—and hinted that this was why he had subsequently been transferred from Major Collision to the Child Sexual Offences and Child Abuse Unit. Pressed to agree that the path of the rolling prints was 'a smooth arc without any noticeable wiggles in it—more or less a straight line but bending somewhat to the right', Courtis would go no further than to say, 'Yes, there was a curve in it.'

Morrissey's aim seemed to be to establish that there was a lot of traffic in the area that night, that any one of those vehicles might have left the disputed tyre mark in the gravel, and that the police reconstruction of the scene, based on its admittedly imperfect paint marks, was worthless. But his cross-examination induced a crazed feeling of restlessness and frustration. Round and round it went, a flood of detail without graspable shape or direction, except in its constant return to the painfully familiar matter of Sergeant Exton's yellow paint marks. Morrissey kept starting a sentence with the word 'now', as if about to bring his line of questioning around in a meaningful curve, but he never reached resolution. There was no relief. My mind lost its grip and slid away into reverie.

'Maybe he thinks,' whispered Louise, 'that if he drags this out long enough the jury will forget that tape.'

Indeed, the Emergency interview had made an impression so deeply disturbing that everything coming after it seemed to be beside the point. By now, close to the end of the third week of the trial, the very words 'yellow paint marks' provoked a Pavlovian response. The jurors glazed over and turned sullen. They rested their chins on their fists. Their eyelids drooped. Their necks grew loose with boredom; they were limp with it, barely able to hold themselves erect. Once I glanced over and saw four of them in a row, their heads dropped on the same protesting angle towards their left shoulders, like tulips dying in a vase.

And hour after hour, as he laboured, Morrissey was tormented by terrific bouts of dry coughing. He barked, he croaked, he sweated and turned pale. Long pauses fell while he composed himself. Justice Cummins coddled him affectionately, offered to adjourn at lunchtime on Friday so he could rest his voice for two and a half days, threatened trouble if he saw him at the football at the MCG. Morrissey was embarrassed. He grinned and ducked his head and said that he would soldier on till the end of the week.

Then, first thing on Friday morning, before the jury was called in, Morrissey told the judge that he had stayed up working half the night and would now be able to finish his cross-examination by lunchtime.

Justice Cummins' brow came down. Overnight, he said sharply, inquiries had come from the jury: how much longer was this trial likely to go on? Some of these jurors were going to work before court, or during the lunch break. They were serious people, applying themselves to their task. They had made arrangements to cancel this afternoon's work, and now they were to be told they would be released by lunchtime. They were not rag dolls to be thrown aside for the convenience of counsel. They had lives to lead. They should be treated properly.

Morrissey stood at the bar table staring down at his hands. He looked offended, even wounded. Why, yesterday the judge had practically tucked him up in bed with a hot-water bottle. Today, he was rapping Morrissey's knuckles with a ruler.

But Farquharson's supporters gazed loyally at their wigged champion. They believed in him. They urged him on. When Louise's mother slipped into court one day to see what her daughter had been raving about, she looked around in surprise and said, 'It feels like a family in here.' The cramped court had become an intimate space, intimate enough for Morrissey—this decent, warm and very endearing man, perhaps sentimental, perhaps a little vain—to identify with his client to the point where, in its paroxysms of coughing, his own body was acting out Farquharson's story. A story that was becoming more fantastical with every passing day.

...

On the Monday of the trial's fourth week, the Crown introduced a crucial witness.

Hostility showed in the rigid shoulders of Farquharson's sisters as the man climbed the steps to the stand. His dark hair was freshly cut. In his jeans, runners and striped short-sleeved shirt he affected a rockabilly jauntiness. But his crisp-featured face was expressionless, his posture tense and wary. His name was Greg King; he was a bus driver; and he was about to be dragged through the sort of public ordeal that most people face only in nightmares from which, gasping and sweating, they are grateful to wake.

'Mr King,' said Rapke. 'Do you know a man by the name of Robert Farquharson?'

'Yes, I do.'

'How do you know him?'

'We grew up together. He's a friend of mine, a mate, a family friend.'

The two mates kept their faces turned in opposite directions. From my seat I could see them in profile, each resolutely avoiding the other's eye.

They were Winch boys. They went to the local primary school a few years apart, and then to Geelong Tech. They did not really become friends until King at twenty and Farquharson at seventeen found jobs with the local shire council. Outside work they played football together, and hung out at the pub or at King's house. By the time Farquharson and Cindy Gambino got serious, King and his wife, Mary, had already started their family, and the men's friendship began to dwindle.

When Rapke asked him to describe the relationship between Farquharson and Gambino, King began to breathe audibly. His voice grew husky. They were always *at* each other, he said. He had urged them to see that as a couple you have to bond, but they kept on niggling and arguing. When they married, they already had two children. King went to their wedding. He and Mary would visit them for a barbecue, or the two couples would go down to the pub for tea. But, as the pressures of parenthood increased, Rob and Cindy argued all the time, particularly about money. Robbie was never happy in his job—not on the shire, not in the Jim's Mowing franchise, not even at the Cumberland Resort. King seemed to be describing a pair of ill-matched malcontents: a grumbling husband, a demanding wife. In his opinion, they had got way ahead of themselves by trying to build a $300,000 house on one wage. They had a habit, he had said in his witness statement, of measuring themselves against what other people had. Farquharson complained to King that Cindy was always buying things they couldn't afford.

'Cindy always wanted the best of everything for the house,' said King. 'She wanted the *best*.'

Hearing this, Farquharson glanced at his sisters and executed a veritable dance of grinning and squinting and shoulder-squirming. Kerri Huntington returned a sardonic nod.

When the marriage ended, King went to see Farquharson at his dad's place once a week or so, 'to comfort him, because we were mates. He was down. He was gloomy. He was angry and upset of what had happened.' One night Farquharson said to him, 'Cindy's seeing someone else, the bitch.' King did not tell him that he already knew this from talk around town. Once, in a dark mood about the break-up, Farquharson spoke to King about driving off a cliff or running his car into a tree.

Again Farquharson swung his head towards his family in the public benches. He rolled his eyes and twisted his mouth into a bitter smile, as if at an outrageous lie.

'What did you say to that?' asked Rapke.

'I said,' muttered King between hard lips, '"Don't be stupid."'

A month or so after the Farquharsons parted, King was driving out of his street on to the highway, heading west to the Winchelsea shops, when he saw Robbie sitting in his white Commodore under a tree on the other side. He was looking straight ahead in an easterly direction, down the road to Geelong. King made eye contact on his way past, but kept going. Farquharson started his car and took off in the opposite direction.

When they ran into each other later that week, King asked him, 'Was that you sitting under a tree? What were you doing?'

'I was thinking,' replied Farquharson, 'about lining a truck up.'

King went home and reported this to his wife. They agreed that it was Robbie 'talking shit again', and swept it under the carpet.

...

One Friday evening in the winter of 2005, a few months before Father's Day, Mary King asked her husband to drive to the fish-and-chip shop and bring home some hot chips for tea. Lucy and Lachlan, their two youngest kids, went along for the ride. King sent them into the shop to order, while he waited outside in the car.

As it happened, Farquharson was in the shop with his three boys. He wandered out and stood by King's open window to chat. He seemed tired and down in the dumps. His mood did not improve when Cindy Gambino drove up and parked. She walked past and greeted the men by name. King spoke to her, but Farquharson would not. When Gambino disappeared into the shop, King rebuked him for his rudeness.

'You have to say hello. Come on, Robbie. You have to move on a bit.'

'No, you don't,' said Farquharson. He was very angry. 'Nobody does that to me and gets away with it. That fucking car she's driving, I paid $30,000 for it. She wanted it, and they're fucking driving it. Look what I'm driving—the fucking shit one. And now it looks like she wants to marry that fucking dickhead. There's no way I'm going to let him and her and the kids live together in my house, and I have to fucking pay for it and also pay maintenance for the kids—no way.'

'You have to move on,' insisted King.

Farquharson said, 'How?'

In the court, a tense pause. Rapke waited, squinting, face upturned. King shifted from foot to foot. He stammered. With an effort of will, he kept going: 'And then he said, "I'm going to take away the most important things that mean to her." I asked him what that would be, and he nodded his head towards the fish-and-chip shop window.

'I said, "What—the kids?"

'He said, "Yes."

'I said, "What would you do? Take them away or something?"

'He just stared at me in my eyes and said, "Kill them."'

From the dock Farquharson looked across at his sisters and violently shook his head. He kept squinching up his eyes and tucking his chin into his collar, in a pantomime of incensed denial.

King stopped to collect himself. He picked up the glass with a shaking hand and took a great swig of water.

'I said, "Bullshit. It's your own flesh and blood, Robbie."'

His voice was barely audible. Farquharson strained to hear, his eyebrows high in his forehead.

'He said, "So? I hate them."

'I said, "You'd go to gaol."

'He said, "No I won't. I'll kill myself before it gets to that."

'I asked him how. He said it would be close by. I said, *What?*'

'He said, "There'd be an accident involved where I survive and the kids don't. It'd be on a special day."

'I said, "What kind of day?"'

'He said, "Something like Father's Day, so everyone would remember it. Father's Day, and *I* was the one to have them for the last time—not her. Then she suffers for the rest of her life every Father's Day."'

'I said, "You don't even dream of that stuff, Robbie!"'

At that moment Lucy and Lachlan ran out of the shop with the chips. King drove them home. His wife was busy cooking the evening meal. She was cross with him for having taken so long. The TV was on, the family room full of the teatime racket of four young children. King told Mary about the conversation. They disregarded it as another bout of Robbie's shit. For several months they thought no more about it.

Then came Father's Day. At eleven o'clock that night the Kings got a phone call from some friends in the town. Robbie had had an accident and the boys had drowned in a dam.

'It all come back to me, the conversation,' said King. He swallowed hard. 'I asked how Robbie was. They said "Robbie's well. He's in hospital." I was speechless. I was—shattered.' Muscles stood out in his jaw and neck. He gripped the rail of the witness stand.

Rapke peered up at him from the bar table. For the next chapter of the story he needed his witness to stay in one piece.

'We'll do this,' he said, 'step by step.'

King's boss at the bus company noticed the wrecked state his employee was in, and started asking questions. King broke down and spilt the beans. The boss, who was a former member of the police force, made some calls. Eleven days later, on the morning after Jai, Tyler and Bailey were buried, two detectives from the Homicide

Squad drove from Melbourne to King's house in Winchelsea. When they had listened to his story, they asked King if he would go to visit Farquharson at his father's place, raise the subject of the fish-and-chip-shop conversation and tape his mate's responses on a hidden recorder.

That same evening, after dark, the devastated King met the detectives at the Modewarre boat ramp, a drought-stricken launching place at the end of an unsealed road a few kilometres east of Winchelsea. In this obscure and tree-sheltered spot, the detectives set him up with a wire. King drove away from the shrunken lake and headed back to the town, with microphones stuck to his torso and a recorder down the front of his pants.

...

The tape that King came away with that night, which the Crown now proposed to play to the jury, was an hour and forty minutes long. The subject of the fish-and-chip-shop conversation was not raised until forty-seven pages into the transcript. Rapke, the prosecutor, had little interest in what he called 'banter between men about football'. He asked Justice Cummins' leave to edit the tape down to the ten pages that he considered relevant—a mere twenty minutes' worth. But Morrissey leapt to his feet. No! The whole tape must be played, for what it revealed about Farquharson's mental state, and about the relationship between the two friends.

Justice Cummins ruled in Morrissey's favour. While everyone moved and stretched, preparing for another bout of intense concentration, Cummins reminded the jury that the evidence was not the typed transcript they had been given to follow. The transcript was only a guide. The evidence was the sounds on the tape. He urged them to pay attention to pauses, to emphasis and tone.

...

The King we hear greet his friends—he is taken aback to find another mate, Mick Stocks, already ensconced with Farquharson—is at first hardly recognisable as the choked figure on the witness stand. His voice is expressive to the point of being musical. *We*, he says, like a social worker or a doctor. How are we? How are we going, mate? All right? He apologises for 'yesterday' but says he has been 'up there' this morning, to pay respect.

'Yesterday=funeral,' scrawled Louise. 'He didn't go?' We sat forward.

But after these awkward greetings, the three men subside into an hour of rambling, murmuring talk. Football, cars, more football. Is it cheaper to drive or fly to Queensland? Football again. The beauty of Las Vegas rising out of the desert: they dream of seeing it. A new cure for snoring, the price of firewood, King's damaged knee and imminent arthroscopy, yet more football. Somehow Farquharson keeps his end up while the others tactlessly compare notes on the sporting and educational progress of local children. On and on it winds, the droning of nasal voices, this visit by men helpless to address the reason for their call: their mate's appalling loss. And all the while in the background, faithful to its task of relieving social anxiety, the television pours out manic energy: screeching tyres, a gunshot, a woman's scream, a police siren, a booming American voice-over.

Farquharson, like the jury, had been provided with headphones, which made him look oddly more adult. The transcript lay open on the chair beside him and he stooped over it, his only expression one of distant scepticism. Some of the journalists seemed to be already writing their pieces. In the family seats the women held themselves erect. Kerri Huntington played a little private game with the cuffs of her cardigan, making them dance and do silent claps. But the dark-jacketed shoulders of Farquharson's brothers-in-law were bowed forward, their elbows braced against their knees and their hands clasped in the churchgoer's posture: the endurance of tedium. I noticed a small, silky brown head between Stephen Moules and Bev Gambino. It was Cindy. She was rocking gently back and forth in her seat.

After a hundred minutes of laborious talk, the good-humoured Mick takes his leave. King and Farquharson are at last alone.

'Hey,' says King in a hoarse whisper. 'I'm sorry.'

'I know.' Farquharson's voice is drab, distant. He sounds weary, forcing himself to be hostly. The TV for a moment goes silent. 'A lot of people didn't come. I understand that. It's a million times harder for me, so you don't have to say nothing. I know.'

The hidden microphone is picking up King's nervous breathing. He seizes the nettle. 'But something's been bugging me, though. Remember? Down at the fish shop? Out the front? That discussion.'

'Discussion? About what?'

'This is what's been eating me up,' says King. He sounds on the verge of tears. 'When Cindy pulled up and you said you'd pay her back big-time. I hope it's got nothing to do with that.'

'No. No way,' says Farquharson. 'No, no, no, no, no. You know I would never—'

'Because listen,' whispers King. 'They're coming to interview me. Tomorrow. I'm freaking out.'

And this—King's first straight-out lie—was the moment at which Morrissey's insistence on playing the whole tape seemed fated to backfire. For the preceding hour and a half Farquharson has come across as dully slumped, battling to be sociable, barely able to inject expression into his speech: a man who has lost his reason to live. But now a shot of adrenalin galvanises him. He shows no surprise at what King has said. Immediately he takes command.

'Right,' he says, his voice at confidential volume but very firm. 'I can tell you. Don't stress. Don't freak out. Just tell who I am, what I represent and all that, I never, *ever* would do anything like that.'

'I've been off work,' murmurs King miserably. 'I shook, and all.'

Farquharson canters straight over him. 'All you have to say to them is who I am. As far as you know, we got along. She's *told* them that we got along. It was just a figure of speech of me being angry. But I would never do anything like that. I've got to live with this for the rest of my life, and it kills me.'

'Oh,' stammers King, 'but that's what's been killing *me*.'

Their voices are low and tense. They must be sitting facing each other, leaning in.

'I've been up there,' says Farquharson, with a muffled force. 'I went through four and a half hours of hell. I looked everyone in the eye and I've told the truth. I'm not lying to anyone. All you've got to do is say, "He's a good bloke. I've known him for a long time. He's always been good with his kids." And if they ask about us, say, "As

---

far as I know, they got along." Or if you don't know something, say, "I don't know that."'

'I'm scared, mate,' says King, dry-mouthed, his voice full of darkness.

'They're not gonna ask ya. Don't be scared. Look at the positive things.' Farquharson's voice rises a few tones, and starts to flow. 'They've interviewed her. They've said she said, "No way known would he do anything like that." What—I'm not a mongrel, I'm not a bastard, I'm not an arsehole, I'm not a cunt. I would never, ever, *ever*. That has never entered my mind. What I meant by paying her back was "One day I'll stand here with a woman in front of you and see how you like it." Say you know me. "He's always spoilt his kids. Taking them to the footy, playing footy with them." All the times you'd be going for a walk and you'd see us going for a bike ride. Heavily involved with the kids and their sport. Look at all the good things you saw that I done. Always say the positive things.'

'Rob, it's driving me crazy, mate.'

'You can't say something like that, because then they'll get thinking…' He trails off, then rallies. 'We did get along. We did, in the end. Look, she doesn't *blame* me. I tell you right now, if I did that on purpose I would've killed myself. I've looked everyone in the eye. I've told the truth. I've had this flu. I had a coughing fit. I've blacked out. That is no bullshit. I've got to live with myself. I've got to.'

'Oh Jesus, mate!' King bursts out.

'*And*,' says Farquharson, 'I loved *them* more than life itself.'

Without using the word, he slides into the subject of suicide. 'That's why Cindy's telling me to be strong. I wanted to go. No one will let me. She's told me I'm backing down if I do. I've had extensive counselling. I still am. I was over-protective. Very over-protective. And I still am. I feel I can't protect them here. I asked her permission and her blessing, and she said no.'

Cindy Gambino listened, leaning forward, her eyes raised to a point on the wall above the jury's heads. Their faces were inscrutable.

The exhausted King is backing away from this fire hydrant he has set off. 'Righto mate,' he says faintly. 'I'm going. I want to go and sleep. I'm bloody...'

'Go and sleep,' says Farquharson. 'Why are they interviewing you? Just for a character?'

'Just a character thing, I suppose.'

'They're only going to ask you what I was like as a person. All you have to do is say, "I've known him for a long time. He's great with the kids, he done this, he done that."'

'All right,' says King. 'I better get home.'

He jingles his car keys, he must be edging towards the door, but Farquharson bores on.

'Look, you can say what you want. That's your business. But if you think negative, you're going to come across negative.' He runs King through it one more time: the sports, the karate, the bike rides, kicking the footy, what a good bloke he is. 'The cops know all that. You'll be right. Just settle. That's all they want.'

'Righto,' says King. 'I'll catch you. See you, Rob.'

A car door slams. A motor turns over.

'Just leaving now,' murmurs King. He is already addressing the detectives, waiting for him back at the dark boat ramp.

...

'My God,' I whispered to Louise. 'Is this like something out of Shakespeare? Double falseness?'

'Not Shakespeare,' she hissed. '*The Sopranos*.'

...

King's recording did not satisfy the Homicide detectives. A month later, on the evening of 13 October 2005, they persuaded him to make a second visit to Farquharson, once again wearing a wire, and press him harder on the details of the fish-and-chip-shop conversation. King, dark-faced with strain, sat next to Detective Sergeant Clanchy behind the bar table while the second tape rolled.

The crunch of boots on gravel announces King's arrival at Kerri Huntington's Mount Moriac house, in which Farquharson, after the funeral, had taken refuge from the ravening attention of the media. But when King presents himself at the front door, a little dog explodes into such wild territorial yapping and growling that, in court, Farquharson and his entire family had to smother their fits of laughter. Kerri Huntington heard herself on the tape: 'Get out, Fox. Get out *now*!' She went bright pink and bowed forward in a convulsion. The rest of the court, reminded of the likeable ordinariness of this family, could not help joining in.

'He's a fiery little thing!' says King.

'Doesn't bite,' says Farquharson. 'Just bloody barks. Let's sit in here.'

Family and dog withdraw. Farquharson tells King about his disturbed nights. His sleep is so broken that he gives up and just sits watching TV. King sees his opening.

'I've been the same, mate. I'm struggling real bad. That conversation, mate. It's killing me.'

This time Farquharson is on the front foot. 'No,' he says, 'but it was never like that. That's what I keep telling ya.'

'Not just "pay her back big-time,"' says King. 'You said to me about taking away what was the most important thing to her. And you nodded your head towards that window in the fish-and-chip shop, mate. I want to get my head clear, because it's fuckin' wreckin' me. I said, "You don't even dream of doing things like that," and Rob, you said to me, "Funny you should say about dreams—I have an accident and survive it, and they don't." That's what you said to me. I want all this stuff off my chest! It's eating me inside like a cancer!'

'I never, never said that,' says Farquharson. 'You're getting it all wrong, all twisted. I meant one day she's going to wake up that I'm not as weak as piss as what she thought—I'm going to *accomplish* something.'

And once more he launches his harangue. His voice is affectless, but still intimate and persuasive, rising at the end of every phrase and sentence, as if listing a series of points in an argument that is laid out coherently in his head. Several times King tries to speak, but Farquharson rolls over him. On and on he goes, tireless, pouring out his explanations, introducing new themes, while King keeps drawing in great, painful sighs that are more like groans; and constantly, in the background, low and persistent, runs the moronic gabbling of the television, its cries and splinterings, and, once, the sharp blast of a whistle.

King's whole purpose, on this visit, was to betray. But there was something strategic, even masterful, about Farquharson's fast-rippling monologue, with its strange rhetorical surges. He sounded like a man talking for his life.

Yes, he was angry with Cindy when she threw up her nose at him. 'I'm driving this good car, and look at *you*'—and now that other cunt was driving it. He was mad at her because she wouldn't sell the house so he could get a better car. His sisters knew she used to treat him like shit. But what King didn't realise, outside the fish-and-chip shop, was that he and Cindy had sorted it all out, that they had become amicable. He would never hurt her, and he definitely would never hurt his kids. Never. Why would someone go from not smacking them to killing them? That's a big gap. Not one person thinks he would do that. It was never there—it's what King has *put* there.

King jacks up. 'It wasn't what I've put there! Come on! Don't blame it all on bloody me!'

All right, Farquharson's not blaming him. He sees now that he should have confided in King, that night, about what he was *really* dreaming of—not revenge on Cindy, but a whole new money-making scheme. He had been thinking for months about buying into a business, a successful yogurt-importing concern worth $300,000 a year that his friend Mark in Lorne might be going to cut him in on, but it was still a secret, so he couldn't talk about it. If King thinks Farquharson could look in the mother of his kids' eyes and tell her a lie and walk away, he'd be an animal. Cindy's belief in him, and his psychologist's, too, is a hundred and fifty per cent. This is what's holding him together—this and his own honesty, his integrity to stand and tell. Tell them the truth. Prove the truth to the end, because that *is* the truth. They've got nothing on him. The police have already told his psychologist that he doesn't fit the profile. When people do things like that, it's a very *planned* thing. Anyway, when people are lying, they fuck up. That lady who poisoned her two kids. They broke her in two and a half hours. *Broke* her. Because she couldn't lie no more. He, on the contrary, has told the truth from the start. He has been steadfast in the face of police interrogation; he will not back down. His three interviews—with the paramedics in the ambulance, with the police in Geelong Emergency, with the detectives at Homicide—were all exactly the same. Again and again he tells King he has misinterpreted everything. He is begging him not to mention any of that. He must wipe it clean out of his head. Wipe it right out. Now.

'I'm going to have to see a counsellor,' says King, miserably. 'Because I can't sleep. It's visions. About what happened. What they had to—what they went through. I'll have to talk about it, mate.'

'For God's sake,' says Farquharson, 'please don't mention that stuff. I'm fearing you're going to say something to incriminate me. The police'll say, "We've interviewed Greg King, he says you're all right, but now he's gone to a counsellor, and the counsellor's said this, and this, and this." And that drags *you* into it. That's what you don't want. I'd have to call Mark and say, "Remember I had a conversation about buying a business?" It goes to another level that's totally irrelevant.'

King makes as if to leave, but Farquharson has him by the sleeve. He's had a freak accident, a tragic accident, and now he's got to live with it. He's not lying. What happened to him is common. Plenty of people have blacked out at the wheel. The trauma team at the hospital all told him there was nothing he could have done. He's not Superman. Even his counsellor's said to him he's got to stop blaming himself. Every day he asks the question, why did this have to happen to me? What have I done?

He ushers King to the door, still talking hard. Remember how he never used to get in fights down the pub when King and the others did? He is upset, he's disappointed, it cuts deep that King should think he'd do such a thing. It's not in his nature. He doesn't want there to be any ramifications.

'All right,' says King. 'I know you were angry that night. And I misinterpreted.'

Farquharson urges King to calm himself by means of the relaxation techniques that his psychologist has taught him to use when he's driving the car. He demonstrates, in a whisper. 'You count. You say, *The tension's gone. The tension's gone. The tension's gone.* Let it flow out.'

Are they already outside in the yard? Night birds pass, with faint, melancholy cries. The chink of keys. A car starts up. But Farquharson talks on and on. He must be leaning down to King's open window, as he did outside the fish-and-chip shop.

'When you drive off from here, you should be able to say, "It's off my chest. He's telling the truth. He's been truthful to everyone, truthful to me." I mean, I'm an honest person. Put it aside. Let it flow out. It's gone. You'll feel so much better. As far as I'm concerned, that's the end of the topic. And it should be for you. You'll sleep a lot better. But if there's any problems, give me a bell before you do any counselling.'

...

People filed out of the court, subdued. Louise and I walked all the way down to Tattersalls Lane with our eyes on the ground.

'I've just lost my doubt,' she said, at the shabby door of the Shanghai Dumpling. 'But not my pity.'

'He wasn't very surprised, was he,' I said. 'You'd almost think he was expecting it.'

She mimicked Farquharson's histrionic trope: 'And I loved *them* more than life itself.'

Students around us were yelling and laughing. We sat in silence. I could hardly meet her eye. To have my residual fantasies of his innocence dismantled, blow by blow, and out of his own mouth, filled me with an emotion I had no name for, though it felt weirdly like shame. Our plates were thumped on to the laminex.

'I'm coming round to that journalist's way of thinking,' said Louise, picking up her chopsticks. 'That he's a selfish, cold-hearted bastard. Who betrayed his children's love and trust in the most horrible way.'

I was straining to hold it at bay. I wanted to think like a juror, to wait for all the evidence, to hold myself in a state where I could still be persuaded by argument.

'Journalists have to work very fast,' I said. 'That must be why they form a detached view so early. We're dilettantes. We've got time to wallow.'

She gave me a wry look. Without another word, we polished off the vegetable dumplings.

...

Was there a form of madness called court fatigue? It would have mortified me to tell Louise about the crazy magical thinking that filled my waking mind and, at night, my dreams: if only Farquharson could be found not guilty, then the boys would not be dead. Cindy would drive home from the court and find them playing kick-to-kick in the yard, or sprawled in their socks on the couch, absorbed in the cartoon channel. Bailey would run to her with his arms out. They would call for something to eat. She would open the fridge and cheerfully start rattling the pots and pans. I could not wait to get home, to haul my grandsons away from their Lego and their light sabres, to squeeze them in my arms until they squirmed. Young boys! How can such wild, vital creatures die? How can this hilarious sweetness be snuffed out forever?

Criminal barristers like to see themselves as free-spirited adventurers, armed with learning and wit, who gallop out to defend the embattled individual against the dead hand of the state. They love to perform. A rill of ironic laughter bubbles under the surface of their discourse. There is something savage in the greatest of them, and their brilliance is displayed to most devastating effect in cross-examination.

Peter Morrissey SC was not vain enough, I thought, to fancy himself one of these dark riders. Still, no woman can ever quite grasp how acutely even the warmest and most decent man cares about what his male peers think of him—even this one who, at a break in proceedings, glanced up into the gallery and saw with a smile of open gladness that his wife was looking down at him as he worked.

...

Greg King was the Crown's star witness. Morrissey could nitpick about road camber and steering-wheel turns and police paint marks till he was blue in the face, but surely it was on the jury's response to King that his defence of Farquharson would stand or fall. Morrissey would have to attack King's memory, his truthfulness, his personal honour, even his sanity. He would have to take him by the throat.

King stood in the witness box in his green-and-yellow-striped cotton shirt, clenching his jaw, waiting for the onslaught.

First Morrissey, in a friendly enough tone, ran him through all the things King had quoted Farquharson saying outside the fish-and-chip shop on that Friday night. King agreed to all of them. Then Morrissey narrowed it down. Was King really alleging that Robbie 'then just stared at me in my eyes and said, "Kill them"?'

'That's correct.'

Morrissey raised his chin. 'That's false, isn't it? You didn't put that to him on either of the two tapes, did you?'

King began to mumble. 'I was too stressed and—'

'Don't worry about that,' said Morrissey sharply. 'You didn't, did you?'

'No.'

Morrissey leaned forward, propped his big footballer's torso on both fists and let fly. Had King then said to Farquharson, 'Bullshit, that's your own flesh and blood, Robbie'? And had Farquharson replied, 'So? I hate them'? That too was false, wasn't it? And when King warned him he would go to gaol, surely Farquharson hadn't really replied that he would kill himself before it got to that? Weren't these very *extreme* statements? Farquharson had never before told King he was going to hurt his children, had he? Hadn't he only ever said that he loved his kids? Beautiful kids, weren't they? They obviously loved their dad, didn't they? Farquharson gave them a lot of affection, did he not? Yet didn't King claim that Farquharson had even told him the *place* and *date* of this cold-blooded murder of his three kids? Three beautiful kids? Yes? Is that what King claimed?

'Yes,' whispered King, flinching and changing colour.

Morrissey reared back and plunged his hands into the sleeves of his gown. 'Did you ring Cindy Gambino,' he asked, in a tone of incredulous challenge, 'and let her know?'

Gambino uttered a single sharp cry, and began to sob aloud.

'No,' muttered King.

No? What about the police? No? The teacher at the school? No? Did King call Robbie the next day and say, 'Robbie, you were saying some way-out things—how are you travelling?'

'No.'

King had had a lot of bad dreams about this, hadn't he, since he learnt of the children being drowned in a horrendous way in the dam? Yes? His ability to sleep was effectively destroyed at that time? And he had visions? Visions meaning waking pictures in his awake mind? Visions he could not control, right? They kept butting in on him, no matter how he tried to close them out? Visions of the children drowning? Yes? Dying? Terribly upsetting visions?

King stood there sweating, gripping the rail of the stand. His face hardened, blanched, turned dark. In these few minutes he seemed to have aged ten years. 'Yes,' he whispered. 'Of the kids. Yes.'

And the visions King had, said Morrissey, were of Robbie being very bad, weren't they? Telling King he was going to kill the children so as to upset Cindy? And these visions remained untreated until King went to get counselling in December 2005 or January 2006?

Untreated. I sat up. Was Morrissey going to pathologise poor

King and his horrible visions?

'You've got your own kids, correct?' said Morrissey. 'You were shocked and upset when you heard about the death of the three kids? And then you struggled desperately to remember the conversation you'd had with Robert Farquharson two months previously? You had a lot of trouble remembering that conversation in any detail, right?'

King, choking, stuck gamely to his estimate. 'I was eighty per cent sure.'

'You claim Mr Farquharson said he would do this on Father's Day? So everyone would remember it? And he would be the one to have the children for the last time, not her?'

'That's what he said.'

'And then every Father's Day Cindy would suffer for the rest of her life?'

'That's right.'

'Did you say, "You don't even dream of that, Robbie"?'

'Yes.'

And yet, said Morrissey, King did not raise the fish-and-chip-shop conversation after that day with anyone except his wife, Mary?

No, he didn't.

Then the children died on 4 September? King made his statements to the police? He made the first secret tape and handed it to the police at the Modewarre boat ramp?

'That's correct.'

'And after *that*,' cried Morrissey triumphantly, 'you went on a *skiing holiday*!'

This was too much even for the battered King. He straightened

---

his back and protested, 'Ye-es! Up to me brother's!'

Morrissey stormed on. After all his secret taping and his *four* statements to the police, did King go into counselling at the Bethany Support Centre to deal with the intrusive visions, nightmares and problems that he was having?

He did.

King knew the Farquharson boys, right? He would never have exposed them to any danger?

No, he would not.

And *because of his upset state of mind*, King had got the details of the fish-and-chip-shop conversation horribly wrong, hadn't he? Up to the point where he said Farquharson had nodded towards his children through the window of the fish-and-chip shop, all right, that was fair enough—but everything else was stuff he had added in his later statements, was it not? Robbie never said he was going to kill them, did he? He never said he was going to drown them in a dam on Father's Day, did he?

Yes, yes, he did.

What he said to King was no more than a separated bloke's grumble outside the fish shop on a Friday night, wasn't it?

No!

And if King had really told his wife all these terrible things when he got home with the chips, then how come Mary King said in her witness statement, and at the committal hearing, that she had absolutely no memory of being told any such thing? Surely their kitchen couldn't have been *that* noisy?

Their house was always noisy.

By the time he came to write out his statement for the Homicide detectives, three months after the fateful Father's Day, King could no longer distinguish facts, could he, from the visions he'd been having in the *very disturbed state of mind* he'd been in since the children drowned?

'It all come back to me,' said King wretchedly, 'in the night I got the phone call.'

Morrissey was on a roll. Robbie's so-called *dream* in which 'the kids go into the dam, I survive and they don't'—where was this dream in the police statements? It wasn't there, was it? It had vanished from King's memory! Would King agree that there was a major, major difference between Farquharson saying on the one hand, '*I've had a dream that I go into the dam and the kids don't get out but I do*' and, on the other hand, '*I'm going to kill them in the dam, it'll be an accident where I survive and they don't*'? One's a dream, isn't it? And the other's a threat, a reality? Did King see the difference?

Yes. King, roasting on the spit, could see the difference.

His memory had been destroyed, hadn't it, by the trauma he had gone through? He'd been treated for post-traumatic stress disorder, had he not? He had even come to see himself, hadn't he, as a victim of crime? Had he, in fact, made a claim for money at the Victims of Crime Assistance Tribunal, on the basis that he was a primary victim of crime?

'I've got a form to fill out, yes,' whispered King.

Morrissey rested his palms on the edge of the bar table, and lowered his voice from the thunder of oratory to a kinder, more conversational level.

'I know I'm crossing swords with you on some things,' he said.

'The reality is that you have been terribly traumatised. And you're not lying about that, are you. It's still something that causes you trouble now?'

'I just want this over,' King burst out, in a voice cracked with tears.

'You're looking for something to finish the pain you're in, correct? In the days after you heard the terrible news that the children were dead, you told the police you were pretty wrecked? You said you had to get it off your chest? It had been going over and over in your head? You couldn't put it all together? You were crying constantly? It was eating you up? It was freaking you out? You shook? It was killing you? You were being placed under intolerable emotional stress? You were scared you were going to have a nervous breakdown? You couldn't sleep?'

'I was under too much stress,' said King obstinately, sensing he was being led somewhere, not sure whether he should follow. 'I was traumatised.'

'You wanted to get it off your chest because that might give you some relief from the horrible tension you were undergoing?'

'Yes.'

'What I'm putting to you,' said Morrissey, 'is that your memory is playing you tricks because of the terrible situation you're in. If Mr Farquharson had said anything *like* the extreme things that your evidence contains, you'd have done something about it, Mr King, wouldn't you—if he really said it?'

'He said it,' muttered King between clenched teeth. Then, in his misery, he broke out again, 'Why would I lie about something like that?'

'You saw it as being of therapeutic relevance to you, to come to some sort of memory?'

King stared at him.

'You needed to remember something in order to get better?'

'It was coming back to me in bits and pieces,' King insisted.

'The trouble is,' said Morrissey, ramping it up again, 'what you've done is to put extreme and terrible words into Mr Farquharson's mouth which he didn't say. The reason you didn't call Cindy, the police, or anyone else is because these extreme statements that you attribute to Mr Farquharson were not made at all!'

'Why would I?' cried King. 'Why would I want to go and do *that* to somebody?'

...

It was four o'clock. The judge excused the haggard witness and sent the jury home. Mr Morrissey's fighting posture loosened and he gave in to his harsh, barking cough. His skin looked pale and waxy. He wiped sweat from his brow with the sleeve of his big black gown. 'I'm worried about him,' whispered Louise. Justice Cummins too, as court rose for the day, gave him several concerned glances. Perhaps this performance of ferocity was violating something in Morrissey. I wondered if he was getting any sleep, what his dreams were telling him, and if he could afford to pay them any attention.

...

Next morning my brother, a chef, chanced to walk past the coffee cart on his way to the Victoria Market. He stopped to say hello, and I introduced him to Bob and Bev Gambino. While the two men keenly compared notes on the beauties of squid and how to clean and cook it, Louise and I turned aside with Bev. I asked her how they were managing. I did not expect a detailed reply, but in her gentle, friendly voice, not dramatising it or trying to impress, she offered one.

'You've got this *mask* all over you,' she said, and made a huge gesture with her flat palms down the front of her person, from forehead to knees. 'You get up. You drive to work. You take the mask off and you do what's expected of you. Then you drive home, and on the way the mask comes back, so you can handle everything that's going on there.'

I looked at her in confusion. I could hardly correct her, but wasn't her image the wrong way round? Wouldn't she need the mask *outside* her home?

'See,' she went on, 'we haven't been able to grieve for our boys. All this has been hanging over us like a cloud for two years. We have counselling. They teach you techniques. But it goes so deep. It cuts you to the bone.'

...

The journalists came bouncing into the court. One of the commercial radio guys slid into the seat beside me. Had we watched *MythBusters* last night? It was about opening car doors under water. Apparently you can't do it till the car fills up and the inner and outer pressures equalise.

I said in a low voice, 'So, what does this mean? About Jai opening…'

He turned his whole body in the seat so that his back was towards Farquharson's family, and mouthed at me, as if to a simpleton, 'It means he's lying.'

I glanced across at Mr Rapke, leaning back in his cushioned swivel chair, one hand clamped around his jaw. He looked like a general in possession of an arsenal packed with weapons so fearsome and so accurate that I contemplated him with awe.

…

Greg King presented himself for the final round of the defence's attack on his credibility. The shirt he had put on that morning bore an image of his ordeal: it was white, with fine black vertical stripes, and printed on its chest was a shatter of black and crimson, like words exploding in a gush of blood.

Today he would be painted by Morrissey as a pathetic figure, a broken man whose nerve had weakened and snapped, whose word could not be trusted—and not because he was a bad person, but because he could not help himself. He had 'mental issues'. He was so demoralised and damaged that he had learnt his statement by heart and simply recited it to the court instead of answering questions afresh. Worse, by allowing the police to wire him he had disgracefully betrayed his mate's trust. Morrissey laid on the pathos with a trowel. Robbie was a pretty lovable bloke, wasn't he? Hadn't he spoken to King in a confiding way, as a friend? Hadn't King himself become emotional and tearful during the conversation, even though all that time he knew he had a tape recorder *running secretly in his clothes*?

King squirmed and sweated. He kept pressing his hands into the small of his back, like someone in pain. Again and again, to explain the sporadic return of his memories, he pleaded stress and confusion. His voice trembled and cracked. 'He's a good mate, you know.' He could no longer hold back his tears.

'He's not a good mate for nothing, is he?' said Morrissey sternly. 'He's a good mate because he's a good *person*.'

'He's my mate, yes,' wept King.

'And you saw him, didn't you, at a footy club junior presentation, with Bailey in his arms, on the Friday night before Father's Day? Wasn't Cindy there too? If there was any truth in your memory of these threats, wouldn't you have warned her that Robbie was planning to murder the kids in two days' time? Your memory of the fish-and-chip conversation is false, isn't it? Isn't it false?'

But somehow, in his strangled, suffering way, Greg King stood firm. He drew it up from the depths of himself one more time, in a hoarse whisper: 'It's true.'

I indulged myself in a long, slow, careful look at the jury. They were sitting erect, focused, with clear eyes and solemn faces.

...

Greg King's wife, Mary, was a slender, long-haired young woman in a fashionable trenchcoat. On the evening of the notorious fish-and-chip-shop encounter, Greg had come back late with the chips and thrown out her timing. The chops were burning. She was short with him. All she wanted was to get the chops off the grill before they were inedible, and feed the four kids. She did not remember being told what Greg and Robbie had talked about down at the shops. She had no memory of being told that Robbie planned to murder his children. She didn't know if Greg had discussed it in detail with her, because she didn't remember. She was busy doing other things. Mime disbelief as he might, Morrissey could not rattle her. She simply declined to engage with him about it. She was phlegmatic, unruffled, a study in refusal; yet where one might have expected her to appear evasive, she showed instead a stolid, housewifely composure.

'I will say,' was all she would concede, 'that my husband's been very upset over the whole matter.'

It was the end of the court morning. As the journalists were getting to their feet, Morrissey shoved along the bar table past his junior's chair and faced us with his hands planted squarely on his hips.

'Those chops!' he shouted, with a scornful laugh. 'How important can a burning chop be?'

...

Louise and I stepped out of the building into weak spring sunlight. We slid round the mob of photographers and found ourselves walking east on Lonsdale Street only a few metres behind Greg and Mary King. We trailed them discreetly for a block.

'How can she not remember?' I whispered. 'Why would she lie about it? Or maybe he didn't tell her? Maybe he feels he should have, and wishes he had, and finally convinced himself that he did?'

'I think she's repressed it,' said Louise. She made a little vertical barrier with her flat hands. 'It must be something she deeply feels doesn't belong in her life. And she just refuses to let it come in.'

'Mind you,' I said, 'wives do get used to not listening.'

The minute the Kings got out of media range, they reached for each other with the habitual gesture of a couple, and headed down the hill, hand in hand, with brisk, firm steps.

...

Everybody knows that memory is not a simple accessible file whose contents remain undisturbed from one inspection to the next. Memory is an endless, lifelong process, fluid, active and mysterious. Nobody should be surprised, then, that King had remembered things in bursts. But what, if anything, did it mean that, according to King's first statement, Farquharson had merely spoken of revenge and nodded towards his boys through the fish-and-chip-shop window, yet in the later statements had said that he hated the boys and wanted to kill them?

I did not think Greg King was a liar. Nor did I see him as the broken-spirited wreck that Morrissey had laboured to conjure up. Still, something in me baulked at the idea that Farquharson would have come out with such an explicit statement of intent. *Hate? Kill?* I tried and failed to hear him.

As it happens, I have kept a diary for most of my adult life. Like any journal-keeper, I have a sharpened understanding of the way memory works. Once in a while, years or even decades after some painful or important personal event of which I have retained the most crisply detailed memories, I get an urge to read what I wrote on the day in question. I hunt out the exercise book and locate the exact date. There is rarely anything surprising in the content: the story is always sorely familiar. But I am often taken aback to find that aspects of the experience that I had clearly remembered in the form of spoken dialogue turn out to have been no more than thoughts or silent insights I had had in the heat of the moment and had recorded as such in the evening. As time has passed, as the occasion has drifted in and out of my mind, my memory has worked, without my conscious knowledge, to make explicit these waves of emotion and private mental activity. It has translated them into passages of direct speech and enclosed them in quotation marks. Yet, though they were at the time 'no more than thoughts or silent insights', and though they were never uttered by me or anyone else as speech, I notice upon rereading them that they still ring true to the tenor of the experience. I can even say, with the authority of hindsight, that they are the most convincing part of the account.

Mild sunlight on the dam. Puffy spring clouds. The paddock is grassy. Its fence is lined with thin saplings. A maroon Commodore, passenger side facing us, is dangling horizontal from a crane, its tyres barely a metre above the surface of the water. Men on the bank study the car as it hangs. A shadowy figure with an unnaturally large head is ensconced in the driver's seat. Down glides the Commodore on its chains, gently, slowly, guided from the bank by wire cables. The sun makes huge spangles on its duco. Just above the water it hovers. Behind the closed window the masked diver at the steering wheel sticks up his thumb, then makes a forceful gesture. The chains slacken and the car drops into the water, flat on its belly. It tips forward at once and begins to sink. The rising water level slices on an angle across the centre of its doors. The diver, visible only as head and shoulders, leans across towards the passenger door and tries to open it. He fights with it, fails, then turns his body more squarely towards it and tries again. It opens a crack, and shuts. The car is going down.

Farquharson's face, watching the video in Court Three, was

stretched into a gape of anguish. He held his handkerchief to his cheeks with both hands. Bob Gambino and Farquharson's brothers-in-law strained to look up at the high screen, but the three wives sat facing rigidly ahead.

Now the diver at the wheel turns his back to the camera on the bank and tackles his own door. He opens it with apparent ease. Water must be rushing in, for the car lurches and tilts to that side. In a few seconds the front half of the vehicle is completely submerged. Its boot sticks up at a helpless angle.

The screen goes black. Then suddenly the camera is inside the car, at roof height, looking down on to the front passenger seat and the interior panel of its door: we are seeing everything again, from a new perspective. The diver's left hand comes into shot and reaches for the passenger door's latch. He tries it, fails, then changes hands, grabs the latch with his right hand and puts all his weight behind his left palm which he slides rearward on the door. It opens a crack. Water gushes in and fills the footwell to the rim of the seat, where a passenger's knees would be. The diver lets go his pressure, and the door clips shut, cutting off the flow. A second of stability. Then another violent surge of water comes roiling up the video screen, a creamy greenish tan, seething with distorted bubbles and flecks of matter. In seconds it obliterates everything but itself. The camera goes on faithfully recording, its gaze fixed on the blurred edge of the car's instrument panel, but then it too is drowned, and the screen goes dark.

This was the first of the police submergence tests.

The diver stepped into the witness stand like a character from an action movie: Leading Senior Constable Simeon Ranik of the Search and Rescue Squad, a tall, powerfully built, dark-bearded fellow with a rumbling voice.

Very little water was coming into the car, he said, until he opened the passenger door. As we saw, water rose to knee level. When he shut the door, helped by the water pressure from outside, the flow almost stopped. As for the driver's door, it was fairly easy to hold it open for a number of seconds. When he took his hand off the door and placed it on the steering wheel, the force of the water rushing in closed the door. By then, the water was up to his waist. He tried several times to re-open the door, but could not get it open. He kept pushing every few seconds while the car sank, using his shoulder; but it was not possible to open it again until he was totally submerged—until the car was filled right to the top of the door.

···

The second test. The car is dropped into the dam and the driver does not touch the passenger door. All he does is open the driver's door and get out.

Seen by the camera on the bank, it is a simple manoeuvre.

Then we see it again through the interior camera, which is fixed high on the rear shelf of the cabin, the vantage point of a kid strapped into a toddler harness. The instant the car hits the dam surface, the diver goes for his own door, shoves it open with his powerful forearm, and scrambles out against a gush of water. He is out, and gone, and the water invades, greenish-yellow with a wild curved top on it. Three beats and the car is full of it. There is nothing left to breathe.

Farquharson wept without sound, wincing, desperately blinking, wiping his eyes, blowing air out between his lips. His family sat
bowed forward, pressing clenched fists to their temples.

Did the diver have any difficulty opening the driver's door, in
this second test?

'No,' said the witness in his deep voice. 'There was water rushing
in and I could feel pressure on the door, but it wasn't adverse. It was
a bit like someone leaning on you.'

...

The third test showed what would have happened had the car gone
down without any of its doors being opened.

Seen first from the bank, gradually, gradually, nose down, on
an angle, heavy and slow, in endless silence the Commodore sinks
into the dam. Its maroon colour loses intensity and turns to rose. At
the very last moment, air bubbles surge in twin streams out of the
disappearing boot. The water closes over it. Huge circles spread on
the delicately flushed and wind-riffled surface.

Then the two interior cameras show their sepia versions, more
blurred and intimate. In the first the camera is strapped to the
headrest of the front passenger seat, pointing across at the driver's seat
and footwell. For a long time nothing happens. Why are we looking
at this? Wait. Something flutters and flickers in the nethermost
corner: water, slipping in round the bottom seal of the driver's door,
and rising towards the level of the seat.

Cut to the second interior camera, the child's-eye view from
the rear parcel shelf. Again, nothing is happening. A minute, two

minutes tick by on the screen's digital timer. Then water begins to pool to left and right of the gear stick. Up it comes, leisurely and secretive, commandeering the space with unstoppable authority, its surface twinkling and wriggling. It rises and rises until it covers the two seat-backs, and engulfs the camera itself. A ridged rubber floor mat floats up towards the lens, soars past it like a stingray. Now the entire screen is water, a creamy grey tinted with green. The car has taken almost eight minutes to fill and sink.

Except for the low roar of the heating system, the court was silent. Morrissey heaved himself to his feet.

When Mr Farquharson's car was recovered from the dam, he said to the diver on the witness stand, a photo showed what looked like a gap of daylight round part of the rear windshield. What if Farquharson's back window had popped its seal? Could its cabin have lost its bubble of air and filled with water *more quickly* than had that of the test vehicle?

It was an attempt to plant in the jury's mind a seed of hope—that the boys might have drowned immediately, with no time for what we were all imagining: Jai battling in the dark to free his shrieking brothers from their harnesses, fighting the boiling chaos to reach the rear door handle, wrenching at the broken latch…

It was true that the police mechanics who inspected the car had found the rear window partially dislodged from its cavity; but this was not part of the diver's knowledge, and he was unable to console us.

...

Louise had not turned up that day: she had an appointment with her orthodontist. I was relieved. I often forgot that she was only sixteen. Did her parents have any idea what dreadful things she was learning in my company? When court rose at 4 p.m., I plodded up to the Sofitel for a disconsolate martini. Next to the high windows I spotted a senior public servant I had known when we were girls at university in the sixties. She closed her laptop and we compared notes on our current work. The mention of Peter Morrissey brought to her tired face an affectionate smile. She had had dealings with him over the years. He was the kindest, the most decent of men, a devoted worker for the underdog. 'He's always appearing for these sorts of people.' She laughed, fondly. 'And apparently he believes they're all innocent.'

...

When I got home I sat out on the back veranda for a while, mumbling to myself, sick at heart. My third grandchild came wandering round the side of the house. He approached me without speaking, turned his back, and stood waiting to be picked up. I lifted him on to my lap. He was only a few months younger than Bailey Farquharson had been when he drowned. For a while the little boy sat on my knee. He relaxed his spine against my chest. Together we listened to the clatter of the high palm fronds, the wail of a distant siren. He glanced up sharply when a flight of lorikeets swerved chattering across the garden. Then he spread his right hand like a fan, inserted a delicate thumb into his mouth, and tucked his head under my chin.

And yet only two hours later, when he and his four-year-old brother disobeyed me at bedtime and went crashing and yelling like maniacs down the hall to the kitchen, rage blinded me. I ran after them, grabbed the nearest arm, and yanked its owner round in a curve. Before I could land a blow, I got a grip on myself. The boys stood frozen in attitudes of flight. Nobody spoke. In a cold sweat I leaned against the cupboard door and took some trembling breaths.

The next morning Louise presented herself early at the coffee cart, looking hangdog.

'I have a confession,' she said in the queue. 'I didn't really go to the orthodontist. I went to a movie. With some friends.'

I laughed. She blushed.

'I just needed a break. What did I miss?'

'Everything, smart-arse. Now you'll never understand it.'

She gave me a pert look. 'Also, I've got no money.'

I shouted her a coffee and we sat down on the concrete bench.

'I realised yesterday,' she said, 'that I'm hooked. I started to rave about where I'd been, but they didn't give a shit. The only thing they wanted to know was, "Well? Did he do it?" The least interesting question anyone could possibly ask.'

...

Nobody said that it was *impossible* for Farquharson to have coughed until he blacked out. The best anyone could say was that it was highly unlikely. But, as Mr Morrissey would point out, the statistical rarity of any adverse event is of little comfort to the person whose number has come up.

People who have blacked out are often referred to neurologists, since a common cause of syncope—a brief loss of consciousness—is a failure of circulation of blood to the brain. So the first of the Crown's two medical expert witnesses was Dr John King, a lean, dry, intensely reserved gentleman in gold-rimmed spectacles, who had been practising as a consultant neurologist at the Royal Melbourne Hospital since 1975.

Dr King had seen many an individual with chronic obstructive airways disease go into a paroxysm of coughing, turn purple in the face, become distressed, and have to sit down; but not a single one of these had actually collapsed on the floor in front of him. He had seen it happen on a teaching video, but never in real life.

In fact, during thirty years in his specialty Dr King would have come across only about six cases of coughing followed by a blackout. In each of these, the patient had reported a blackout to a GP who, wanting to rule out serious conditions like epilepsy, had sent him along to Dr King for a neurological check-up. Off the top of his head, Dr King could not remember even one of these six cases who did not have lung disease. He had diagnosed cough syncope in them only after getting from the patient a credible history, particularly one corroborated by an eyewitness.

How brief was the loss of consciousness in cough syncope?

Oh, very brief, said Dr King. Unlike an epileptic fit, where the patient can be unconscious for up to three or four minutes and is often confused and without memory for half an hour or so, an episode of cough syncope lasts only five, ten, twenty seconds. Afterwards the patient is usually rapidly orientated, and can recall what happened just before he passed out. There exists, too, something called a pre-syncopal episode, where the paroxysm of coughing can lead to a feeling of being very unwell, light-headed, dizzy. The sufferer will perhaps sit down and try to control the cough. Vision may narrow. Stars may be seen. But a blackout can also occur suddenly, without warning.

Mr Morrissey asked whether cough syncope could be accompanied by compulsive activity. Was it beyond the realms of possibility that a person might maintain his grip on a steering wheel, or move a steering wheel to direct a vehicle in a certain direction?

Not in a purposeful sense, said Dr King. He may fall on the steering wheel and make some convulsive movements, but generally the movements seen in a person with cough syncope are merely 'repetitive twitching of the limbs'.

Morrissey had dug deep and come up with some case studies from American medical journals. According to one of these, dated 1953, chronic pulmonary or respiratory diseases were associated with seventy-five per cent of cases of cough syncope—in other words, only three-quarters of them. In 1998, the *Aviation, Space and Environmental Medicine* journal had described the case of a forty-one-year-old US Army helicopter pilot who was driving home from training with his unit. He had a mild cold, with a cough. On the road he coughed forcefully, experienced tunnel vision and light-headedness, and passed out. His car hit a tree. He was unconscious only for seconds, and recalled the incident immediately. He reported no headaches, shortness of breath, loss of bowel or bladder control, chest pains, tremors, nausea, vomiting or amnesia. His medical history was notable only in that he was a smoker and overweight. He had no chronic airways disease. A third case involved a healthy forty-five-year-old with the flu who had suffered a cough syncope episode. Had the neurologist read all of these documents? Yes, he had, replied the impassive Dr King.

Morrissey was driving Dr King back against the wall, but there was a sense of strain in the cases he was quoting, a sort of thinness. They felt distant, sparse, dredged up. I looked at the jury. They were concentrating hard. The faces of most were unreadable. But one of the older women was listening with her head tilted back, the corners of her mouth pulled into her cheeks, her eyes narrowed to slits: the expression that in ordinary life prefaces a click of the tongue and a sharp 'Come off it.'

Ms Forrester, re-examining, drew from these same case studies the fact that most of the subjects had identified themselves as heavy smokers. The American chopper pilot had recently been subjected to G-force in the course of his aviation training. Dr King shrugged calmly. He knew nothing about the effect of G-force on cough syncope. But he pointed out that most people who reported incidents of cough syncope were in their forties and fifties, so that thirty-six, Farquharson's age at the time of the crash, was perhaps at the lower end of the range. The twitching seen during cough syncope, he repeated, was 'involuntary and purposeless'. A person in such a state would not be capable of the purposeful steering of a car.

At this, the journalists en masse leaned forward to their notebooks, and the ABC television reporter sprang up and darted out of the court.

. . .

Professor Matthew Naughton, the Crown's main expert medical witness, was the only man I had ever seen wear a pink tie with a tweed jacket. Rimless spectacles hung round his neck on a black cord. His turned-up nose made him look young, but he had a real mouthful of a title: Head of the General Respiratory and Sleep Medicine Service in the Department of Allergy and Respiratory Medicine at Melbourne's Alfred Hospital. Mr Rapke led him through a CV of such vast scope and lavish detail that the journalists could hardly keep straight faces. The reporter beside me, stifling laughter, printed on my notebook, 'Are you clever?' But, as soon as Rapke's examination began, Naughton showed himself to be soberingly quiet and modest.

Cough syncope, he said, is a recognised medical syndrome—a very brief loss of consciousness that follows an episode of intense coughing. The medical literature has described it for half a century in middle-aged, overweight males who are usually heavy smokers with underlying heart or lung disease. The mechanism most people accept as its cause is repetitive coughing that causes pressure within the chest. This pressure impairs the flow of blood on its way back to the heart from the lungs, so that the heart, when it contracts, has less blood to pump on its forward way.

'I have trouble getting my head around this condition,' said Naughton, 'because it's so nebulous. When I look through the literature on cough syncope, I find an absence of good quality scientific rationale to back up the validity of the condition. In twenty-five years as a medical practitioner I have never personally seen it.'

He had asked his respiratory colleagues at the Alfred Hospital 'in a casual manner' whether they had experience of cough syncope. They all knew of it as a condition, but there was only one case that any of them were personally acquainted with—a young man who suffered from the severe and chronic pulmonary condition cystic fibrosis and a neurological condition that impaired blood supply to his brain. The nurses on the respiratory ward were aware of his vulnerability to cough syncope and had to try to manage it.

Naughton had also consulted the physiotherapy staff at the Alfred. Part of their work is to test for the presence of a germ called pneumocystis that is common in the HIV population—people who, apart from their HIV-positive status and some breathlessness, are healthy. These patients are asked to inhale a hypotonic saline solution, which causes them to cough vigorously for up to thirty minutes. A physiotherapist who had administered this disagreeable-sounding treatment about once a week for ten years told Naughton she had not seen a single case of cough syncope in all that time.

'Do people with normal lungs, hearts and brains,' asked Rapke, 'suffer cough syncope?'

'I have never seen a case in which that has occurred,' said Naughton. 'Nor have I seen, in the modern medical literature, objective descriptions in which people have actually witnessed and monitored a person having cough syncope in which there has been normal heart, lung or neurological function.'

Now Rapke sharpened the focus. He asked Professor Naughton to imagine himself clinically faced with a man aged about thirty-seven, moderately overweight, a smoker who said he went through a packet roughly every three days. He was generally in robust health, but had been suffering for about three weeks from an infection which commenced in the upper respiratory tract, then developed lower down, and was being treated with antibiotics. An ECG taken 'after a certain incident' revealed no heart abnormality, a systolic reading of 140, and a rapid pulse. Seen immediately after the incident by paramedics and doctors at a hospital, he was not observed to be coughing. He had taken fluids within two hours of the incident. At the time of the incident, which he said occurred while he was driving, he was in a seated position. After the incident he was generally coherent and seemed to be lucid. He had been immersed in cold water, but had got himself out of the water, waved down a car and conversed with its occupants.

Morrissey jumped to his feet. To say that the man was coherent and lucid, but not that he was also delirious and *a babbling mess*, was misrepresenting the true situation!

'I won't intervene,' said the judge. 'Go on.'

No underlying medical illness was known or detected, Rapke continued smoothly. Blood tests showed no alcohol or drugs in his system. The patient claimed that as he was driving on a cool, even cold night, he had a coughing fit at the wheel of his car, and blacked out. Based on these facts, what was Professor Naughton's professional opinion of the likelihood that the driver of that car had suffered an episode of cough syncope?

The professor hardly allowed a pause. 'Extremely unlikely.' From Rapke's description, the man's heart and lungs were in reasonably good health. He did not appear to be disabled by breathlessness. He was plainly not dehydrated. A dehydrated person who coughs would be more likely to experience changes in the pressure inside his chest— maybe not a blackout, but a dizziness that doctors call pre-syncopal.

Naughton was quiet and lucid. Rapke stood still and let him go on uninterrupted.

The interior of the car, said Naughton, where the hypothetical man said the coughing fit had overwhelmed him, would have been much warmer than the air outside. Cold can often trigger coughing, but this man did not cough after the event, although he was exposed to cold air and wearing wet clothing. Also, at the time he claimed he had started to cough, he was seated. A lot of our blood volume is in our abdomen and legs: cough syncope is more likely to occur if someone is fully upright.

Certainly he had a common-or-garden variety respiratory-tract infection. These happen every day in society, yet people with colds are not having cough syncope on a day-to-day basis. A single episode of cough syncope in a relatively warm environment, and one that was not replicated, struck the professor as highly unusual.

What if this hypothetical man, two days before the crash, asked Rapke, had been observed to have a severe coughing fit while on his feet? If he had gone red in the face, but had recovered once he was invited to sit down?

The fact that man had *not* passed out only consolidated the professor's opinion. All of us in this room, he said, could cough to the point at which the colour of our facial skin changed.

He would expect a person with cough syncope to recover consciousness within seconds. He might feel confused for a few moments. Naughton had read reports of people becoming 'flaccid' when they lose consciousness: he let his head and shoulders droop forward, and flopped his hands apart, palms up, on the rail of the witness stand.

'In that period,' asked Rapke, 'would the person be capable of any purposeful movement?'

'Not if he was unconscious!'

What did it mean to say that the diagnosis—even a provisional one—of cough syncope is done 'on history'?

'We're dealing,' said Naughton, 'with an extremely rare condition. Ideally we like to have a collateral history—at least one observer who witnessed the person cough and black out. But there is no definitive test that confirms or refutes cough syncope, apart from a classic description.'

'The accuracy of the diagnosis is, then, solely dependent on the history?'

'A hundred per cent,' said Naughton.

'But,' said Rapke, 'if you've got only the patient saying it happened, how does one test the diagnosis?'

'It's impossible to test. It relies on the individual providing an accurate history of what went on.'

...

Mr Morrissey himself was still struggling with spasms of harsh, dry barking that threatened to overwhelm him, but he was soon roughing up Professor Naughton with skill and gusto.

'You're not an expert in cough syncope? Did you tell the prosecutors, when they came to you for an opinion, that you've never seen it, never written about it, never diagnosed it, and didn't know the way an episode would unfold if it happened? Yet they still called you as a witness?'

Naughton protested. 'I've completed a training in respiratory disease where these conditions are discussed.'

But Morrissey made him out to have swotted up on cough syncope very recently and shallowly. Had he not read only one textbook and one article on the condition? Did he even know how to take a history of a cough syncope episode?

Naughton bristled. 'I am educated about cough syncope,' he snapped. 'I do take a history of cough syncope when it's presented to me. Because of its rarity, I don't profess to be an expert in it.'

Well, had he read the list of cough syncope case studies that the defence had provided him with?

'I did my best,' said Naughton, 'but they're often not electronically available, and they take some time to locate. A lot of that data is many, many years old.'

Even so, said Morrissey, didn't the data contain case histories of people without chronic airways disease who had been diagnosed with cough syncope while driving cars? Didn't Naughton read the study of the four heavy-goods-vehicle drivers who had been involved in fatal crashes? They didn't have chronic airways disease, but doctors were prepared to diagnose cough syncope on the histories they had provided. Didn't this show that it *was* possible for a man without such a disease to have a coughing fit while driving and black out?

Naughton was beginning to gnaw and purse his lips, but he maintained steady eye contact with Morrissey. 'I would rephrase that,' he said. 'I would say it is possible for someone to *provide a history* of having had cough syncope in the absence of chronic lung disease.'

What about the provisional diagnosis of cough syncope made by the Emergency Staff Specialist at Geelong hospital on the night of the crash? Wasn't Dr Bartley, who unlike Professor Naughton had the benefit of being on the spot and taking a history from Farquharson face to face, fully entitled to make that diagnosis?

'That's his call,' said Naughton.

What if a bloke came to Naughton and said, 'Look, I'm twenty-eight. I don't smoke. I play football. I'm a legend. But *I've* had an attack of coughing and blacked out'?

Naughton shrugged. He couldn't exclude the possibility, but he would be very surprised indeed to hear of such an unlikely thing.

But Morrissey ushered Naughton down a fire escape of unlikelihood, step by step. 'Since it could be possible, though extremely unlikely, with a person who's twenty-eight and has no health problems, you'd agree with me that it's less unlikely if he were a smoker? Even less unlikely if he were thirty-seven rather than twenty-eight? Even less unlikely if he'd had an acute respiratory-tract illness for three weeks? Even less unlikely if he'd suffered from paroxysms of coughing during those three weeks? And less unlikely still if he'd been witnessed to have a bad gripping coughing attack where the watcher thought he was going to have a stroke and told him to sit down?'

Naughton assented in a wary, affectless tone to each step.

But then Morrissey got down to what he riskily called 'an actual episode'. On the Thursday before the crash, Farquharson had reported to his friend Darren Bushell, a Winchelsea shearer known to everyone as DB, that he had had a coughing fit in his car a few days earlier. He told DB he had blacked out at the wheel of his car outside the Winchelsea roadhouse; when he came to, he found his car had driven twenty metres further towards some rocks.

Mr Rapke sprang to his feet. 'That is based on an assertion, not a witnessed event!'

Morrissey pulled his horns in. Had Naughton not noticed this report of Mr Bushell's in the documentation he had been provided with? No? Still, if this incident were accepted as a proved fact, wouldn't it have a massive impact on Naughton's opinion?

'It would have an impact,' said Naughton.

And had the prosecution told the professor that, three weeks after Farquharson's car went into the dam, a man called Zane Lewis had come forward saying, 'I had one of these'?

'Bloke down our way,' whispered the reporter from the *Geelong Advertiser*. 'Ran his car into a fence and said he'd had a coughing fit.'

'I object!' said Rapke. 'That's not fact at all. There's no evidentiary basis for that whatsoever.'

'*Had* one of *these*?' said Justice Cummins, picking up the words in tweezers. 'It's not something you get off the supermarket counter. Is he an expert in neurology? Or an expert like this professor? Or is he a layperson? Is he expressing a medical diagnosis? What are you talking about?'

'Would it have been of interest to you, Professor,' said Morrissey, corrected, 'in your consideration of the nature and scope and existence of cough syncope, to meet someone who said he had a coughing fit and drove off the road after blacking out?'

'Yes,' said Naughton politely. 'That would be of interest.'

...

Court rose for a short break. Some of us stayed in our places, updating our notes. Mr Morrissey's junior, Con Mylonas, got out of his chair and wandered along the bar table towards the press box. He was a small, dark man with pouty lips, who wore his wig low on his forehead. The word among the journalists was that he had been a brain surgeon before he came to the law, and had been taken under Morrissey's wing. He stopped in front of me. I looked up nervously.

'What's your take on this guy?' he said in a confidential tone.

Did he mean Farquharson? Why the hell was he asking me? I stared at him in alarm. But he jerked his head at the witness stand that Professor Naughton had just vacated.

'I don't know.' I blurted out the first thing that came into my head. 'He's biting his lips a lot. What do you think?'

He smiled genially, and strolled away. Baffled, I turned to Louise; but she and the young journalist from Geelong were doubled over like schoolgirls in a fit of silent hysterics.

...

For the rest of that afternoon Morrissey hammered away at Naughton. Hadn't he jumped too early? Offered his opinion before he had properly informed himself? Wasn't he now too proud or vain to admit he had been wrong?

Naughton rolled with the punches, continuing to work his lips and teeth. Eventually he got a grip. For twenty years, he said, he had regularly attended conferences. Some of these were focused purely on cough. Cough syncope had not been included as a condition that respiratory physicians should be routinely aware of. He kept a close eye on the medical literature as it came through. In the last fifteen or twenty years he hadn't seen anything on cough syncope. References he had found were from the 1980s. He was yet to be convinced that there were physiological reasons to explain cough syncope in an otherwise healthy person who does not have any chronic lung, heart or brain disorder.

He offered a brief, clear lecture on the four levels of evidence in medicine. 'As I read the data here,' he said, 'we're running on the lowest, most anecdotal level to support a diagnosis of cough syncope. I'm not saying it doesn't exist. I'm just saying it's rare, it's poorly defined, and most of the time the episodes are not witnessed.'

'So in short,' said Morrissey with a light scorn, 'you'll believe it when you see it? You're as good as the scenario you're given?'

'Absolutely.'

'Rare conditions do happen, though? It's not much use to a person when they get a rare form of cancer to be told, "It's all right— it's rare"? The fact that it's rare doesn't tell you it can't happen? Just that it's unlikely to happen?'

Louise, who had been studying the jurors with a pale concentration, leaned over and whispered, 'Even when he wins a point, he does it in such a way that the jury doesn't seem to notice.'

There was no imaginable resolution. Barrister and witness would prowl on forever, in this debate. Neither would be able to land a knockout blow. Again, in the dying fall of the cross-examination, the glaring fact presented itself: no one but Farquharson knew what had happened in the car that night, and, by now, perhaps not even he knew.

...

In a few deft strokes Rapke drew everything back into shape. While the bruised Naughton reasserted his professional integrity, Morrissey swung sideways in his chair and turned his face towards the jury, histrionically suppressing a sceptical smile.

Morrissey set great store by the vivid phrase 'babbling mess', describing Farquharson's state when he flagged down the two young men on the roadside and begged them to take him to his ex-wife, but Rapke drained it of power: when it was traced back through the transcript, it was found to have originated not from the mouths of Shane Atkinson or Tony McClelland, but in a question that had been put to them by Farquharson's counsel at the committal hearing in Geelong.

Lastly, Rapke dispatched the defence's case study of four heavy-goods-vehicle drivers who were on the record as having experienced cough syncope immediately before they were involved in fatal smashes. Naughton pointed out that the truckies had each given 'a classic description' of cough syncope; that none of them had had prior episodes of it; and that all four episodes were unwitnessed.

And were those four fatal smashes the subject of police investigation?

They were.

'Thank you,' said the prosecutor, and sat down.

These casual coups that Rapke pulled off made the spectator in me want to stand up and cheer. At the same time a chill ran over me. While Morrissey slugged away with a big heart on his sleeve, Rapke sat hunched in his chair, unruffled, peering up at an angle into an invisible light that seemed too strong for his eyes.

I went to my local shopping centre to buy some vegetables. The friendly woman who ran the greengrocery asked me what I was working on. My answer upset her. She covered her mouth and her eyes filled with tears. I stood at the counter while she wiped them away. Then she told me something that surprised me.

'My husband,' she said, 'had a coughing fit once and went off the road.'

She called his name and he emerged from the storage area. He was the sort of man Morrissey might have described as 'a barrel-chested individual': in his forties, thickset, carrying a bit of weight, used to long days of physical labour. His wife told him what I wanted to know. He looked at me narrowly.

'Come out the back. We can sit down.'

We picked our way between crates and bags to a battered formica table. He listened while I outlined, in the most neutral terms possible, Farquharson's account of his crash.

'I can tell you what happened to me,' he said. 'It was about four years ago. I was driving my HiAce van—it's a manual—along the south-eastern freeway in the middle of the afternoon. My daughter was with me. She was about thirteen. Quiet time of day. Not much traffic. Four lanes going each way.

'I remember starting to cough. I remember slowing down to about sixty or seventy. I cut left across two lanes, to pull into the emergency lane, and I blacked out before the impact. After that I don't remember anything till I heard my daughter saying, "Dad!" I came to slumped over to my left side, towards her. I only knew there'd been an impact because she was saying, "You hit the rails!" She'd grabbed the wheel and the car had swerved back to the right, across four lanes, and ended up in the median strip.

'As I was coming to, I could hear sounds but I couldn't see. You know when you're on top of a hill and you can hear traffic far away? It was like that. I reckon I would have blacked out for about a minute. The vehicle would have been out of control. I wouldn't have been able to brake or accelerate. And I came out of it *slowly*. My daughter shook me. I could hear her voice, miles away. It got clearer and clearer. She was saying, "We hit the rail!" and I was saying, "No, no, we couldn't have." Then I got out on to the median strip and had a look. I saw the damage. That's the first time I believed what she was telling me. The front left indicator had got sideswiped against the guardrail of the emergency lane.'

He stared past me.

'I'm trying,' he said, 'to picture this bloke shutting his kids' door. Saying, "We'll be right, mate". Jumping out. Nah. This guy should've drowned. No way could he have got out, if he'd just been unconscious. I remember waking up and needing a few minutes to focus. To be in a mental state to make a decision—like with this bloke, to pull the door shut—I dunno—and I had my daughter shaking me.'

I asked him what his state of health had been. He said he had had flu in the preceding week. He had no lung disease and had not smoked for eighteen years.

'One thing I remember clearly,' he said, 'is that when I started coughing and couldn't stop, my very first thought was to get off the road—because of my daughter. My utmost concern was my daughter beside me. That's why I pulled to the left—to get off the road.'

He expressed incredulity that Farquharson had got out of the car and left his boys in it. 'You'd stay with them, wouldn't you? You'd fight to get them out? You'd go down fighting to get them out?'

I told him about the police evidence that there had been a thirty-degree turn of the steering wheel. He pulled towards him a crushed sheet of paper with a list scribbled on it: chillies, cucumber. Impatiently he turned it sideways. He drew a rough circle and marked ninety degrees at three o'clock.

'He couldn't have been doing a hundred,' he said. 'In a turn that sharp, the tail would swing out. It would have skidded, or even rolled, when it hit the drain. He must have been going much slower than a hundred when he turned the wheel.'

He drew a diagram of his own vehicle's progress, circled the point in the emergency lane where it had struck the guardrail, and said firmly, 'I have no recollection whatsoever of this. The GP told me the coughing puts pressure on the blood vessels in your chest, and that cuts off the oxygen to your brain.'

We sat in silence, looking at his sketch on the scarred tabletop.

'The insurance paid up,' he said.

Then he breathed out sharply through his nose, and threw down his pencil.

'One thing I know for sure,' he said, getting to his feet. 'My van slowed down. The van. Slowed. Down.'

...

At my early morning Pilates class someone asked me how the trial was going. I said it was swinging this way and that. I told them about the fathers I had met who stated categorically that in Farquharson's position they would have gone to the bottom and drowned with their kids. The four of us agreed in very low voices that this could only be a fantasy. As we worked with our pink and yellow weights, an unpleasant forty-year-old memory came to me. I was walking along a street in Werribee with one of my year-twelve students when a savage dog leapt over a gate and rushed at us. Next thing I knew, I was standing behind my student, clinging to her back, while the owner dragged the dog away. In a second of primal terror, of which I have no memory, I must have pushed the girl between me and the danger.

'A teacher wouldn't get away with that these days,' someone said. We laughed.

Then the youngest woman present told a story. One Easter, on a family camping trip, she was wading into a calm lake with her three-year-old son on her hip and his six-year-old brother paddling alongside them on a boogie board. The bigger boy screamed, 'Mum! A snake!' He turned his board and thrashed for the bank. The mother, waist-deep and hampered by the heavy toddler, saw the snake's tiny head rippling towards her. *Drop the kid*, she thought, *and get out of here*. She struck at the snake with a foam floatie and it veered away, but fifteen years later, confessing the blind urge to save herself, she lay on the Pilates reformer with her feet in straps, trembling with shame.

...

'To know a man's car,' according to the American novelist E. L. Doctorow, 'is to know him. It is not useless knowledge.' And surely, to see your wife and her lover flying around in the newish car you had paid for, while you had to clunk along in front of the whole town at the wheel of an '89 VN Commodore Berlina with 387,000 on the clock, second-hand tyres, a faulty rear-door latch, rust in the back window seal, and an infuriating habit of cutting out on hills would be mortifying to many a man. 'The car,' said James Jacobs, the Winchelsea mechanic who had struggled to keep the vehicle roadworthy, 'was not a shining example of its model.'

Who knows what midnight doubts had assailed Jacobs over the past two years? He was a skinny, dark man, whose eyebrows arched high into his forehead, giving him a bright, bird-like aspect. He spoke softly and very fast, all on one note and without expression, but he was extremely, almost anxiously articulate, and precise to the point of being pedantic. He had first met Farquharson about a year before the crash. 'Acquaintance through mutual friends,' he said, 'would be the best way to describe our connection.'

The Commodore did not impress him. 'It was in a fairly worn state, quite a high mileage vehicle, typical with the age of the car. I would suggest it had maybe sporadic maintenance. The main thrust of my work was to try and rectify its cutting-out and driveability issues.' Farquharson was 'frustrated' that his wife had ended up with the newer car while he had to persist with the old one until he could afford to replace it. He did not want to spend money on the 'shit' car. Once or twice he had paid Jacobs in kind, by mowing his lawn. Jacobs had done his level best with the Commodore. Over several months he had worked on its brakes, fitted the roadworthy but mismatched front tyres that Farquharson turned up with, and installed a new crank angle sensor (the part that stops the motor from cutting out, commonly a source of bother in this model). The driver's side rear-door mechanism, which had been giving trouble, he found to be worn and rusty. He lubricated it; it left his premises working.

In late July 2005, about six weeks before Father's Day, Jacobs test-drove Farquharson's car, with Farquharson beside him. He took it five or six kilometres eastbound out of Winchelsea towards Geelong, past the dam, up the overpass and down the other side, then did a U-turn and drove back into town. This was the route Jacobs habitually took on test-drives. It was 'a very standard piece of road', and he knew it well. On the way back up the overpass, westbound, doing about ninety, Jacobs noticed that the motor was still misfiring. He had to slacken speed to stop it from cutting out.

He also observed, when they reached the top of the overpass and headed down the Winchelsea side, that Farquharson's car had a tendency to want to wander to the right—an easily correctable but palpable rightward urge towards the middle of the road. 'I took my hands off the wheel because I could feel that I was having to keep some left-hand pressure on it. I could feel the car start to gently move across—it would not have crossed the white line before I corrected it, but it certainly would have got close to the centre of the line.' The vehicle had shown no signs of correcting itself before Jacobs put his hand back on the wheel.

Jacobs put this down to 'minimal road camber'—the left lane of the road at that point tilted slightly towards the dam, he estimated, instead of the other way as it should—but he also suggested that Farquharson ought to have the Commodore's wheels aligned, a process Jacobs did not have the equipment to perform. Farquharson had the common misconception that wheel alignment was the same as wheel balancing, which Jacobs had already had done when the tyres were replaced. The mechanic was too diplomatic to correct him on the point: 'I do not recall that I elaborated on it,' he said.

Now Mr Morrissey launched a slow, laborious, energy-thieving cross-examination of two police officers, Senior Sergeant Robert Leguier of the Mechanical Investigation Unit, and Senior Constable Wayne Kohlmann of the Forensic Services Department in Macleod, about the pre- and post-crash condition of the car in all its scrupulous detail. We heard again that the keys had been found in the ignition, that the ignition was off. The headlight switch was off. The heater was off. Because the car had been submerged, the investigators could not say for certain whether or not the headlights and tail-lights had been on at impact, or had been turned off in the water. This much was clear; but to anyone ignorant of automotive terminology, the mechanical evidence was almost as taxing as the yellow paint marks. The sheer bulk of technical minutiae induced a hopeless stupefaction. I had to flail at myself to stay alert. Some of the jurors appeared to be nodding off. Even the judge looked blank and stunned; he took off his glasses and fiercely polished them. One journalist near me skimmed the *Age* television guide. Another was doing Sudoku under the desk. The hands of the high clock seemed to slow and stop.

...

Then, on the Friday morning of the fourth week, just as our concentration seemed to have flagged past the point of no return, a short, quiet, terrier-eyed man in a dark suit stepped into the witness stand—Detective Sergeant Gerard Clanchy from Homicide, the officer in charge of the investigation. The evidence that the Crown was about to present through him would drag the story away from tail-light filaments and side-mirror housings, and thrust it back into excruciating realms of human behaviour, where reason fights to gain a purchase, and everyone feels entitled to an opinion.

Major Collision formally handed over the Farquharson investigation to Homicide early on the Tuesday morning after the crash. By lunchtime, Clanchy and his partner, Detective Senior Constable Andrew Stamper, were knocking at the front door of Farquharson's father's house in Winchelsea. A media pack swarmed outside the front gate. Farquharson was not arrested; he was asked to accompany the detectives back to Homicide headquarters in St Kilda Road, to be formally interviewed about the deaths of his children. He got into the back seat of the unmarked car. His sisters' forceful and repeated offers to travel in the police car with him, or to drive him to Melbourne themselves, had been firmly repulsed by Clanchy: this we know because Stamper, who sat in the back seat beside Farquharson, was wearing a covert recording device.

I heard Louise expostulate under her breath, 'How dare they?' I too felt a shudder: so there was nowhere to hide.

In the dock Farquharson bowed over the transcript. His sister Kerri kept shaking her head with a small, contemptuous smile, which faded as the tape rolled on.

Once they have cautioned their passenger, Clanchy at the wheel rarely speaks, but Stamper rambles on in a sprawling, blokey style. He questions Farquharson casually, empathises with him about marriage break-ups—he's been there himself and it takes a lot of getting used to. It's tough, isn't it, when you turn that light off at the end of the night, mate, and the kids aren't there? Specially, says Farquharson, when he's never had an accident or never been in trouble before or anything. Did they blue? asks Stamper idly. Did it ever get…untidy, or was it just verbal? Peeling off huge, unabashed yawns, he asks Farquharson if he's eaten, had any sleep. Farquharson volunteers that he has had to ask people what day it was. Does he realise there's a media car right behind them? says Stamper. The whole circumstance of what's happened is why the media's jumped on it, chimes in Clanchy from the front; all they're after is the truth. Farquharson speaks in sporadic bursts. His voice is muffled, and faint. He's never been in trouble before and it's daunting. He doesn't think he's gonna like all this questioning. He doesn't think what? He said he doesn't think he's gonna like all this questioning. He's got nothing to hide. He loves his kids. He would never do anything to hurt them. He's just so upset he couldn't get them—he tried. He's only got two arms, two legs. If anyone's tryin' to make out it was intentional, that wasn't the case at all. Sorry? says Stamper. If anyone's tryin' to make out it was *intentional*, that's not the case at *all*. For long periods in the ninety-minute drive there is no sound but the engine's smooth hum, a steady rushing, like a river pouring towards the edge of a cliff. Is Farquharson looking out at the flat landscape sliding past the window, the tired mounds of the You Yangs? His children have been dead for barely forty-eight hours. They are not yet in their graves.

As they approach Homicide in St Kilda Road, with the media still in pursuit, traffic holds them up. In the idling car the two detectives begin to close in on him. 'If something horrible's happened, if you've done something horrible, you can tell us.' Their voices, quiet but urgent, overlap Farquharson's low, nervous gabble like the intensifying chorus of a song. 'All we want is the truth. However horrible or bad that might be. All we want is the truth. If there's a secret there, Robert, tell us. Tell us. Please tell us.' Why isn't he screaming? Women in the public row of the court softly moaned and shifted in their seats.

A handbrake creaks. Breathing. Car doors slam in a void. Men's shoes thud on concrete stairs. The whine and clash of a heavy door. Does he want a drink of water, a cup of coffee, tea? Take a seat. It's quarter past two.

…

I looked at Louise. She was as white as the wall.

'This is so over,' she whispered. 'I can't stand what it'll do to his sisters.'

But just as the video of the official interview was about to be played, I saw the two sisters get up and march out of the court with slow, formal steps that indicated a protest.

…

The bare, fluoro-lit room is empty but for a small, stocky man in a lime-green Adidas T-shirt. He sits sideways on a chair with his back slumped against the wall and one forearm resting on the table. His short brown hair is wavy, thinning and going grey. His eyes are set in deep, fatty sockets. He appears not to have shaved. His head is bowed. The slack curve of his spine gives prominence to the plumpness of his belly and chest. There is something piteous about his deflated posture. But when the door opens he straightens up and turns to face the two detectives, who enter briskly with notebooks, pens and paper cups of coffee, and sit with their backs to the camera.

Clanchy is a neatly built man in a pink shirt, with thick, prematurely grey hair in a pelt-like buzz cut. Stamper is taller, shambling, with rounded shoulders and dark hair. Farquharson says he does not drink tea or coffee. He accepts only water. On the table stands a flat box of tissues. One of them is sprouting from the slot.

At the first mention of the fact that his boys died on Sunday night, Farquharson closes his eyes for a second, in a moment of private pain. Then he sighs, and launches once more on his story.

When he speaks he keeps his eyes on the melamine tabletop. He has an anxious, hangdog look, like a schoolboy. Now and then he flicks a glance at his questioners from under his brow. When he relates the events, he illustrates his account with eager movements of his small, well-shaped, very clean hands. Sometimes he rubs one bare forearm, or audibly scratches his thigh or his armpit. At certain moments, when the questions come in a rush, he blinks rapidly, or licks his lips. He whisks his fingertips across his face, and glances at them. Once he presses his palms together, then wipes them on his trousers. When he speaks of his love for his sons, his over-protective attitude towards them, he shakes his head and clasps his hands. When he explains that his marriage ended because his wife, though she still *loved* him, was no longer *in* love with him, he distinguishes between these two states by flexing his bent wrists and knotted fingers to left and right. At the mention of his ex-wife's new man, his jaw takes on a grey, tense look. The anti-depressant he has been on for twelve months, he says, has put everything in his brain back into perspective: he makes a delicate bridging gesture with the fingertips of both hands. When he refers to his cough, he taps his chest with one palm. Asked again if he had ever thought about hurting himself, he says, with a bitter smile, that he had a little glimpse of that at the start, but it passed. Several times he places his clenched fists on the table. His knuckles are white.

The questions in the interview transcript are numbered from 1 to 613. At number 323 they put it to him squarely: did he deliberately drive off the highway into the dam? No, he says, very quiet and firm. He did not. He had a coughing fit, blacked out, and found himself in water. Did he help with the boys' seatbelts? He doesn't know. It's all just a big blur. He's got nothing to hide.

Clanchy and Stamper swerve away to his mortgage, his maintenance payments, his medication, never raising their voices, always polite, always thoughtful and patient, always looping back to the question of what happened in the water. Under their sustained pressure, Farquharson flares out into passages of rhetoric. He feels pretty shithouse. The boys were his *life*. His *world*. He throws up his hands and lowers his head. His chin stiffens and goes grey; his mouth turns upside down and his voice trembles. He wouldn't even go to Queensland for a holiday because they would miss him and he would miss them. They were his world, his whole life. Even his counsellor will tell them that. He never went and bothered meeting any other women because he wanted his kids for himself. Everything he did was for them, his whole life. And he had two arms and two legs and he couldn't save 'em. He always wanted to *protect* them. Cindy always told him he was *over*-protective. Watching them like a hawk 'cause there could be cars on the road. If they stood up on the slide, he would bolt over. Sit down, sit down! Come down properly—don't fall—flying underneath with his hands out to stop them so they didn't hurt themselves—but he couldn't save 'em. He blacked out. That's the honest truth. He's got no lies—no reason to lie. He'd do anything to have them back—he's got to live with this for the rest of his life, that he couldn't save his kids. His voice thickens. He is on the verge of tears. He looks up under his brow, angry, hurt, unfairly accused. He gabbles out again his mantra of helplessness—he had two arms, two legs and he couldn't save the three of them. How was he supposed to do it? He tried and tried and tried.

A pause.

Clanchy takes his chin out of his palm. How *did* he try, though?

Farquharson waves both arms at shoulder level. Well, he went around and he—he went and swam to the road to get people to help him, 'cause he—he just can't recall everything—everything just went like *that*. He snaps his fingers fast, three times.

Mm, says Clanchy.

He wouldn't lie, 'cause if he lies, what's he gonna do, live a life of guilt?

Does he feel guilty?

Yeah, well anyone would. He feels bad. The counsellors he's seen have told him he shouldn't feel guilty, that it's a freakish accident. He's very concerned about what's gonna happen. He's never been in trouble before. He's never done anything—*anything*. He throws out both arms in a large, heart-exposing gesture, then brings his palms together and makes a series of rhythmic, double-handed thrusting movements as if thumping down facts on the tabletop: he believes he's a very good citizen in life; he's a family man who's looked after his kids and everything like that. So it's pretty bloody hard and he doesn't know what he's thinking and what he's not thinking, at the moment. But he's telling them the truth. He's not lying to them. He's got no reason to.

What did he have on, in the car?

Just lights. The radio, it could have been music, he doesn't know. The boys were wearing T-shirts so he turned the heater round to where it's red, where it's warm.

When his son opened the door, asks Stamper, did Robert see water come in?

Yeah, he thinks so.

Where was it?

Um, on the floor. He won't say too much about that, 'cause he can't 'pecifically—

Why did he close Jai's door?

Farquharson pauses, looks at the detective with an expression that could mean either *Why do you reckon?* or *Is this a trap?* Because water, he says, was getting in.

How hard was it to close the door?

It could have been really hard, but he can't say, because it was just all so quick. Again he snaps his fingers.

When he got out of the car, did he have to swim up through water, or how was it?

He thinks so, but he can't recall. He thought for some stupid reason that they might have only been in a little bit of water, or rocking on a ledge, and he managed to get out but it was going down before that—he doesn't even know how, he doesn't know.

Did he see the car go down?

Yeah, he was trying to swim round the other side. He thinks he was under water when it went down, he remembers being under water, he remembers that. He thinks he remembers it nosediving. He got out and he looked to try and see what he could do, and he knew he couldn't do anything.

After the car went down, did he dive to try and find the car, at all?

He tried, it was, he thinks it was really black and—

Stamper presses him, quiet and patient. *Did* he dive down to try and find the car?

Farquharson thinks he did, he can't tell 'pecifically. He knows he went down somewhere but he can't recall where, it was all so quick.

But didn't he tell the other police, earlier, that he dived down?

Yeah, he went down to try and look and try and find it. He couldn't do anything so he went back up.

Why couldn't he do anything?

Because of the pressure.

What does he mean, the pressure?

Well, it was all under water. He knows he went to try and do something. What he doesn't know is if he succeeded, or seen the car or not.

He's said something about the pressure. It's a word he's used several times, the pressure.

Well, says Farquharson, that's what the counsellor at Geelong Emergency said—that he wouldn't have been able to do nothing because of water pressure and everything.

Stamper doesn't want to hear what someone else suggested

might have happened. He's asking if Farquharson himself remembers whether he dived down.

Yeah, he did go down, because he remembers swallowing a little bit of water. He had a jumper on, and—

Does he remember finding the car underwater?

Farquharson stammers, he jabbers. He doesn't think he did. Then he thinks he did. Then he doesn't think he did. He's sorry, it's not a question he can really answer.

Clanchy wonders, casually, about the date of the anniversary of his separation from Cindy.

It's coming up, but it's totally irrelevant. Farquharson's happy with the fact that Cindy doesn't want to be with him. He's accepted all that. All he knows is that they were his kids—

So it's not quite twelve months, is that what he's saying?

Pretty close. She's moved on; he's moved on.

When's the divorce going to be finalised?

In about a week.

So. His divorce is pending? And the anniversary of the separation's also very soon?

He's not even sure of the date.

Did he give the boys any drugs at all?

No. He did not.

Who's his mortgage with?

Westpac.

All right. Does he need a drink? Go to the toilet?

He shakes his head.

Now they suspend the interview. The little room, with its garish white light, becomes calm. They ask him to sign authorities for the

___

release of his records from the Geelong Hospital, from his GP and his counsellor. It can be seen that all three of the men at the table are left-handed. Farquharson grips the pen as a boy might, awkwardly, between forefinger and middle finger. They point to the correct spots, and he signs.

...

Before court rose, Farquharson's sister Carmen returned. She slid back into her seat and established commanding eye contact with him in the dock. She mouthed instructions, perhaps about his clothes; she made stabbing downward gestures with one forefinger. Oh, I thought, he could never have pleaded guilty, not against this tide of relentless loyalty. My own brother has four elder sisters and one younger; all his life I have watched him deal with this. If he doesn't fight back, a treasured boy can wind up as a man with women in his face.

Louise and I bolted out the side door of the building and down Lonsdale Street. *I believe I'm a very good citizen in life*. We could hardly look at each other. At the lights she peeled off to the station. I kept going to a bar at the top of Bourke Street. I ordered a shot of vodka. Strangers near me were gossiping loosely about the trial.

'I heard he's got a girlfriend,' said a young woman in a suit.

I was thunderstruck. Had I missed something that obvious?

'A blonde,' said the woman, in an authoritative tone. 'She accompanies him to court each day.'

A blonde. It could only be his sister Kerri. What idiot had twisted up that piece of nonsense? I leaned rudely into their conversation.

'"Accompanies him to court"? He's in custody, for God's sake. They bring him up from the cells every morning in handcuffs.' I thrust out both arms, elbows stiff, wrists in shackled position. Offended, the woman and her companions moved away.

Why on earth was I angry? Did I think I owned this story?

It was a fresh spring evening, but in spite of the vodka I walked home from the train in a stupor of cold and horror. How could he have seen the water coming in? Wasn't it pitch dark? In the kitchen I stumbled about trying to cook. I kept making mistakes and dropping things. Nothing I made resembled food. I gave up, wrapped myself in a blanket and lay on the couch. Night fell. How much longer would this go on?

Seconds. That was all it took for Farquharson's car to veer off the wrong side of the highway, flatten an old timber-and-wire fence, cross a stretch of paddock, clip a tree and plunge into the dam. What more could be said about that splinter of time?

The young reconstructionist, Acting Sergeant Glen Urquhart, took the stand equipped with a protractor and a calculator the size of a shoe. He was one of Major Collision's civil engineers, tall, fair and broad-shouldered, with an almost comically noble head and reasonable expression.

'He looks like Chris Grant,' I whispered to Louise.

'Who?'

'Western Bulldogs.'

She shrugged. Like Jai, Tyler and Bailey, she followed the Bombers.

Urquhart had got to the dam just after midnight and, while the car was still submerged, had conducted his own torch-light walk-through of the scene. On the bitumen he found no marks of skidding or yawing that would indicate the path of a car that had been out of control. In the grass between the roadside and the dam he spotted the pair of tyre marks already familiar to us—rolling prints, with no sign of the churning or ploughing that emergency braking or loss of steering control would have caused. He traced the prints to the dam's bank, where headlight debris and a broken branch showed him that the vehicle had clipped a tree on its way into the water.

Back up at the roadside he saw the famous yellow marks that Sergeant Exton had sprayed in the gravel at the point where the car was thought to have left the road. The angle of these marks struck Urquhart as too great, but he thought their position was correct, and concluded that the car must have veered off the road at a sharp angle.

He saw the car when it was hauled out of the water. He noted the positions and the condition of its various controls: ignition off, handbrake off, heater off, headlights off. His listing of these details, in the court's deep silence, was like a series of calm blows.

He paused and let out a long breath through tubed lips.

He saw the three dead children. He described the postures in which they lay. The only sound, apart from his voice, was a terrible sob, almost a muffled scream, from Cindy Gambino. One of the women jurors glanced across at her, her face creased with distress. Kerri Huntington rubbed her eyes with the flat of her hand. Gambino, her mouth twisting, leaned towards Moules, rested against his shoulder, his chest. She was almost in his arms.

Next, with the aim of producing a three-dimensional scale plan of the scene, Urquhart instructed Senior Constable Courtis to set about measuring it, using a piece of equipment called a total survey station or Geodimeter.

Three weeks later Urquhart drove down the overpass in a car of the same model as Farquharson's—a 1990 VN Commodore, whose wheel alignment was within Holden specifications—to video what the vehicle would do if he raised his hands from the steering wheel at the point where Farquharson's car was believed to have swerved off the road. These tests, he said, showed that nothing in the camber of the highway would have caused a car with an unconscious driver to veer towards the dam. Farquharson's car could have diverged sharply to the right only if he had steered it.

Wait, said Rapke. Hadn't the Winchelsea mechanic noted, when test-driving Farquharson's car down the overpass, that at this point of the road the car had a tendency to 'move gently across to the right'? Yes, said Urquhart, but there was an enormous difference between a tendency to drift to the right and the sharp angle off the road that he had measured at roughly thirty degrees. For the car to have left the road at such an angle, the steering wheel would have had to be turned two hundred and twenty degrees.

With a magician's flourish, at which people could not help smiling, Rapke produced from under the bar table a steering wheel mounted on a three-dimensional metal frame and marked at certain points with strips of black gaffer tape. Urquhart set it up on the rail of the witness stand, and demonstrated that to turn it two hundred and twenty degrees, 'either your arms are going to cross, or you have to release one or both hands.'

Urquhart had used an 'internationally accepted' computer software program called PC Crash to create six cartoon-like simulations of how the car would have behaved at three different speeds—sixty, eighty and a hundred kilometres per hour—and with different steering inputs. The court lights were dimmed, and like kids at a matinee we watched the little car zoom down the overpass, swerve to the right across the oncoming lane, and dash across the paddock to the dam, leaving, according to its speed, a simple set of rolling prints, or an extended yaw, or a dramatic sideways skid.

For the car to have travelled between road and dam along the path that the rolling prints showed, said Urquhart, three distinct steering inputs would have been required: the initial sharp one to the right, to take the car off the bitumen; then a brief straightening; then a second input to the right.

If the first sharp input had remained constant, he said, the car could not possibly have left the tracks that the police had found.

Obviously, said Urquhart, because the car had hit water it had left no landing marks that would have allowed a precise calculation of its speed. But before its wheels lost contact with the bank it had left no evidence of high speed: no skid marks, no sign that it had gone into a yaw. It did not bounce. It did not bottom out. It did not gouge the grass. There was no break in the rolling prints. They were continuous all the way to the dam. Thus Urquhart believed that the car had been travelling at between sixty and eighty kilometres per hour, probably closer to sixty.

...

'Herman the German,' I heard one of the tabloid reporters mutter as we shuffled out for lunch. 'Could there *be* a bigger calculator?'

'I hate a bloke who thinks he knows his job,' said Bob Gambino, across the street at the coffee cart.

Was this some sort of country workingman's joke? Louise and I laughed nervously.

It was a while since our last encounter with Bob. He told us that a special ceremony had been held in Winch the previous weekend, at which Cindy had formally inaugurated an annual football trophy called the JTB Award: Jai, Tyler, Bailey. Coffee in hand, Bob settled in for one of his drawling ruminations. 'Cindy and Rob always had the child locks on,' he said. 'It wasn't done on purpose…Yeah…I was surprised Morrissey didn't go in harder with Kingy. Rob's lawyer at the committal went through Greg. He was cryin' and that. But Morrissey said he didn't want to go in any harder, because Greg was so delicate.' He touched thumb and forefinger together in a zero. 'He thought he might snap. He didn't want to be responsible if Greg, um…'

'Went into meltdown?' I said.

'Yeah. If Rob really said, "I hate 'em, I'm gonna kill 'em," well, those are hard words. Why would he need to be wired? How could you misinterpret *those* words?'

He scanned the street, at his leisure. We waited.

'They'll appeal,' he said at last. 'If there's a guilty verdict they'll appeal. They need a good reason. More evidence turnin' up. Or the sev—the severity of the sentence.'

We looked at him, confused. He stood with his hands in his pockets and his feet wide apart, like a farmer.

'Couple o' people on that jury,' he said, with his vague, beneficent smile, 'look like people we know!'

'Hard to tell what they're thinking,' I said. But I was only trying to make conversation.

For two whole days Acting Sergeant Urquhart was mauled on the stand. Morrissey blazed away at him, shouting, whispering, sledging, sometimes merely arguing in an ordinary tone of voice, working to wring some shred of reasonable doubt from the mass of technical information that Urquhart had laid down.

What on earth was the point of surveying the crime scene— sorry, Morrissey meant the *potential* crime scene—if the scanner Major Collision used was not capable of computing the *slope* of the terrain? What use were its measurements if all it could do was calculate the terrain as if it were *flat*? Why didn't Urquhart measure the camber of the road? Why didn't he collect the wire or the posts from the flattened fence? Why had he changed his tune about which of the famous *Exton marks* he had used as a starting point for his calculations? First he said he used the left one, then later he said he'd used the right one. He was incompetent, wasn't he? Negligent? Wasn't he supposed to have an *honours* degree? And how ridiculous and outrageous was it that he had stopped the traffic in both directions on the Princes Highway for—how long? Fifteen minutes? Did he mean to say that *the whole of Victoria* was held up while he shot his pointless, meaningless steering-test videos? He took his hands off the wheel, yes, but what was to show he hadn't been steering with his knees? And why didn't he conduct his steering tests on Farquharson's actual car? He didn't drive Mr Farquharson's car, did he?

'No,' said Urquhart. 'It wasn't driveable. It was caked in mud and water. It was beyond salvage.'

'Being caked in mud and water,' snapped Morrissey, 'doesn't set it apart from many vehicles in the city of Melbourne.'

The court rocked with laughter. Men in the jury lowered their grinning faces. It was impossible to tell if their masculine empathy was directed at Morrissey, or Urquhart, or Farquharson himself.

Urquhart was obliged to acknowledge various police mistakes. Not only were the Exton paint marks on the wrong angle, but they were not even parallel. The wheelbase of Farquharson's car was too wide to have left both tyre marks in the gravel. Only one of them could be correct. Urquhart dug in, though, when Morrissey urged him to agree that Farquharson's vehicle could have left the road at 'a much gentler angle' than the one he had calculated. On this point he would not give way.

'What about a series of tiny little steering inputs?' said Morrissey.

Urquhart smiled wearily and shook his head.

Figures were scattered about like confetti: angles, arcs, radii. The word *infinity* was mentioned. Every now and then Justice Cummins would protest: 'We did all of that this morning, Mr Morrissey. Let's not start again. We've gone over this, Mr Morrissey, for a day and a half.'

Then Morrissey screened a five-second segment from Channel Nine news of the roadside gravel, shot in daylight on the Tuesday after the crash, which showed the yellow paint marks clearly present. He compared this footage with the Peters and Courtis photos of the gravel that were taken on the Tuesday, in which the marks appeared smudged, and forcefully alleged that one of the police officers, in an attempt to conceal Exton's mistake, must have scuffed out the paint with his boot.

The jury was sent out.

'From the Sunday night to the Tuesday,' said Justice Cummins, 'it was not a controlled scene. Paint can disappear for a hundred reasons, but the TV on the Tuesday, on a clear calm day, showing the lines of paint, and then the photograph not showing them, clearly ups the ante. An allegation has been put that needs to be met.'

'What is shown in number one of the Peters photos,' said Rapke, 'is a photographic distortion of what you see in the Channel Nine footage. There has been degradation in the two days since the night of the crash, but there has been no interference.'

'It's not merely a matter of police corruption for the sheer joy of doing so!' cried Morrissey. 'It's—'

'No,' said the judge sarcastically, 'it's just police corruption to frame a man wrongly for the murder of his three children.'

Morrissey raised his voice. 'I'm not going to back away from putting to them that somebody's interfered with it! I'll be putting it very strongly!'

'You've already put it,' said Justice Cummins. 'You've had a long, hard day. There's a nice old saying—"Appeal judges are men who in the cool of the evening undo work that better men do in the heat of the day." Let's have the cool of the evening to think. Let's do it tomorrow.'

...

As the Crown case worked its way into the home straight, some of Farquharson's supporters seemed possessed by a cheerful confidence that verged on the manic. After lunch one day, when Morrissey swept past her through the narrow glass-paned doors, heading back into the fray, Kerri Huntington sang out after him, 'Go, tiger!' She turned to the rest of us with a cheeky giggle. 'That man,' she said, 'makes me laugh.'

On and on went the gargantuan struggle between the two big men. Morrissey accused Urquhart and his fellow officers of all manner of trickery and dishonesty. He challenged him on complicated slabs of what he had said in earlier evidence. He dragged him back and forth across fields of minuscule detail. Hour after hour, while cop and counsel danced like medieval angels upon the head of a pin, I grew stupider and stupider. Surely one did not need a science degree to understand how the car had gone into the dam? I kept glancing at the older men in the jury, the ones who looked like retired tradies or maths teachers in their loose, comfortable T-shirts or plain zipper jackets. Did they too feel this thickening of the brain, this blunting and blurring of mental capacity? Could it be that some atavistic force in me was trying to sabotage my intellect, to block its access to calculations that might demonstrate Farquharson's innocence? What on earth could one take seriously here? Did a modest manner, an air of patient seriousness, the ability to crack a gentle joke, mean that a witness was trustworthy? What if I were one of those tired, frightened jurors, sequestered by an oath from the comfort of work and family, browbeaten by oratory, craving the release of laughter or tears? Would I be dreading the moment when this tinnitus-like racket would have to be disentangled, unpicked, coaxed into a pattern of meaning, so that we could see what was really there, weigh it up, and arrive at a judgment on a fellow human being? What if Farquharson's guilt or innocence was a mystery beyond reckoning? Was anyone going to explain the meaning of the words 'beyond reasonable doubt'? And, if they did, would I still have the nous to grasp it? Or had these five gruelling weeks stripped me of every vestige of native wit?

Calm down. I was not on the jury. I had made no vows. I was only an observer. Nothing life-altering would be required of me. If sitting here became completely intolerable I could pack away my notebook and pen, make my bow at the door, and rush back into the world, where it was spring, where the sun was mild, and the plane trees on Lonsdale Street were putting out their pale fuzz of green.

...

Indeed, as soon as Rapke rose to re-examine Urquhart, a window seemed to open in the courtroom and a stream of fresh air to pass through. I could not tell if it was the simple clarity of what he was saying or the light, dry timbre of his voice, but things flung about in disarray by Morrissey's mighty blitzkrieg quietly resumed their proper places in the landscape. A calm settled, a sense of proportion. No, I did not need to be a scientist in order to picture what had happened between the road and the dam that night.

...

Near the very end of the Crown case, while Detective Sergeant Clanchy was still on the stand, Morrissey screened again the passage from the formal interview at Homicide in which Farquharson, in a voice thickened by tears, denied the detectives' direct accusation and gave his finger-snapping account of how he 'tried and tried and tried' to save his boys. 'I believe I'm a very good citizen in life. I'm a family man who looked after his kids and everything like that. I'm not lying to you. I've got no reason to.' For a second time we saw his indignant tears, his protestations, his strange, emphatic hand gestures on the tabletop. Could Morrissey possibly think this looked good? Yet women in the family seats were crying. Noses were blown, quivering breaths drawn.

Years later, when I read Marilynne Robinson's novel *Home*, I found a description of that moment: 'It was the sad privilege of blood relations to love him despite all.'

...

The jury left the court, and Mr Morrissey made a second no-case submission: he argued that the Crown case was so weak and so circumstantial that it was incapable of reaching the standard of proof required. While he argued on in a low voice, murmuring, sometimes almost whispering, Justice Cummins listened with his head propped on one fist at a dreamy, attentive angle. When he reasoned with Morrissey, his voice too was very soft. Farquharson strained forward to hear, his face dark and clenched above his neatly knotted tie. Kerri Huntington kept changing position in her seat, irritable and frustrated. At the other end of the bar table, Mr Rapke lay back in his tilting swivel chair, one hand clasped around his jaw, watching and waiting.

Justice Cummins spread in front of him several sheets of paper, from which he read a summary of the evidence so far. He brought out of it a narrative that turned the blood to ice. As a matter of law, he ruled, there was sufficient evidence to make a case.

Mr Morrissey would have to gird his loins and launch his defence.

The Crown, in its duty to lay all relevant facts before the court, had called forty witnesses. Its case, swollen by Morrissey's exhaustive cross-examinations, had stretched out over five whole weeks. Morrissey must have done the bulk of his work in those marathon sessions; the defence, he said, had a mere five witnesses lined up. He would lay out its case in two and a half days.

Next morning, before the judge and jury entered, Morrissey got up from the bar table and turned his big body to the seats into which the journalists were filing.

'I know what *you* want!' he shouted with a challenging grin, hitching up the shoulders of his black robe. 'But my client's not going to be called to give evidence. Nope. Mr Farquharson will *not* be called to give evidence!'

He swept his eyes with satisfaction along the row of faces. It was a point of honour for us not to betray surprise or disappointment. We took our seats with decorum, and he plumped back into his swivel chair.

Everyone by now was very tired. The group dynamic of the jury seemed to have stabilised. They entered less formally, sometimes with the fading smiles of people who had been laughing, but they arranged themselves always in the same configuration. Was it a pecking order, or an urge to seek comfort in habit?

As he did every day, for the comfort of counsel, the tipstaff set out along the bar table several tall, clear plastic jugs of water. The eye rested with relief on those evenly spaced columns of purity.

...

The first defence witness was a big, smooth-headed, solemn man in his fifties, Dr Christopher Steinfort. He practised in Geelong as a consultant physician in thoracic and general medicine. He was the Director of the Geelong Hospital's lung function laboratory, and of the Geelong Private Hospital sleep laboratory. Unlike the Crown's medical experts, Dr Steinfort was across cough syncope in a hands-on way. He was here to challenge the accepted view of it as a condition of almost mythological rarity.

Since 1995 he had been keeping a documented database of everyone he saw in his private practice. A search of the 6500 patients currently on his database, he said, had turned up thirty-odd cases of syncope, and among those, about fifteen of cough syncope.

Already this year several cases of it had come to his attention.

A GP had rung him about a chap in Geelong who, while driving his kids to a football match, was overcome by coughing. His car ran off the road, turned over, flipped on to its side, then flipped back and finished up wedged against a fence post.

One woman was sitting having a cup of tea in front of her TV when she started to cough. Next thing she knew she was flat on the floor, with very nasty bruises to the face. Steinfort had admitted her to hospital. She did have pulmonary fibrosis, he added.

And since the Farquharson case became known, quite a few people had come forward to say they had been diagnosed with cough syncope over the last ten or fifteen years, often after a car accident.

Legal Aid had passed them on to Steinfort, who had interviewed them at length. They had all been suffering from a flu-like illness. They had taken time off work and gone to bed with aches and pains, coughing, sore throat and runny nose. They were all men, aged between thirty-five and sixty-five. Two had mild, untreated asthma. One had vascular disease connected with his smoking, so he probably had lung disease as well.

But wasn't the whole point of this, I thought, to explore the occurrence of cough syncope in people who didn't have lung disease?

How was it that Dr Steinfort disagreed so fundamentally with the two Crown medical witnesses, Dr King and Professor Naughton, about the rarity of cough syncope? This was due to a referral bias, said Steinfort, a filtering system. Because of seniority, King in particular, as a neurologist, would tend to have very complex cases referred to him, rather than patients who merely coughed till they keeled over. But Steinfort, down at Geelong, worked at the coalface. Back in the year 2000 one of his patients, while doing a lung function test, had actually blacked out from coughing right in front of him. The man buckled at the knees. Steinfort grabbed him just before he hit the ground. From that day on, the doctor always kept a grip on a patient's shoulders when he administered such a test.

Since May 2006, Dr Steinfort had seen Farquharson five times. He had taken a detailed history, and run his patient through a battery of tests. Farquharson said that he smoked up to twenty cigarettes a day—three times the number smoked by the 'hypothetical' driver Rapke had described to Professor Naughton. Farquharson told Steinfort that he had had 'multiple dizzy spells' at work and at home, and that he had coughed, at times, to the point where his vision darkened; Steinfort called this a 'grey-out'. He had reported to Steinfort a 'witnessed' coughing fit at work during which he had lost consciousness. He had been for years what Steinfort described as 'a horrendous snorer': his throat was reddened by it. He was overweight. Steinfort had advised him to lose ten kilos, which he had been unable to do, and to sleep on his side rather than on his back. A diagnostic sleep study showed that on average his sleep (and no doubt that of his former wife, I thought with a pang) was disturbed twenty-six times an hour, which put him in the moderately severe category of sleep apnoea. But he did not report sleepiness during the day, so Steinfort had discounted falling asleep as a cause of the accident.

...

Mr Rapke's cross-examination was courteous and leisurely. He pointed out that Dr Steinfort was not only an expert witness for the defence but also Farquharson's treating doctor: that he 'had Farquharson's interests at heart'. With the delicate scalpel of a literary critic, he worked his way through Steinfort's clinical notes on his consultations with Farquharson. He stressed from every possible angle that cough syncope is diagnosed on history, and that if the patient's truthfulness is in doubt then the diagnosis cannot be trusted. Then he shone a glaring light on Farquharson's account of his coughing fit at work, witnessed by his supervisor Susan Bateson—an account that for Steinfort's benefit Farquharson had exaggerated, giving him to understand that in Bateson's office he had blacked out. Yet Bateson herself, before this court, had stated that he had sat down, recovered at once, and worked the rest of his shift. Rapke piled up the contradictions between this embroidery of the facts and the testimony of other witnesses to whom Farquharson had clearly stated that he had never before passed out from coughing. He got Steinfort to agree, in a rather small voice, that in Farquharson he might have been 'dealing with a man who was not a reliable historian'. He did the maths and presented Steinfort with the fact that, for all his claims to broad experience, only an incredibly small percentage of his patients—lower than .008 per cent—had cough syncope without underlying lung disease. And surely, he suggested, *a loving father* would not drive his children down the highway at night if he really was suffering from an untreated condition that made him liable to black out without warning.

Listening to this suavely reasoned dismantling was giving me a pain in the stomach. Morrissey objected to what he called an 'oppressive cross-examination', but Steinfort stayed calm. He was an excellent witness, steady and thoughtful. His manner, when he restated his firm belief that Farquharson had experienced an attack of cough syncope, was undefensive, even humble. I remembered the greengrocer slumped across his steering wheel on the freeway. What if, despite everything, Dr Steinfort was right?

When I glanced at Louise, I found her gazing at Rapke in silent admiration.

···

That lunchtime, at the coffee cart, I ran into an old ratbag of a lawyer I had known since the seventies. The years had not been kind to him.

His smoking fingers were stained yellow, and his cheeks were scored with vertical lines. I introduced Louise. He studied her bright, wary face with pleasure.

'So,' he said. 'How did Farquharson strike you, on the stand?'

'They didn't call him,' I said. 'And they're not going to.'

His jaw dropped. 'They're not calling him? What'll the jury think? "What? You're not gonna look us in the eye?" The only thing you can do, when you've got nothing, is put the guy in front of the jury and let him eyeball them!'

We watched him skulk away in his sagging suit and unpolished shoes, muttering cynically to himself.

'Would you have called him?' I asked Louise.

'No way.'

'Neither would I.'

...

David Axup, the defence's second witness, was a traffic analyst who had visited the dam—even Mr Morrissey had slipped by now into using the term 'crime scene' without correcting himself—and come up with his own scale plan. Axup had spent 'thirty-one years and one month' as a member of Victoria Police, and retired in 1992, at the rank of Chief Superintendent commanding the Traffic Support Group. His bulky CV was studded with the names of university courses and Asian countries. Some of the officers currently working in Major Collision had been supervised in their academic work by him. He now ran his own traffic analysis consultancy, with expertise in collision investigation and reconstruction.

The jury sat up and paid Axup full and serious attention. He was a wiry, well-turned-out fellow in a beautiful blue-grey tweed jacket, with delicate hands and a Kiplingesque moustache. When he smiled his face wrinkled dramatically: in a western he would have been addressed as 'Oldtimer'. He must have had experience as an expert witness: he had brought with him to the stand a small wheeled suitcase such as lawyers trundle, out of which, to illustrate a point, he would extract a child's palm-sized toy car. He seemed a figure of benign authority; but under the softly drooping moustache his mouth had a pugnacious set to it, and his voice was as grating as a dragged chain, loud yet oddly hard to hear.

Morrissey dived in crisply, and within minutes Axup had made a categorical statement: Urquhart's famous two-hundred-and-twenty-degree turn of the steering wheel? Impossible. At sixty kilometres per hour a car steered like that would have spun out. 'It didn't happen. It didn't leave the marks.'

Marks. The light went out of the jurors' faces. A reporter scrawled on my pad, 'Yellow paint mark syncope! Instant and total blackout.' We snorted behind our hands, but soon, while Axup confidently set sail on a sea of *steering ratio*, *friction value*, *critical radius*, *cord*, *middle ordinate*, tapping at times on a big black calculator and pouring out figures in his harsh voice, a familiar stupor enfeebled me. A visible wave of resistance rolled through the jury. Their eyes dulled. Their backbones went limp. Yawns tormented them. Two of the younger ones leaned their shoulders together weakly. Justice Cummins took his glasses off and scrubbed at his eyes and forehead; he clenched his jaw, rubbed his cheeks with both hands. I thought, he is sick to death of this, and so is the jury. Louise passed me a note:

'This witness is deeply unpleasant. Inflexible and pedantic. Makes Urquhart look more engaging, thus, convincing.'

Farquharson's family was made of sterner stuff; this was their man and they sat straight-backed. Once, when Axup grudgingly allowed Morrissey's estimate of a crossfall—'It's…close'—Kerri Huntington flashed me an indulgent smile. But even when Morrissey made sharply telling critiques of Major Collision's surveying methods at the scene, Axup blunted their point with his long-winded replies. He was most at ease when asked a question to which he could respond with a lecture.

Hadn't Major Collision been remiss in not collecting the pieces of the broken fence and keeping them for analysis? What was the potential relevance of the fence? 'It may be,' said Axup, 'that if in an investigation it becomes relevant to determine a possible force…in terms of doing that damage with the fence…which could be equated with…a velocity when we know the speed of the vehicle…or when we know the weight of the vehicle…' Several times he seemed to lose his thread, or to miss the point of Morrissey's question. Offered a protractor, he fumbled with it in a growing silence, then held it up awkwardly and rasped, 'It's not a very good one.' Everybody laughed. Morrissey skated airily past the embarrassing moment— 'They don't make 'em like they used to!'—but the witness suddenly looked fragile. His harsh voice began to seem poignant, a shield whose metal had worn thin.

Morrissey toiled away, drawing from him an attack on Urquhart's calculations. If the reconstructionists had used the geodimeter to measure and record the rolling prints as distinct from the yellow paint marks, could they have produced a diagram showing the course of any other visible marks? Yes, said Axup, but in fact their scale plan showed only the yellow paint marks. If the geodimeter had been used to record faithfully the path of any visible rolling print, would it have been possible to calculate the angle of departure of those prints off the bitumen edge? Yes, it would, said Axup—quite easily.

This did not sound good for Major Collision. The uniformed officers seethed in their seats behind the Crown end of the bar table. Urquhart scowled down at his notes, scribbling, his face crimped with suppressed fury. Senior Sergeant Jeffrey Smith, one of the men who had interviewed Farquharson in Geelong Emergency on the night of the crash, sat with elbows on knees, his lined, black-browed face dark and closed. Shoulder to shoulder in their firm-fitting blue tunics, they presented a wall of dense male power. They looked hard, tired and angry; mutinous, deeply fed-up.

...

In the rush to the door at the morning break, Kerri Huntington grinned at me.

'Can you understand this technical stuff?' I said.

She raised her eyebrows and nodded.

'Were you good at maths?' I said. 'I can't follow it at all.'

Slowly and clearly, with exaggerated lip movements, she spelled it out: 'He's going against what the *other* bloke said.'

Morrissey strode past us, rambunctiously cheerful. 'They should just admit they made a mistake,' he roared, 'instead of rubbing it out with their *boot*!' He paused to mime a scrubbing action with one outstretched foot. 'There shouldn't even *be* accident reconstruction-ists at *all*!'

Twenty minutes later, on my way back in, I walked past a small interview room off the echoing hallway and glanced through its glass-panelled doors. The whole Crown team was crammed in there, Rapke and Forrester seated at a laptop, the others standing behind them and craning in over their shoulders: a cinematic arrangement of figures in buzz cuts and wigs, emitting a crackling aura of purpose.

...

When Mr Rapke rose to tackle Axup, his opening questions sent a surge of adrenalin coursing through the thick stupor of the room. What was the *issue* that existed in this case? What was the actual area of *dispute* between the prosecution and the defence? At last, at last—the point! The jurors' eyes cleared; they sat up.

Rapke cross-examined with hands in pockets, eyes down on his papers, so that, when he did raise his head, squinting, lifting his top lip off his teeth, his gaze would hit the witness in the face, like a slap. He shot Axup's persona full of holes. He filleted his CV, bringing out the fact that his training in accident reconstruction consisted of a six-week intensive course in Illinois twenty-one years ago, and that he had no tertiary qualifications in either maths or physics. Did Axup understand the Crown's hypothesis about the car's progress, and had he developed an alternative to it? In a series of silvery manoeuvres, Rapke coaxed the erstwhile cop to a position almost identical to that proposed by his former student, Acting Sergeant Urquhart: that the car could not have travelled from the road to the dam on the arc of those rolling prints without three distinct steering inputs. In its elegant way, it was a massacre.

Morrissey, re-examining, could only attempt damage control. Would the terrain *necessarily* move a vehicle in that situation? No. Would the impact with the fence *necessarily* move the vehicle? No. *Must* there have been three steering inputs? No: it was only hypothetical. Axup climbed carefully down from the stand and left the court, towing his wheeled suitcase behind him.

Between witnesses, Morrissey made a little legal jest to Justice Cummins. The judge laughed, then sat smiling down on the barrister, fondly, like a father.

...

Cam Everett owned the property on which the dam lay. He was a tall, slim, smiling fellow with a head of greying curls. He was a professional firefighter, he said, not a farmer. His sheep were 'just lawnmowers'.

In the last eight years, seven cars had come off the highway and through the fence on to Everett's land. At least two of them had been heading from Geelong to Winchelsea. One bloke's vehicle had landed upside down under a tree; Everett thought he had fallen asleep at the wheel.

On the night of Farquharson's crash Everett had stayed at the scene for an hour, then gone home and sat on the veranda to watch the rescue. Later, when he heard all about what had happened, he drove his Nissan Patrol down the overpass at a hundred kilometres per hour and took his hands off the wheel at three different spots—'just a curiosity thing.' On each occasion his car drifted to the right, as far as the central white line, before he corrected it. 'The whole road,' he said, 'goes to the right.'

Loping out of the court, he flashed a warm grin at Farquharson, who met his eye with a wry grimace.

...

Last up on the Friday of the trial's fifth week was an expert in medical and forensic photography from RMIT University, a good-humoured American in a reefer jacket and elastic-sided boots. Associate Professor Gale Spring was asked, first, to compare stills from the Channel Nine video footage of the yellow paint marks with certain of Sergeant Peters' aerial photos, and to confirm the degradation of the marks that the defence argued was visible. Second, he was to pronounce upon the reality or otherwise of some mysterious 'pale marks' in the long grass—possible tyre tracks that Morrissey accused the police of having purposely ignored in the 'tunnel vision' of their investigation.

Spring stunned us with a lecture on the different provenances of the photos—video and still digital camera—and the effects of compression on these two formats. We struggled to evaluate his comparisons of the intensity of daylight, the positions of the sun, the angles of shadow in the different images—of black marks, pale marks, black dots, yellow dots, a splodge and a smaller splodge, bits and pieces of grass. From his laptop he manipulated the images on the high screen, zooming in, blowing them up, shrinking them down, until we did not know whether we were coming or going. He compared pairs of photographs—'gee, the screen is bad'—and made declarations of such audacious certainty about what was 'really there' and what was 'an artefact of the photographic process' that I stared at him in wonder.

'Are they there, whatever they are,' asked Morrissey about the strange pale marks in the grass, 'or are they a trick of the camera?'

'They're not a trick of the camera at all. They're as real as any of the other areas we've seen.'

But how real was that? Morrissey's long bow strained close to snapping. Why didn't the whole court burst out laughing? When I looked at the judge I thought for a second that he was working to keep a straight face; but no doubt it was a trick of the light.

And as the cheerful photography expert clomped out of the court in his Cuban heels, the spectre I had been trying to ignore for five weeks rose up before me. Sergeant Exton's famous paint marks in the gravel were a red herring. The angle of them did not matter at all. Whether they had been scuffed out or degraded was neither here nor there. The only things that mattered in all this technical palaver were the steering inputs, and all the rest was noise.

...

When I stumped home at the end of that fifth week, I was surprised to find that the world beyond the trial was still carrying on its humble existence. Rain must have been falling while I sat in court: my tanks were more than half full. The big pittosporum tree over the back fence was about to burst into blossom. Junkies had held up the corner shop. Kids from the flats had crashed a stolen car on to the railway line. And my grandchildren reported that a runaway horse from the racecourse had been recaptured in our street by a neighbour, an old strapper, who had approached it with a carrot in one hand and an apple in the other. The modest glow of these facts filled me with gratitude and relief.

The defence had one last arrow in its quiver: a social worker and grief counsellor from Geelong named Gregory Roberts.

As it happens, a close friend of mine worked for years as a grief counsellor at the Peter MacCallum Cancer Centre. She is a subtle and serious person, and the things she told me about her work made it clear to me that she and her colleagues performed an essential and deeply humane service. But Roberts, said Morrissey, was apparently something more than an intelligent comforter. He would testify that Farquharson's unnatural-seeming conduct after he got out of the dam, his bizarre responses to the calamity, lay 'within the normal grief/trauma reactions of a suddenly bereaved parent'.

The only witnesses who are permitted to express opinion before a jury are people acknowledged to be experts in their field. Before the jury entered the court that morning, and before Gregory Roberts was called, Justice Cummins questioned Morrissey on Roberts' formal qualifications. They seemed, he said, rather sparse for an expert witness. What gave him more authority than an ordinary member of the community?

An ordinary person might find it surprising, argued Morrissey, that Farquharson had left the dam, declined an offer of help and kept asking people for cigarettes. An ordinary person might well be...*put off* by Farquharson's insistence on being taken straight to his ex-wife. But Roberts, it seemed, had a breadth of experience with people in the grip of sudden bereavement, and he had two concepts— 'traumatic grief' and 'hyper-focus'—that would sweep these odd behaviours back into the fold of the normal. 'Traumatic grief' was a relatively recent concept, and only very limited research had been done on it, yet it was already listed as a diagnosable condition in the *Diagnostic and Statistical Manual–IV*.

Justice Cummins looked askance. He allowed Morrissey to call Mr Roberts, but excluded a second grief counsellor, Leona Daniel, an older woman who had been summoned to Farquharson's bed in Geelong Emergency at 10 p.m. on the night of the crash. Daniel had observed his terrible distress and done her best to console him.

'The prosecution,' said the judge, 'has never suggested that your client hasn't exhibited grief. What is said is that he killed his children. He's not charged with not crying.'

Farquharson listened, his face darkening. He did not enjoy hearing his psychological state discussed. He looked older; his hair was longer, and turning grey. From time to time he would glance at his family with a crooked frown of indignation.

In came Roberts, a small, fragile-looking man with the bird-like head and dark, trimmed beard of a Renaissance courtier. He worked, he said, for Hope Bereavement Care, as well as SIDS and Kids in Geelong, a service that offered support for anyone affected by the sudden and unexpected death of a child. When Morrissey used the phrase 'bereaved fathers', Kerri Huntington began silently to cry, wiping her eyes with her fingertips. Her sister Carmen went pale and wept, and Farquharson himself pulled out his hanky, blinking and blinking, his mouth upside down. In full view of the sisters, one of the journalists folded her newspaper into a pad and started on a crossword.

Four days after the boys died in the dam, Gregory Roberts had been called to give support to Farquharson. Morrissey would ask the counsellor, now, to work his way through the events of the fatal night, starting with Farquharson's escape from the dam and ending at the police interview in Emergency. Roberts would name and interpret each stage in the language of 'traumatic grief', the emerging field in which he was researching his PhD.

Getting out of the dam, said Roberts, the person would be disoriented. There would be elements of shock, a high level of fear. His adrenal levels would be rising. The *fight mode* would be his efforts to get the children out of the car. When that was unsuccessful, the *flight mode* would have kicked in—he would seek to flee.

Though Rapke had shot down the phrase, Morrissey resurrected it: what did it mean that witnesses described him as 'a babbling mess'?

That would be the effect of disorientation, especially when one remembers that he had been unconscious. When your adrenalin is surging, you don't make a lot of sense. Even if you are able to give information, you can come across as robotic and emotionless. Workers experienced in this field, said the grief counsellor, do not find it at all strange for a person to make the blunt statement 'I've just killed my kids'. It is part of the *surrender mode*, even though the reality of the statement might not have quite hit home.

His obsession with being taken to Cindy?

When a child dies in the presence of only one parent, said Roberts, regardless of whether the parents are together or separated, there is very strong urge to contact the other parent. People in trauma often suffer from information overload. They can become what's called *hyper-focused*. Very single-minded. They disregard any other information that is put to them. Trained people know that in such a situation someone has to take charge—to acknowledge what the hyper-focused person is saying, but guide him firmly towards what really needs to be done. Shane Atkinson and Tony McClelland, the two young men who stopped for Farquharson on the road, could not have been expected to know this. They succumbed to his hyper-focused demands.

The fact that Farquharson refused their offers to dive down after the car, and would not use their phone to call 000?

Farquharson's system was already overloaded. He was unable to absorb or even register any extra inputs. By the time they had taken him to Cindy, when he appeared to her to be delirious, he had entered what was called in the literature *the outcry phase*. Some of the reality of what had happened was starting to become apparent. The presence of Cindy, 'a key attachment figure', was likely to bring up more emotion.

Farquharson's failure to join in the rescue attempts at the dam showed that he was already quite exhausted. Adrenalin levels do not stay high for long. He had moved into *dissociation*, a state in which he started to block out what had happened, to become detached, and to step back.

His repeated demands for cigarettes, so enraging to the other men at the scene?

Trauma experts know that under stress the body craves stimulants. This is not rational or conscious. It is a physiological fact, and Roberts had witnessed it many times.

How was it that Farquharson had been seen in tears by two civilian witnesses, while various police officers, particularly the two who had interviewed him in Emergency, had been taken aback by his lack of distress?

This, too, was standard—well within the typical range of trauma and grief. Most civilians faced with a police officer, paramedic or doctor (figures Morrissey called *men in uniform*) will fall into a very respectful way of talking; and people dealing with an overload of information tend to resort to behaviours already ingrained in them. Plus, in a state of 'traumatic grief', and in what Roberts further called 'complicated grief', people go emotionally numb. Their moods fluctuate. There is a shrinkage in their ability to think rationally: a condition called 'cognitive constriction'. Things they do can seem illogical to observers.

...

This testimony filled me with scepticism, yet I longed to be persuaded by it—to be relieved of the sick horror that overcame me whenever I thought of Farquharson at the dam, the weirdness of his demeanour, the way it violated what I believed or hoped was the vital link of loving duty between men and their children. And, as I listened, the phantom of failed suicide shimmered once more into view. Nobody in this whole five-week ordeal had yet said anything that could lay it to rest.

...

Perhaps Morrissey had warned his witness that the judge had been reluctant to acknowledge him as an expert in anything, for Roberts' analyses were offered in the faintly piqued tone of someone whose amour-propre has been stung. When Rapke got to his feet, he did not temper the wind to the shorn lamb. Before the blast of his cross-examination, the witness's spine seemed to ripple and his head to bob and tilt on the slim stalk of his neck.

Yes, Roberts was aware that Farquharson had a history of depression and that he had been taking anti-depressants for a time. Roberts' impression was that the Farquharson marriage break-up had been 'amicable', and that their focus had been on the welfare and happiness of the children. Farquharson, he said, showed no animosity at all towards his former wife. Yes, Roberts had heard the allegation that Farquharson had made threats to kill his children in revenge against Gambino, but he had not taken this into consideration, because his opinion was 'around traumatic grief', a condition that he had noted in Farquharson from their first contact. He had made no presumption of guilt or innocence.

It soon came to light that since 9 September 2005, Roberts, in his role as grief counsellor, had seen Farquharson, weekly or fortnightly, seventy times.

'Did you say seventy?' asked Rapke.

The judge leaned forward on both elbows: 'Seven *oh*?'

Yes.

'In those seventy counselling sessions,' said Rapke, 'you, for the purpose of requiring him to confront what had happened and deal with his grief and his bereavement and his "traumatic" grief and his "complicated" grief, had him talk about the events of the night?'

Well, no, said Roberts. If Farquharson had gone into detail, he would have steered the conversation away from it—in fact, he would have brought it to a halt. From the beginning he had had instructions from the victim liaison people in Victoria Police that his brief was to focus on grief and bereavement. He was to avoid any in-depth conversation about what had happened on the night.

In the wry silence of the court somebody clicked her tongue. A thought-bubble floated above the jurors' heads: 'What the hell *did* you talk about?'

'Fair enough,' said Rapke, pressing forward. 'What did he tell you he did on the night?'

'He told me he was driving home from Geelong, had a coughing fit and blacked out. He woke up, found himself in the dam. He tried to save the children several times. He got out of the dam, flagged down a car, got to Cindy, went back to the dam, then found himself in Geelong Hospital.'

'What did he tell you he did, to try and save the children?'

'Again, I would have stopped the conversation if it went into detail. But he said he made several attempts to save the children. It involved diving down.'

'Did he tell you that he tried to get the boys together?'

'No. I heard that on the taped interview with the police.'

'He's suggesting,' said Rapke drily, 'that as part of his rescue attempts he tried somehow to *marshal* the boys in the car for the purpose of getting them out?'

'It appeared to be, yes.'

The journalists slid their eyes sideways in expressionless faces.

Rapke bounded on. Would Roberts expect Farquharson's responses to trauma on the night to have been the same, whether he had killed his children deliberately or by accident?

In a person who had done such a thing on purpose, said Roberts, yes, the same trauma reactions would have been expected, but that person would also have shown more agitation, more angry outbursts, more allocating of blame to others—and perhaps a complete flight from the scene.

And what about the fact that at no stage did Farquharson ask what had happened to his children? If they had been found? If they were safe? Had they been rescued? Were they dead? And the fact that all he did ask about was himself? What's *my* position? What's going to happen to *me*? All that was normal too, was it?

It was.

The jury sat rigid. Nobody breathed.

Rapke spread his fingertips on the bar table. 'I have to ask you this question, Mr Roberts, and I hope you'll forgive me—but has there been any event in your life which has made you particularly empathetic towards Mr Farquharson?'

Roberts' head wavered on his thin neck. 'No.'

Rapke raised his chin, squinted his eyes, and said in a low, polite, clear voice, 'Have you lost a child?'

'I have.'

'Thank you,' said Rapke, and sat down.

Morrissey let the ghastly pause stretch out and out.

'No questions arising, Your Honour,' he said at last.

The defence case was over.

While the court's attention swung to the judge, Roberts crouched down in the witness box to gather up his things. He walked out, holding his head high, a wounded, discarded, yet suddenly dignified figure.

...

'How'd you like that last question?' shouted Morrissey at the journalists, as we filed out for lunch. I did not hear anybody answer.

Louise and I darted across Lonsdale Street.

'God,' she said, 'that was brutal.'

'Yeah, but the guy had obviously taken everything Farquharson told him at face value. Rapke had to blow that open, surely?'

'Couldn't he have asked him, "Was there anything you saw in his post-offence conduct that struck you as indicative of innocence?"'

'Oh, come on! They can't ask a witness that, can they?'

But we were shaken. Rapke, our hovering falcon, had swooped into the muck with the rest, and savagely drawn blood.

From the queue at the coffee cart we saw Kerri Huntington walking down the Supreme Court steps with Gregory Roberts. Surely, I thought, a counsellor has to do more than feel empathy for a client and teach him 'techniques'. Doesn't a counsellor have to take it up to him? Tackle him right where he lives? Even across four lanes of traffic and a row of parked cars, we could see him nodding, the placating tilt of his small, fine head.

...

The ideal closing address, I imagine, is a brilliantly condensed recapitulation of the trial, a sparkling argument with a spin that clears the jurors' heads and engages their hearts.

For that, you have to watch TV.

In this court, the exhausted jurors sat in their box for four more days, some still dutifully taking notes, while first Rapke, then Morrissey, ran a précis of the evidence past them.

Rapke addressed the jurors quietly, as if he considered them his intellectual equals. He proposed two possible views of the matter, both classed as murder: first, that the killings were the product of a sudden, aberrant impulse, perhaps triggered by a psychological disturbance and exacerbated by Farquharson's despair, anger, frustration and loneliness; and second, that they were the culmination of a desire and a plot, hatched months earlier, to take revenge on the wife who had rejected him.

He laid out the evidence in categories, with a level efficiency. He gave full weight to Farquharson's anger, his humiliation and depression after the breakdown of his marriage, but then turned them to his own purpose: the darkening of the accused man's thinking. He pointed out the lack of fit between Farquharson's differing accounts of the events to different people, his calculated embroideries with their wonky hems and ragged edges.

He made the excruciating suggestion that, while Farquharson was refusing offers of help from the two young men on the road, his children might still have been fighting to unbuckle their seatbelts in the sinking car, surviving for brief moments in an air lock. At this,

---

Farquharson covered his face with his handkerchief and sobbed.

Rapke read out passages from the Homicide interview. Even in the barrister's unhistrionic rendition, Farquharson sounded flustered, hollow, terribly evasive and woolly. He kept glancing across the court at his sisters. He shook his head. He scowled. Kerri Huntington's sharp profile, under the fleece of curls, remained attentive and still.

But not even Rapke, with his sinewy syntax and his steel core of logic, could inject adrenalin into the most soporific material of all: the engineering evidence, the physics of the way the car had left the bitumen and gone into the dam. It had been worked to death. While he reasserted with vigorous clarity the propriety and competence of the Major Collision investigation, the jury sagged and flagged. Some of them blatantly yawned, as did Morrissey once or twice, leaning back in his leather chair.

During the summary of the medical evidence, a dark-haired young juror in the front row of the box rested her head, in a posture of unendurable fatigue, on the shoulder of the woman beside her. Just when I thought she had fallen asleep, she roused herself, and exchanged a tiny private smile with the other woman. It shocked me. They looked like people who no longer needed to put on a show of concentrating, people who had already made up their minds.

But when Rapke turned to the testimony of Farquharson's mate Greg King, when he defended that witness's integrity, his mental stability and his motives, the whole jury snapped back to life. Plainly they cared about King, or, at the very least, found in him a crucial strand of the story. Rapke took apart the material in King's secretly recorded conversations; he guided the jury through the escalating

urgency of Farquharson's utterances with a psychological sophistica-
tion that made the heart quail.

And when he surged into the final curve of his argument—the
sheer statistical improbability of the defence version of events—
the jury sat engrossed. What were the odds, asked Rapke, that a
man without lung disease would suffer an attack of cough syncope,
this condition so rare and so unprovable? That a paroxysm would
overcome him at the one spot, on that thirty-seven-kilometre journey,
where a car could leave the highway, slip neatly past the end of
the guard rail, and travel across almost flat terrain into one of the
only two dams in the immediate area? Then, that a car with an
unconscious driver could miraculously maintain a steady arc, flatten
without changing course a fence strong enough to rip its front panel,
and swerve to clip a tree? And most extraordinary of all, ladies and
gentlemen, what were the odds that these things could happen to a
man who, only two months earlier, had confided in his mate that he
had dreamed of having an accident that involved a dam?

...

Next morning I was sitting in the front row of the media seats when
Farquharson was brought past me into the dock. He glanced up.
Our eyes met. Startled, I smiled. He tried to return the greeting, but
managed only a teeth-baring grimace that did not reach his eyes. I
remembered the day at the Geelong committal hearing, a year earlier,
when he had held open the heavy court door for me. The smile he
had offered me that day was awkward and shy. Now he was a man
accustomed to being stared at, and sketched by court artists, and

hustled along in handcuffs. I was shocked to catch myself thinking: *You poor bastard*. Was there something about him that called up the maternal in women, our tendency to cosset, to infantilise? Perhaps he had made use of this all his life. Or perhaps he was trapped in it, helplessly addicted to being coddled. A tough American public defender I know, a woman, on first hearing the charges against Farquharson, had said to me, 'If I was appearing for him, I'd try to make his family see that loving him doesn't mean they have to believe he's innocent.' As he shuffled past me into the dock and sat down with a guard on either side, a wild thought came to me. What if he could turn to his sisters, right here in front of everybody, and shout to them across the court, 'Okay. I did it. *Now* can you love me?'

...

While the Crown in its closing had taken a dry, intellectual approach, the defence lunged straight for the heart. For two whole days, with his back to the press seats, Morrissey yarned to the jury in his warm, matey way, like a man buttonholing a stranger in a pub. Throughout this loosely constructed address, Farquharson gripped a big blue hanky in his hand. At direct mentions of his boys he covered his distorted face with it, and shed bitter tears.

A benign light bathed the world that Morrissey conjured up: Winchelsea, a sun-splashed hamlet whose residents were focused on family and work, on sport, on the schooling of their kids. It was a *nice* community, populated by decent, law-abiding folk who loved their children and shared an attitude of respect for authority. Sometimes 'a circle of pals' drank together quietly in one of the town's few pubs, or at a makeshift bar in a neighbour's back shed. Farquharson, he said, was one such Winchelsea bloke—'an Anglo-Saxon country-town man'.

Anglo-Saxon? Surely the name Farquharson could only be Scottish. Then it dawned on me. Anglo-Saxon is code for stiff upper lip. An Anglo-Saxon bloke might well appear emotionally repressed at a time of great trauma.

Morrissey complimented the jury on their deep knowledge of the case. They were now equipped, he said, to understand details that the ignorant newspaper reader out there would find 'a bit funny'—the car's ignition and headlights being turned off, Farquharson leaving the dam and going to his wife. In a clever rhetorical move he praised the police for the 'hardness', the 'toughness' of their interview with Farquharson. They were experienced officers. They had brought psychological pressure of a perfectly legitimate kind to bear on Farquharson. The defence was glad they had pushed him, because look at the answers he so honestly and cooperatively provided! Those answers had completely undermined the case against him—and now the Crown was stuck with them.

Marital separations are always difficult but, as separations go, he said, the Farquharsons' was 'the least aggressive and nasty ever on record'. Cindy Gambino, though she had lost her love for her husband and left him, was 'magnificent at all times'. Never once did she use the kids against him.

He brushed aside the import of depression. To distinguish Farquharson's sadness at his mother's death in 2002 from the genesis of blacker moods, he called sentimentally upon the jurors' own experience of family loss: 'Everyone's got a mum and all of those

---

mums are going to die one day. And anyone who's lost a mum knows that it will be a sad day when it happens.'

Thus Morrissey drained the darkness from the background of the story. All its mythic shadows were dispelled. He airbrushed out Farquharson's anguish and humiliation, his wounded jealousy, his angry fear that he would be ousted as a father by Stephen Moules. Farquharson's sadness was real, sure—but it was the sort of sadness that Avanza could help with. Everybody around him saw that he was coming good. The man with *real* mental problems was that tormented soul Greg King, who at the behest of the police had so appallingly manipulated and betrayed his friend.

Time and again, to describe what he called the Crown's 'theories' as distinct from the defence's 'facts', Morrissey used the word *weird*. This weird, nasty theory that Farquharson could have pre-planned the crash—it was ludicrous, 'a crock'. All Farquharson's actions with his boys implied a future. Two nights before Father's Day, at the footy awards, didn't King see Farquharson cuddling little Bailey in his arms? This doomed baby he was supposedly going to drown in a dam? And Mr Rapke's horrible picture of the children fighting for breath in an air pocket as the car sank? It was a fantasy. There were no air bubbles. The rear window popped out. That car went down like a stone.

As for Professor Naughton, the Crown's medical expert—he was so ignorant of the reality of cough syncope that it was incredible he had ever been called as a witness! In a sinister macho voice Morrissey mocked the Crown's claim that Farquharson was in a seething rage about getting 'the shit car': 'A man can only take so much. Now I am going to murder three children.' The threat that

Greg King heard Farquharson make, in the 'innocuous' fish-and-chip-shop conversation, he parodied in a gangster snarl: 'No one does that to *me* and gets away with it.' The investigation on the night was a farce. He pilloried the Major Collision officers by adopting a Mr Plod the Policeman voice when he quoted them or summarised their evidence. Acting Sergeant Urquhart was Buzz Lightyear, a nice sort of bloke who had no idea. Sergeant Peters had lied through his teeth. There was absolutely no evidence of conscious steering. Indeed, there was every chance that ten-year-old Jai might have grabbed the wheel—he was a responsible, alert kid, capable of reacting to a crisis by trying to help.

The Crown case was 'a fairy story—the myth of the bad daddy who killed his kids'. It was 'glib, glib, glib'. Farquharson was not some monster. He was not an iceman, not a brooding, angry, rage-filled person at all. He was a traumatised Anglo-Saxon guy. He was just—*Rob*. He had been dealt a hard hit. The time had come to find him not guilty—to let him go on with whatever life he had.

I scanned the jury. They were wide awake, sharp-eyed and concentrating, but their faces were blank. Louise studied them too. She scrawled on my notebook, 'I don't think this is working.'

In the lobby, when court rose, I pushed open the door of the ladies' toilets and found Farquharson's sisters in there with the younger women of their party, crowding together at the hand basins and the mirror. Someone was saying, '*He* was a *prince*.' 'Yes,' said Carmen tartly, 'but princes can turn into frogs, you know.' They all burst out laughing. I ducked behind them into a cubicle, and waited there while they merrily refreshed their make-up and bouffed up their hair. I wished I could stand close to them. They sounded so confident. Were they cracking hardy, working to keep each other's spirits up, or was I the one with the wrong end of the stick?

...

Late that afternoon my old barrister friend and I met on the steps of Parliament House, and spent an hour drinking gin and tonic in the Regency-striped armchairs of the lounge at the Windsor Hotel.

'You've heard the closing addresses,' he said, neatly arranging his feet in their polished brogues. 'Which way would you jump?'

'I don't know,' I said. 'What if there's doubt, but only a cigarette paper thick? Is that reasonable?'

He closed his eyes. 'What kind of answer's that, woman? This is real life. Hard decisions have to be made.'

I drank in glum silence. Why did lawyers always make me feel so stupid? I wanted to ask him about gut feeling. I knew he would say it had no place in a court. But what *was* it? Wasn't it really a kind of semi-conscious reasoning, shaped by the many weeks of evidence? A lightning-fast, instinctual matching up of the phenomenon in question against every similar one you had ever come across, in all your life's dealings with other people?

...

Everyone could see that the jurors liked Justice Cummins. He had a way of acknowledging their fear, and soothing it. Whenever he spoke directly to them, their weary faces would soften. Even the usually expressionless men would turn to him, smiling, like students of a

teacher who had earned their trust. Their duty, now, was to deliberate on the facts of the case and arrive at a verdict; but first the judge
would give them careful instructions about the law as it applied to
the facts. This address is called the charge, and it is the part of a trial
most vulnerable to the critical eye of the Court of Appeal.

Cummins launched his charge on the final Monday morning.
He spoke with energetic expression, moving and swaying on his
throne-like chair, leaning forward, rearing back. He inhabited
rhetorically, one by one, the conflicting testimonies, the competing
submissions the jury had heard over the long weeks of the trial. Once
or twice he had to pause, as if to control emotion.

Soon Louise nudged me. 'Look at Rapke.' The prosecutor's
glasses were folded on the table in front of him and his cheek rested
on a hand that threatened to go limp and drop his head among his
papers with a crash. As we watched, he settled back into his leather
swivel chair with his chin tucked into his collar and his starched
white jabot poking up in a curve, and sank into a frank slumber. His
junior, Amanda Forrester, swung to him, to whisper a comment. She
froze, then quietly turned away. Soon she too closed her eyes and sat
with head on hand, her face in repose younger and sweeter.

Cindy Gambino sat between her parents. Since the last time I
had talked with them at the coffee cart, Bob and Bev Gambino had
faded further into their quiet country selves, coming and going with
a nod or a smile. I admired their reserve, their composure. What did
they hope for in secret? How deep did it run, their fidelity to their
daughter's support of her ex-husband, in the bereavement they all
shared? Farquharson listened keenly to the judge's long address. At
the mention of his son's names he flinched, and his jaw swelled with

stifled tears. At times he would pull an angry face, or jerk about indignantly in his chair. Meanwhile, Gambino sat in the shelter of her parents. She leaned her elbows on the rail and held a white hanky to her nose and mouth, as if her tears would never stop leaking. At painful moments of the story her face went into spasm and she put her hands over her eyes. Finally the three Gambinos got up and discreetly left the court.

At every break, Farquharson's family would throng into the paved courtyard, chattering and smoking, bringing take-away coffee and standing about in the patches of sunlight that narrowed as the day dragged on and shadows formed in the colonnaded corners. The journalists politely left the open spaces to them, and clustered murmuring in more remote spots. The girl from the *Herald Sun*, in her little black ballet slippers, opined that the verdict would come fast, and would be not guilty. A cold shudder ran through me: oh, wait! I haven't worked it all out yet, and I don't know how I'm going to! I shifted away from her certainty, and hid in an alcove pretending to read a magazine. When I looked up, the others had gone back in. I ran across the flagstones in my soft-soled shoes, past a woman standing near the only bench still flooded with afternoon light. It was Farquharson's sister, Carmen Ross. Her weary husband, slumped on the bench with his arms folded on his chest, had fallen asleep in the remaining warmth. She stood facing him, watching over his rest. She raised one hand against the sun, to cast a small patch of shade on to his bare, greying head. He did not stir. As I crept by, she put out a forefinger and delicately touched his brow.

...

At the end of the second day, when Justice Cummins had concluded his charge and painstakingly fine-tuned it, the jury of fourteen was whittled back to the requisite dozen by means of a random ballot. The judge's associate drew numbers out of a wooden box: two of the women were liberated. The judge expressed his regrets to them, but they hardly bothered to conceal their elation. In its final configuration, the group looked compact, business-like—a twelve-person outfit, stripped back and ready to rock.

How terrible it must be for counsel to see the jurors' backs as they retire. Morrissey's lips were white. Seven weeks of struggle, and now these twelve strangers of unknown sympathies and reasoning power would take the reins.

'The wait for the verdict,' said Justice Cummins gently to Farquharson, who sprang to his feet, 'is the hardest part of the trial. I suggest you try to bear up.'

Farquharson nodded to him, courteous and present. For the first time I saw him as he might have been in ordinary life, at work, at school. It touched me. Again I felt shocked, as if this response were somehow illegitimate.

...

All Thursday we waited.

Families and journalists drifted around the echoing corridors, staying well within call. Carmen Ross sat at the long table in the hall and laid out games of patience. Another woman worked quietly at her crochet. The word among the journalists now was acquittal, though no one could quite articulate a reason. I was glad that nobody asked for my opinion. The responsibility of making a decision seemed beyond me.

Mid-morning the sun came over the roof of the building and we headed for the fresh air. But a door burst open on the other side of the courtyard and disgorged a bunch of people in bright casual clothes, dressed for spring. It was the jury. The frowning tipstaff shouted to us, 'You can't come through here!' We withdrew to the corridor and gazed at them through the glass-paned door. They milled about in the sun, laughing, shifting from foot to foot like guests at a barbecue. Many of them were smoking. They seemed cheerful, and free. They did not look like people who might be about to send a man to prison for the rest of his life.

Halfway through the afternoon a passing man called to us over his shoulder, 'They've sent out some dry-cleaning.'

The day ended without result.

On the train home I texted my scornful barrister friend. 'The jury were laughing. What's that mean?'

He replied at once. 'Their laughing is unnerving. But in the end their decision is a purely rational one, devoid of sympathy and emotion. Rather like solving a maths problem. At least so they are told by the judge. And that is how it should be. In other words, the decision is made without ANY consideration of the consequences for Farquharson.'

'Big ask.'

'In no other way can I explain the levity of which you speak.'

. . .

On the Friday I took to the courtyard some unfinished knitting, an old green scarf, and tried to get it moving again. My hands were sweating and my tension was uneven, but it helped to have something to do. The journalists drew together, looking each other in the face more openly. There was a comradeliness. They shared food, brought each other coffees without being asked. Someone reported that Rapke was not here: it was the festival of Simchat Torah; he had to go to shul. We kicked the Farquharson story this way and that. Had Rapke made a big enough hole in the defence's medical evidence? Would the jury give a shit about the mistakes in the yellow paint marks? We wondered about Farquharson's mother, what kind of woman she had been, whether it was the loss of her presence alone that made Cindy Gambino call that house 'the morgue'. Strange hours, with no end in sight, analysing and speculating in the sun, feeling our hearts beat faster than usual.

Just after two o'clock, one of the *Herald-Sun* journalists beckoned wildly from across the courtyard. We ran down the hall in a pack and jostled into our seats. Morrissey forged in. He went straight to Farquharson in the dock, and high-fived him. Police officers slid into the pew behind the bar table. People we knew and others we had never seen before sat tightly crammed, upstairs and down. The judge strode to the bench. We bowed. He said, in a low voice, 'I urge people, whichever way the verdict goes, to try to contain their emotion.' A sickening hush. The jury entered. Their faces were grey. One woman was squeezing a fistful of soaked tissues. Another had a hand over her eyes. The foreman worked his mouth, chewing the insides of his cheeks.

Each dead child was named and the charge of murder read.

At the first 'guilty', Cindy Gambino let out a piercing, animal wail. Guilty. Guilty. Court officers rushed to her aid. Beside her a pale face swayed and dropped: her mother had fainted. Bev's sons carried her to the door. The court swarmed with people turning and gasping and pressing. Screams and sobs echoed in its high white ceilings. Farquharson must have been whisked away to the cells: the dock was empty. In the uproar, Morrissey turned towards the media seats and faced us in silence. He stood like a beaten warrior, feet together, shoulders stooping, hands clasped in front of his genitals. His face was chalk, and on it was a tiny, rigid smile.

The judge cleared the court. The tipstaff pushed the journalists out the door. In the courtyard, paramedics trundled Bev Gambino past us on a gurney, flat on her back, her face a greenish white. Gambino was already in an ambulance. Kerri Huntington crouched on a bench, elbows on her thighs, smoking hard and staring up at the crowd with loathing. I veered close to her and muttered a clumsy word. She scorched me with a look. In a corner of the yard, beside the men from Major Collision, Amanda Forrester fumbled for a cigarette. The cops, in their paratroopers' loose pants and heavy black boots, were a study in self-command. If they were triumphant they declined to show it. But Forrester's vivid, white-toothed face, gushing smoke, shone with a fiercely suppressed satisfaction. A man behind me said, 'What a courageous jury!' A prosecutor I knew squeezed past. He too was restraining jubilation, but he said to me, 'You don't know how much shit we cop, as prosecutors. Having to cut a path through all that lying.'

The journalists were reluctant to part. 'Oh,' they cried, 'that was the worst I've seen. It doesn't get any worse than that.' They hugged each other and rushed away. One of the young women was six months pregnant; her face had turned yellow, and she stood still with one hand pressed against her belly. The boy who was covering his first murder trial touched my arm and stared at me, white-eyed, unable to speak.

At my elbow Louise the gap-year girl had been observing the pandemonium with her customary dry reserve, though her cheeks were faintly flushed. 'I'm out of here,' she said.

'What? You're leaving?'

'Text you later.' She hugged me, slid into the crowd and vanished. She knew when she had had enough.

I found the veteran journalist, and put out my hand to say goodbye. My face must have been a sight, burning red. She looked at me hard, with an ironic smile.

'You didn't see this coming, did you. You're shocked, aren't you.'

'Yes. I'm shocked.'

She drew me away from the others. 'When *I* first came into court today,' she said, 'I was filled with wave after wave of *rage*. You see this is what these men *do*. This is the most appalling, savage, cruel revenge a man can take on a woman—to make out it was *all her fault*.'

From the train home I sent Louise an over-emotional text: 'Don't be alone today after what we just saw.'

She made no reply. I felt foolish, but not surprised. I saw that unlike Morrissey, unlike me, she was a person with sturdy boundaries. I tried to imagine what she would have said, had she answered. Probably something philosophical. Something hard-nosed, in Latin. *Dura lex sed lex.* The law is hard, but it is the law.

That night, at bedtime, I found the unfinished green wool scarf on the floor where I had dropped my bag. I picked it up and saw that, when the call for the verdict had come, I had stopped halfway along a row. It occurred to me to preserve in some way the moment of decision. I marked it with one red stitch. Then I knitted to the end of the row, and cast off.

After the high-pitched drama of the verdict, the plea hearing three weeks later, on 26 October 2007, was quiet and slow. The air in the court seemed thick, almost gluey. Mr Rapke argued that a crime so cruel, by a man who showed no remorse, could be fitly punished only by three life sentences with no chance of parole. Remorse, replied Mr Morrissey, could hardly be expected from a man who had pleaded not guilty and still maintained his innocence. Justice Cummins listened patiently to the submissions, but the heart had gone out of the thing. Every word spoken rang with a weary, perfunctory note.

Then Carmen Ross—a registered nurse, we now heard, who worked in aged care—took the stand to sketch the life story of her wretched brother. A sweet-faced figure in a white embroidered blouse, dark pants and a large, practical watch, she was clearly the matriarch of the family, and she spoke with authority, twisting a small white hanky in her hands. Rob was the youngest of four, she began, and he was born three months premature.

Twelve weeks early, forty years ago. Doted on, coddled. Was this the missing piece?

He was a treasured baby, she said: lucky to survive, fragile, over-protected, smaller than he should have been. He had trouble with his eyesight. He was not robust, not smart, but a battler; not much good at school, but a struggler. He grew up to be a 'quiet, patient person', a team-player in sport. With a smiling affection that at times almost tipped over into tears or laughter, she painted a picture of a faithful, decent, hard-working man, passionately devoted to his children. 'I *like* him,' she said, 'as a person.' All the while Kerri Huntington sat grim-faced, a hard block of introverted rage and pain.

...

On the evening of 28 October 2007, between the plea hearing and the sentencing, Cindy Gambino appeared on *60 Minutes*. I taped the program. It was a riveting and complex piece of television, and in the years that followed, I watched it many times.

Gambino sits in an armchair in a living room, wearing a pretty rose-pink blouse and stroking a framed photograph of her children. Her interlocutor, a young man, seems awe-struck in the presence of a woman so bereaved; and indeed there is something majestic in Gambino's demeanour, the slow flood of her tears, her sighs and stubborn refusals, the long pauses she allows to fall while she considers her replies.

'Most parents who've never lost a child,' she says, 'can't fathom the thought of it. They get to a certain point in their thoughts and they just go, "Nuh. Not goin' there."'

'What she can't fathom, can't accept,' declares the interviewer in voice-over, 'is *the truth:* Robert Farquharson, the man she married, the father of their children, is a convicted killer, and is now in gaol.'

'This is too incomprehensible,' says Gambino. She starts to cry. 'I can't believe that this person would hate *me* that much to want to murder his own children, who he worshipped the ground they walked on. I don't *believe* that…He loved me. I know he loved me.'

The interviewer risks it: 'Did you love him?'

Complex expressions flitter across Gambino's face. She comes up at last with a pellet of popular wisdom. 'I think there's a difference between love and being in love. I loved him, but I was never truly *in* love.'

A few seconds from a wedding video: against the sun-yellow interior walls of a country church, the newlyweds peel away from the altar and parade arm-in-arm down the aisle. A beaming Gambino glides like a princess in full fig, head high, her veil flowing back from a Russian-style coronet. Alongside her scurries Farquharson in a dark suit and mullet, round-shouldered, unsmiling, a little tame bear.

We see home videos of the three boys playing together in a bath. They blow out birthday candles, crawl among wrapping paper on Christmas morning. In a labour ward Gambino holds out to the camera the newborn Bailey, a wobbly, cloth-wrapped parcel that she handles with consummate authority. In these unstaged moments she is simply a young mother: her face, without make-up, shows the fragility of a woman fresh from an encounter with the numinous, her cheeks scoured, her skin pearly with fatigue.

'After fourteen years together,' intones the voice-over, 'they separated.'

Gambino quotes herself: 'I don't love you, and I can't do this any more.'

'How did Rob take it?'

'He took it hard. He felt like he'd walked away with nothing. He basically took his pillow, and a television, and his clothes, and went back to his father's house. He was devastated, of course.'

The program gives a careful version of the transition. 'Just as Cindy was breaking up with Robert, another man came into her life—Stephen Moules. He was a concreter who met the couple while working at their house. He became confidant to a miserable Robert, but at the same time he was falling in love with Cindy.'

Fair-haired Moules, looking younger and finer-featured than he had in court, describes his attempts to 'counsel' the troubled couple; but once Cindy made it 'blatantly clear' that she didn't want the marriage any more, and when he saw that Farquharson wasn't prepared to put in 'the correct efforts' to put it back together, Moules 'saw it as a lose–lose situation'.

In the blue-tinted *60 Minutes* re-creation of the events at the dam, Moules is a furious hero. While Farquharson in his blanket begs him for a cigarette, Moules curses him, strips off, and begins to dive.

'He nearly died,' says Gambino to camera, 'just doing what he did.'

'Very brave, what you did,' says the round-eyed interviewer to Moules. 'Very brave.'

Impassive Moules deflects the praise. 'That word would be a lot more justified if I had've found them…I know if I was in that situation, I believe if *my* children weren't here today, *I* wouldn't be here today, 'cause if I couldn't save them, I'd huddle around them'—he makes an eloquent gathering gesture—'and I'd say, "Well, we're goin' together, kids. And that's all there is to it."'

'When the verdict came,' says the interviewer to Gambino, 'you wailed.'

Her tears begin to flow. 'I wailed 'cause—'

'For Robert or for the kids? What?'

'Both—the honour of my children. I don't want my children to be remembered as "those three little Farquharson boys murdered by their father"…That's not honouring my children. I wailed because it was not the verdict I wanted.'

'How do you want the world to see him?'

A long, hard-working silence. The tears stream down her polished cheeks. In a curious, graceful movement she places her hands palm to palm across her chin. She tips her head to one side with a sob and a strained smile, and murmurs, 'Free?'

'Cindy,' says the interviewer sternly. 'All the evidence that was presented in the court—that the ignition was off, the lights were off, that Rob was in control of the car as it left the road—'

She shakes her head. 'Means nothing to me.'

'A jury of twelve unanimously found him guilty.'

'Means nothing. They don't know Rob. They don't know him from a bar of soap.'

'In your mind,' says the interviewer, with the ponderous solemnity for which the program is famous, *did he do it?*'

She tips up her chin, lets her heavy eyelids droop. 'No,' she says, very softly.

'He's innocent?'

She pauses. Something like a shadow brushes her face, and

is gone. 'I believe he is.' Her voice is barely more than a whisper. 'I believe this is a tragic accident.'

...

Gambino did not come to court on 16 November 2007, the day Farquharson was sentenced. His family and supporters arrived in force, with large badges pinned to their lapels: ROBBED, they read, and IN ROB WE TRUST. But no sooner had Justice Cummins begun to read from his slender document—'You had a burning resentment...You formed a dark contemplation'—than the people with the badges got to their feet and marched out of the court in a body, leaving Farquharson forlorn in the dock. His hair was greyer and his cheeks thinner. He looked pale, even ill. As he listened to the judge's harsh telling of his story, and to the fierce moral condemnations it laid down, he made grimaces of the kind one would see on a teenage boy being called to account in front of the class: he threw himself back in his chair, flexed his eyebrows ironically, shook his head, blew out air between pressed lips. At the phrase 'no remorse' he let his jaw drop and his mouth hang wide open. His responses were so inadequate to the gravity of the situation that it hurt to look at him.

And in the end, the sentence wiped all expression from his face. There was no mercy. Three life terms, one for each dead boy, and no parole.

In the deep, shocked silence, a young man rose in his seat at the back of the court and started a slow clap. He had beaten his palms together no more than three times before the big tipstaff was on him and hustling him out through the glass-paned door.

The court was stood down. People got to their feet and moved in two dense streams towards the outside world. Dazed, I stayed in my seat. All I could think of was the fact that Robert Farquharson would never again get behind the wheel of a car.

Late that evening a text came from my old barrister friend. 'Too much,' he wrote. 'It will not survive appellate scrutiny.'

• • •

Presuming upon our friendly encounters at the coffee cart, I sent a letter to Bob and Bev Gambino. I asked them if they would introduce me to their daughter, so that I could request an interview. In the most delicate way Bev gave me to understand that this was out of the question. But she said that she and Bob would always be glad to see me if I was ever down Birregurra way.

I wrote to Carmen Ross and Kerri Huntington, asking if they might be prepared to speak to me. Carmen Ross declined in a firm but gracious card. The Farquharson family, she wrote, was putting all its energies and efforts towards the appeal process and the welfare of their brother. When Rob was found to be an innocent father who had had a tragic accident, they might perhaps consider my offer.

An email came from Louise. 'I saw Justice Cummins having a coffee up in Bourke Street, and Carmen Ross in Degraves Street. I may or may not have violently blushed. I felt a strange rush of guilt for even existing. It was the same awe and fascination I had in court, like they're very sacred and mysterious people.'

• • •

A month or so later, driving home from Anglesea, I took the inland route through Birregurra. Bob and Bev welcomed me warmly and sat me down at the kitchen table for a toasted sandwich and a cup of tea. I stayed an hour or two. We talked of this and that. Their discretion was faultless. Nobody cried. Sometimes we laughed. They would not let me leave without a bag of silver beet and potatoes from their garden.

'We don't work out there much any more,' said Bev. 'Jai and Tyler used to help us with the mowing and the digging. It's just too painful without them.'

Bob told me that on the day of their grandsons' funeral in Winchelsea, twenty-five kilometres from Birregurra, three white doves were released into the sky. Days later, a tired and bedraggled white bird flew into their yard and took refuge under the eaves of their back veranda. They fed it. It was there for a fortnight. One morning they went outside and it was gone.

On 1 April 2008 I heard that Farquharson had lodged an appeal against his conviction. I picked up the phone and called Mr Morrissey. He was in a fluster, halfway through another trial, but boomed in his matey, rackety voice that he had come up with fifty-one grounds. The judge had definitely made errors in his charge to the jury. Plus, what about the violent brawl Greg King had got into, at a Winchelsea pub, in the December before Rob's trial? This would have reflected on King's credibility as a witness—but the coppers had delayed charging him for ten months, until the Farquharson trial was over. I mean come on, ten months' delay in hearing a pub brawl? And by the way, who was that really clever-looking fair-haired girl who sat beside me at the trial? Gap year! She was smarter than the whole bloody jury put together. If she ever wanted to do work experience she should give his office a call.

...

A pub brawl in Winchelsea? That peaceful village full of law-abiding citizens? Eventually I saw the charge sheet. After a 'heated discussion', in the presence of wives and children celebrating Christmas Eve, two men set upon two others, and half a dozen more joined in. It sounded like the sort of free-for-all where blokes run across pool tables to get amongst it. The investigating police officer observed that the assault followed a series of earlier incidents between two feuding groups of locals, in which the victim had played no part. He was not known to his assailants; his mistake, while he consumed 'approximately five cans of Jack Daniels and Coke', was to be seen talking to the wrong man at the bar. He was punched and head-butted, even after he had run from the building. 'It would appear,' wrote the police officer fastidiously, 'that a pack mentality prevailed.' Under the heading 'Reasons', one of the arrested assailants told police that he had been trying to find his thong. Another said 'I just jumped on top.' Greg King, charged with having punched the victim in the stomach, said, 'I did the wrong thing.'

King had no prior convictions. When he came before a Geelong magistrate on a charge of unlawful assault on 20 November 2007, a few days after Farquharson got his life sentence, the police handed up a letter recognising his cooperation in the Farquharson case. The magistrate, declaring that this letter had had no effect on his decision, sent King home with a twelve-month good behaviour bond and a $750 fine.

...

Cindy Gambino was by now a public figure. During 2008 and 2009 I followed her fortunes at a distance. She drifted through *Woman's*

Day and *New Idea*, dull-eyed and overweight, helplessly acting out her grief. Her interviews were reported in the tabloid language that can reduce the purest human anguish to a pulp.

Any woman could see that in her stubborn refusal to condemn Farquharson she was fighting to hold back an avalanche of misplaced guilt that no mother would survive. The people who loved her must have had to tiptoe around her, muffle their own emotions, cradle her in her protective delusion. How long could she hold out?

I understood now what her mother, Bev, had told me outside court one day—an image that at the time had seemed to me topsy-turvy: 'You've got this mask all over you. You get up. You drive to work. You take the mask off and do what's expected of you. Then you drive home and on the way the mask comes back, so you can handle everything that's happening there.'

But the cracks in Gambino's carapace were beginning to show.

As long as she clung to her belief that the crash had been an accident, she could not claim Victims of Crime compensation. She lodged, and settled for an undisclosed sum, a damages claim against the Transport Accident Commission for severe psychiatric injury. Then she turned to Farquharson's assets. These amounted to a mere $66,000, but on 14 May 2009, in a Supreme Court decision, Justice Cummins ordered him, under the Sentencing Act, to pay her $225,000 in compensation for her pain and suffering.

...

On 1 June 2009 I climbed the steep stairs from Lonsdale Street to the old Court of Appeal. In the vestibule Mr Morrissey smiled at me. His big face was waxen.

'You must be very tired,' I said.

He made a wordless sound and closed his eyes.

'Are you in despair?'

'Not despair,' he said hastily. 'No. But look—it's like the ancient myth. Orpheus, having to go back down to the underworld. That's what it's like. And I lack the musical talents of Orpheus.'

I followed him through the big doors. Green Court was a higher class of room than Supreme Court Three, recently refurbished with thick green carpet and tilting seats of green leather, and subtly lit by elegant wall-mounted lamps.

Farquharson hobbled in on crutches. A journalist told me he had had a coughing fit in prison and fainted. He had fallen off a chair and fractured a bone.

The appeal hearing had been slated for two days. Compared with the smoothly confident Mr Rapke and his junior, Douglas Trapnell SC, Morrissey was as jumpy as a student undergoing an oral exam. Three judges sat in a row above him, in scarlet robes with huge white fur cuffs. Their wigs were not the grey, dead-rat ones of the lower court, but foaming and globular, as pale as raw cauliflower, with a texture reminiscent of brain tissue. Their voices rang crisply, and their questions were challenging, pointed, and at times impatient. They gave no quarter. The quality of their listening was ferocious. There were no witnesses: the whole thing was a blast of argument and analysis, awe-inspiring in its thoroughness.

On the second day, Morrissey hit his stride. He was less flustered, more calmly forceful, much more in command of the content and tone of his discourse. Late that afternoon, long after I had lost my grip on the technical details of the argument, I began to be aware of a mysterious movement in the room, a fluid shift. At first I thought I was imagining it. I did not discern it with my intellect, but sensed it along my nerves. It was a slow, submarine surge, like the turning of a tide.

It would take the judges months to publish their decision.

...

A couple of weeks after Farquharson's appeal was heard, *Woman's Day* ran a three-page 'news exclusive' on Gambino, in which she ominously raised the stakes.

She told her faithful journalist that she had written several times to her ex-husband in prison and begged him to accept a visit from her. A photo of one of her letters, in a hand as unformed as a teenager's, appeared beside the interview. She could not understand why he would not want to see the only person on earth who understood his pain. What had he been thinking on the day of the accident, and in the months before it? Was all this her fault because they had separated? She prayed that she had not made him hate her that much. She had defended him to the world. Didn't she deserve answers to her questions? Why wouldn't he see her?

Farquharson had agreed, through his sister Kerri, to see her after what would have been Jai's fourteenth birthday; but when the time came, he said he was not ready.

A reply came at last, she said, but not from Farquharson. It was written by his counsellor, Gregory Roberts, the social worker who had given evidence for the defence about the new concept of 'traumatic grief'. Farquharson, he wrote, was missing Cindy's cooking and struggling with prison life. Roberts offered a stark account of Farquharson's horror in the sinking car, his agonised scream when he could not free his boys. But the counsellor was adamant that Gambino would not be able to see Farquharson. He was in a fragile emotional state. A visit from her would be too damaging and destabilising.

Gambino was incredulous. What did Farquharson imagine life was like for her, out in the real world, where practically every day she had to drive past the children's school, or the dam? How was she supposed to mother her two-year-old son, and the new child she would soon give birth to? She had not changed her mind— Farquharson was not a killer. But she needed to ask him face to face why he had not given evidence at his trial, why he had not seized his only chance to tell everyone what really happened. All she wanted was to look him in the eye.

Her face in the magazine was a vision of ruin: its doughy pallor, its heavy-lidded eyes and expression of sullen entreaty. From the dock during the trial Farquharson had silently implored his former wife to look at him. Now it seemed that the counsellor, in his helpless empathy, was doing everything in his power to shield Farquharson from the challenge of that gaze.

Around this time, I received through my publisher a letter from a stranger. She wanted to tell me that her daughter's small children had been burnt to death in a house fire, after their parents' ugly divorce. Suspicion hung over the former husband, she said, but the coroner had returned an open finding. The grandmother, in her anguish, might have been speaking for Gambino:

'What's worse?—living with suspicions and various possibilities and never knowing the truth, or living with the truth of something too horrible to contemplate?'

...

On 17 December 2009, six months after the hearing, the Court of Appeal handed down its decision. The judges had sieved Mr Morrissey's fifty-one grounds down to a mere handful. They found, most importantly, that Justice Cummins had erred in his directions to the jury, in particular about how they were entitled to evaluate the complex layers of Greg King's testimony. Also, by failing to disclose King's pending assault charge from the pub brawl and the fact that the police intended to provide a letter of support for him, the Crown had deprived Farquharson's defence of a chance to discredit King as a witness.

The Appeal judges laid out in one careful page the circumstantial evidence against Farquharson. They made it clear that it had been open to the jury to find him guilty beyond reasonable doubt. Still, the errors had deprived him of a fair trial. The Court set aside his conviction and ordered a retrial.

Four days before Christmas 2009, Robert Farquharson was released on bail.

...

How would it feel to be out of prison, back under your big sister's roof, on a beautiful summer night? I imagined Farquharson roaming barefoot through the Mount Moriac house, taking a beer out of the fridge, maybe sitting on the back doorstep and listening to the crickets. At bedtime he would stretch out to rest between fresh cotton sheets, and lay his head on a clean pillow.

Meanwhile, his sons were lying in their own little beds, in a couple of scrubby acres on the outskirts of Winchelsea.

n February 2010 I was invited to give a talk about non-fiction writing at the Wheeler Centre in the State Library. Someone in the audience asked my opinion of the Farquharson verdict. I did not think it was the moment to talk about it. I confined myself to the observation that the only person who knew the truth wasn't talking, and changed the subject.

The retrial was scheduled for May 2010. I heard around the traps that Mr Morrissey might not appear for Farquharson this time. Everyone at the criminal bar liked Morrissey. They were worried about the effect on him of this long ordeal. 'Oh, I don't envy him,' said one barrister I knew. 'Defending such an unpopular client—it's the worst of the worst.' 'He should run a million miles,' said another, 'but I bet he won't.'

On 10 March 2010, when I walked into Supreme Court Eleven to listen to Preliminary Argument, the first person I saw, looming over his junior, Con Mylonas, was Peter Morrissey, his forehead shining, his wig tilted to the back of his head. At the other end of the bar table sat the new prosecutor, Andrew Tinney SC, a wiry, silver-haired man with a solemn address. A journalist told me he was to be seen on Lonsdale Street clad in lycra and cleated cycling shoes, and that he coped with his work worries by riding to Frankston and back before breakfast. Beside him he had the combat-toughened Amanda Forrester, Rapke's junior from the first trial.

The man on the bench was Justice Lex Lasry, a tall, rangy fellow in his early sixties who had been a judge for barely two years. I had once watched him, when he was at the criminal bar, coolly dismantle a murder charge against a young woman whom a whole city had believed to be guilty. He was widely admired for his work as a QC in international human rights, and liked for the fact that he played drums in an amateur band.

These preliminary sittings of the court took place well before a jury was empanelled. New witnesses were carefully questioned and the rules of engagement were negotiated. Farquharson listened intently between his guards, chin up, eyelids fluttering. Morrissey came out swinging. Justice Lasry ruled in his favour to exclude any evidence in which Farquharson was heard to express intentions of suicide or self-harm. The Crown case, said Lasry, was not that the events of Father's Day amounted to a failed murder-suicide; it was that the accused had meant the children to drown while he survived. Lasry agreed, too, to scour the evidence of a term that had freely besprinkled the first trial: *depression*, a medical condition about which, he said, many people in the community know a lot less than they think they do. What he feared, if he should admit evidence from lay witnesses about depression, was that the jury might take it upon themselves to speculate about an imagined link between depression and motive for murder. Speculation of any kind was anathema.

Justice Lasry proposed to say to the jury, once it was empanelled, 'Any gaps in the evidence are not to be filled with guesswork.' Fat chance, I thought. Still, judge and counsel worked together to draw out of the story, without rucking up its texture, the long black thread of Farquharson's 'depression'.

...

At lunchtime one day Mr Morrissey asked me for a word. He ushered me into a little interview room off the vestibule, and gestured to a chair. We sat facing each other across a table. He did not remove his wig.

'Someone's sent me,' he said with an ominously charming smile, 'the video of a talk you gave at the State Library.'

My heart went boom. 'Did I drop a clanger?'

'You did. You said, "Only one person knows what happened in the car that night, and he's not talking."' He leaned forward on both elbows and subjected me to a power-darkened look. 'Our case is that my client *doesn't* know what happened in the car that night. Because he was unconscious. By offering that opinion in a public forum you were undermining my client's right to silence. I think you might be in contempt of court.'

Contempt of court? Me? I broke into a cold sweat.

If I did not get that video off the internet within two hours, Morrissey went on, still forcefully holding my gaze, he would go to the judge and get a court order. He might even use my smart crack to support an argument for adjournment, on the grounds that adverse publicity would deprive his client of any hope of a fair trial.

Of course I was not responsible for posting the video, and I had no idea how to get it down. Galled most of all by the thought that Justice Lasry might think me an idiot, I ran out of the building, red-faced, phone in hand. The Wheeler Centre people had it sorted in thirty minutes. Still shaking, I texted my old barrister. He replied at once: 'My dear. You were in contempt only on the most pedantic interpretation of your words. It's a nothing. A trifle. You merely said something unfavourable to Mr Morrissey's case.'

So Morrissey had bullied me, and I fell for it. The chips must be down.

And soon the word flashed among the journalists: Gambino had changed her mind. She had withdrawn her original witness statement and made a new one. Only when I watched judge and counsel nervously planning tactics for handling her before the jury did I realise, with a thrill of dread, how wild she must have become, how terrifying—what havoc she might wreak upon the court's delicate edifice of reason.

had ignorantly imagined the second trial proper, when it opened on 3 May 2010, as a canter across old territory, with a few shifts of emphasis, a fresh angle here and there—an up-dated production of a modern tragedy whose characters and plot and poetry were so familiar to me that it had lost its power to devastate. But from the first moment the very air in the court felt different. There was grit in it. The benign courtesies, the comradely sharing of the crowded space were no more. In the jostling for seats in the body of the court that day, in the banishing of Farquharson's supporters to the upstairs gallery, in the hostile glances and ostentatious turning of backs, my usual morning nod to the lawyers was rebuffed at the defence end of the bar table by a clutch of belligerently blank faces. It dawned on me that I was being sent to Coventry by Mr Morrissey and his whole team. Without my gap-year girl I was a shag on a rock. I backed away, hurt, to a seat remote from the action. A court in a long trial is a desert island. We are all castaways. Why make enemies?

But soon I would find my new spot to be an excellent one, so close to the dock and the glass-paned rear doors that, as witnesses were dismissed and headed out of court, mine was the last face they saw before they reached the exit—except for Farquharson's, which most of them avoided looking at. In their relief at being off the hook they would shoot me a secret beam of fellow-feeling. One of the medical witnesses, forbiddingly severe on the stand, sent me, on his way out, a tiny smile that sparkled with ironic self-deprecation. In the strained atmosphere of a court the merest glance from a stranger carries serious psychic freight. I had been declared a non-person by the defence, but for the first time I felt that I belonged in that room, that I had earned the right to be there.

I tried to be the first stranger each day to step into the high, white space of Court Eleven. Its tranquil order moved and comforted me. Everything gently shone. Counsel's chairs and microphones waited in rows down the long table. Cool air streamed in from some mysterious source. The tall flasks of water, each encircled by a cluster of polished glasses, stood ready on blue mats.

'Nice in here, isn't it,' I said to the tipstaff.

'Think so?' He surveyed his handiwork with a pleased smile. 'Yep. It's nice. That is'—he threw out one hand towards the bar table—'until all *this* starts.'

...

Morrissey fought to have the judge exile Gambino and her parents to the perspex-screened gallery upstairs, where Farquharson's family now sat; he wanted to protect the jury from the 'pageant' of suffering he said she was likely to present. Justice Lasry was working like a Trojan not to load the dice against the accused, but he would not come at this. So, when the new jury filed in, pale with dismay that their lives were to be put on hold for at least eight weeks, Morrissey in his opening address gave them fair warning: in cross-examination, even if she was distraught, he was going to take Gambino on. The point was not to beat her up. It was to get answers that would help the jury in their deliberations. When he pressed her on certain questions, he said, they would need to be quite strong in their role. Only a wooden-hearted person would not feel sympathy for Gambino, and he did. But this was not the Oprah Winfrey show. His job was to ask questions, and that's what he was going to do.

...

It was the Friday morning of the retrial's first week when Cindy Gambino was called. As she passed me on her way to the witness stand I saw that she had run a purple rinse through her long brown hair, and that she was not the only person in the room wearing purple. Meaningful dabs of it shone here and there, scarves, jackets, blouses. Even the Homicide detective's tie had a purple stripe. I whipped off my faded lavender cardigan and stuffed it into my bag.

The calm that Gambino showed seemed natural, not the effect of medication. Once or twice she flicked a glance at Farquharson. Asked if he was the natural father of the three boys, she bared her side teeth at him in a quick snarl. The unspoken things that had shadowed her original version of their relationship and his character she now brought to prominence in a most unflattering light.

Even at the time of their marriage, she said, when they already had two children, she knew in her heart that she did not really love him. She had to fight past his reluctance to have a third child. Farquharson was very protective, very possessive, but he never called her or their kids by their Christian names. His nicknames for the boys were Wobber, Bruiser, Bub. Cindy herself he addressed as Big Mama or Fat Mama; he would grab her by her private parts. As Jai and Tyler grew bigger, Farquharson used to get into play fights with them; he would stir them up till they got angry and lashed out at him. Yet he left the disciplining of the children to her. He would not smack them: he said that if he got really angry, he did not know how far he might go. He whinged and moaned a lot, she said, always complaining that he was tired. She was not physically attracted to him. Their intimacy faded and died. She was drawn to Stephen Moules, but despite Farquharson's suspicions she was not having an affair with him. The marriage went downhill fast. She ended it in November 2004 and he went back to live with his father. During an argument at her house after their separation, Farquharson pushed her hard against a wall. She locked herself in her bedroom and called the police. Later he came over and apologised, but she did not forget it.

Football was the main conduit between Farquharson and the boys. In the first trial this was painted as something hyper-paternal, a passionate commitment on Farquharson's part that he had boasted of and worn as a badge of virtue. Now Gambino shrugged it off as 'his thing'. She had never denied his request to take the boys over to his father's house, but added a stinging detail: 'He never really asked to have them that often, and the children never ever asked, "Can I go and see Dad?"'

After she ended the marriage, Gambino said, Farquharson started to call the boys by their proper first names, and stopped the tormenting play. She quoted her favourite aphorism: 'You don't know what you've got till it's gone.'

On the Wednesday evening before Father's Day, Farquharson phoned Gambino after tea. They spoke for twenty minutes. It was a conversation that Gambino was no longer permitted to say had made her fear that he was suicidal. He was very down and out, very 'woe is me', very 'glass half empty'. He hated living at his father's. He wanted their unfinished house to be sold so he could buy himself a place to live, and a new car. He would never get ahead while he had to keep paying maintenance. He said he was looking at starting some sort of business in Queensland. Gambino told him he could not do that—he could not leave his kids.

...

The story of the night at the dam belonged to Gambino by right. Led by the new prosecutor, Mr Tinney, she launched on it in a clear voice, spreading her well-kept hands in expressive gestures. At the first trial she had dragged it out of herself with a raw, agonised restraint, and people in the court wept with horror and pity. Now, like her hair, the story was coloured by an element of self-consciousness. Her account had become a recital, with the rhetorical figures and grace notes of a tale polished by many a telling. How could it have been otherwise? No narrative can remain pure. Often she spoke with a simple directness. Her tears, when they fell, were sincere. But in spite of Justice Lasry's hint that the prosecutor might 'slightly increase his degree of control', Tinney gave her the green light, and she enriched her account with the sort of emotional detail that causes judges to scowl and journalists to bend to their notebooks. While she ran up and down the paddock in the dark, she said, she was screaming hysterically, 'Please, God, not my babies, please don't take my babies, please, God.' Until that night, Stephen Moules had never 'admitted any feelings' for her, but when he reached the dam and ran to her, he took her in his arms and said, 'Baby, it will be all right.' And she characterised Farquharson's demeanour, as he stood watching the rescue attempts with his arms folded on his chest, in a phrase that curdled with contempt: 'like he'd lost his pushbike'.

...

Morrissey glided into his cross-examination with a pair of recorded telephone calls. These had been captured, several weeks after the children drowned, by a bug that the police had put on Farquharson's phone. Gambino would have to listen, before a roomful of strangers, to two deeply revealing conversations of which she had no memory. Perhaps it was the intimacy of the exchanges that made her pull the faces she did, at first, while the tapes rolled: the grimaces of a woman who has been married to a man she did not respect, a man who needed a mother more than a wife.

She calls Farquharson at nine o'clock one morning, a fortnight after Father's Day, and asks him what he remembers of the accident. Her voice is quiet and matter-of-fact, but Farquharson has surely been dreading such a call, for his tone is put-upon, and the high-quality audio registers the fact that he is lightly panting: his heart rate is up. He rattles out the account he has told to everybody: the coughing fit, waking up in the dam, Jai opening the door, the water coming in, his efforts to 'go round the other side'.

'Jai opened the door,' muses Gambino. 'Shit.' She must be sedated, she is so slow and thoughtful, like someone hearing for the first time an interesting but only vaguely surprising fact. 'How did the kids get out of the seatbelts, do you know?'

'Not all of them would have had their seatbelts off.'

Would have? How come he didn't already know? Hadn't he asked?

'They all did,' says Gambino. 'I asked Gerard Clanchy.'

'What?' Farquharson's voice rises. 'They must've undone Bailey or something.'

'Yep. So I reckon Tyler's undone Bailey.'

Starting to panic, he shifts oddly into the present tense. 'Because how can—how can I reach him from where I am?'

Dully she soothes him. 'I know, I know, I know it wasn't you, *they* know it wasn't you. I think the kids have undone their seatbelts and tried to get out.'

'Oh *no*.' He breaks into racking sobs.

For the first time it hit me that he must have fantasised their dying as instant and total annihilation—boom, gone—as in a cartoon or a dream.

She tries to keep talking, in her rational, unexcited voice, but he weeps on. In the far wifely reaches of herself, she begins to lose patience with him. 'Come on, don't get upset. I just need to know what you remember.'

He gets a grip, he sniffs, he sighs, but his voice trembles and he bursts out crying again. 'How am I gonna get through all this?'

'You'll get through it, Rob, you will.'

'They were the love of my life. I never, ever could hurt them.'

'You know how much *I* wanted them,' she says, with a flare of rivalry.

'I'd never, ever hurt them.'

'I know that!' she snaps. 'You don't have to keep saying that!'

'I feel like I've gotta try and justify myself to everyone,' he says, breathing hard. 'To the police. I've got this feeling they want to put me away.'

She asks him further questions that he struggles with and fails to answer. After each burst of his revved-up gabble she emits a short, soft hum of attention, or lets a pensive silence fall. This must be worse for him than if she were sobbing or raging: she sounds authoritative, like someone to whom he owes but cannot give an explanation. He protests that her questions are traumatising him.

'But there are things I need to know,' she says mildly. 'As their mother.'

They agree that the two young blokes who picked Farquharson up on the roadside should have tried to get the boys out instead of driving him to her place. Why hadn't they stayed with the car? This suggestion—so frightful and unjust—that the outsiders, Shane Atkinson and Tony McClelland, are to blame seems for a moment to soothe something in both of them. Then Gambino cuts it off with a brisk realism. 'But it doesn't matter. There's no point in talking like that now.'

Listening from her seat, Gambino darted one desperate look at Farquharson. Journalists corkscrewed to stare at him. While the technician cued the second tape, jurors put their heads together and compared notes, muttering.

...

Ten days later, Farquharson calls her late in the afternoon, 'just to say g'day.'

Somewhere outside a rooster is crowing. A dog barks. She can't talk properly, she says. The medication has made her tongue swell. He speaks at length, entirely about himself. Anything she says, in her thick, drawling voice, he tops, or appropriates. She's had a bad week? So has he. She has to make a statement to the police? Imagine what *he's* had to do. She has calm days and then really shitty days? That's like him. Her mum's been having panic attacks, can't face going back to work? That makes it hard on *him*. All those things affect *him*, 'cause he's affected everyone's lives and it's on *his* shoulders too. How much more torture are they going to put him through? It rips his guts out that people would think he'd ever in his wildest dreams do something like this. It fuckin' hurts big-time and he suffers. Anyone knows he wouldn't do it.

How was it, she asks with a dreamy curiosity, that the car's headlights came to be turned off? He stammers and fumbles. He doesn't know. He doesn't remember *anything*. Probably when it first happened he thought he was in a ditch. So he stopped the car, just in case it was a fire.

'A fire?' I said to the *Age* reporter beside me. 'That's new.'

'I came across a bad car crash once,' she whispered. 'I was the first person there. There were people in the car, they were unconscious, and the motor was still running. The first thing I did was reach in and turn off the ignition. I didn't think. It was automatic.'

Outside the house the rooster is squalling. They pay it no

attention. Each of them confesses to thoughts of suicide. They don't use the word. They call it 'giving up'. But people tell them the kids would be beside themselves if they knew. She assures him that there is no evidence, that they have nothing on him. They compare griefs. He can't smile, he says; he can't laugh. If she laughs she feels guilty in seconds. She defers to him: his suffering, she says, is tenfold of hers. She has lost three children, but unlike him she doesn't have that guilt behind it—not that she's saying he should…

Gambino in the court got a fingertip grip on the gold cross round her neck, and cried in great gaping silent sobs. Tinney and Forrester flashed her glances of anxious inquiry. The tall blonde woman from Victim Support shifted to a seat behind her, watchful, ready to move.

But the voices on the tape slide into the dull, rambling familiarity of two people who have once been husband and wife, parents together. Farquharson tells her he has a new phone. They marvel that the SIM card of the one that went into the dam still works. Many pauses fall. Their silences are more comfortable than speech. Neither of them seems ready to break the contact. Perhaps, I thought, the children can still exist as long as their parents are in each other's company.

Then she tells him that, though it has hurt them, she has left her parents' house and gone to be with Stephen Moules. She used to be confident, but she has turned into a 'timid, mild, insecure little being' who doesn't want to be left alone. Stephen is now her security.

At the mention of his victorious rival, Farquharson slips back into a doleful, guilt-tripping mode: 'And *I* gotta ride this stuff out on my own.'

Still, she draws the conversation to an end with something like tenderness: 'I know in my heart of hearts you would never harm those boys.'

'Ohhh, no way known.'

'You got to keep on fighting for the boys' sake.'

'I keep thinking of you,' he says.

'I think of you, too. I defend you. I do defend you.'

…

Morrissey rose. Gambino sat regarding him with narrowed eyes, her jaw set hard.

'Are you very angry with Robert Farquharson?'

'Yes.'

'Did you bare your teeth at him?'

'Possibly.'

'For the state you're now in, do you blame Robert Farquharson?'

'Correct.'

'You hate him?'

A pause.

'I hate him for what he's done to my life.'

'And it's your wish that he be convicted of murder?'

A long, long pause.

'Correct.'

At that moment the audio-visual technician who was trying to cue Gambino's *60 Minutes* interview hit the wrong key. Tinkling music rang out and on the high screen we saw the three little boys naked in their bath, moving and smiling in clean water. Gambino let out a stricken cry. I saw Amanda Forrester drop her head into her hands. Justice Lasry's face went very long and grey.

As soon as Gambino had got herself in hand, Morrissey hauled his gown on to his shoulders and opened fire.

He invited Gambino to list the psychiatric and medical conditions for which she was being treated—severe major depressive disorder, chronic adjustment disorder, chronic anxiety, heart palpitations, calcified shoulder, neck and back pain caused by stress—and the medications she had been prescribed: Effexor, Clonazepam and, for her physical pain, the Codalgin Forte on which she had accidentally overdosed when Stephen Moules was away. Quoting page after page of transcript, he forced her to contrast her statements at the first trial with things she was now alleging. She had changed her evidence, hadn't she? Did she not tell *Woman's Day* in 2007 that she didn't blame Farquharson? Was she not now deliberately exaggerating the bad things about her marriage, putting a bad spin on things which in the past she had viewed as perfectly innocent? The way she described him at the dam, for example—that was just a deliberate piece of spite, was it not?

Gambino squared up to him. She answered with rudeness and aggression. She drew heavy, affronted sighs. She widened her eyes and sarcastically wobbled her head. She frowned, glared, muttered under her breath as if cursing. The judge sent her out for a moment's break. When she returned, he leaned forward and said to her gently, 'You must grapple with what's put to you.' Chastened, she replied, 'I'll do my best, Your Honour.'

Next Morrissey announced that he would play something horrific: the audiotape of the 000 calls that Gambino had made from the water's edge. It was heart-breaking, he said, it was highly destructive and dangerous to the witness. But it had to be done, to show her unreliable state of mind when she accused Farquharson at the dam of behaving like someone who had lost his pushbike. Justice Lasry urged Gambino to leave the court while the tape was played to the jury. She rebuffed his concern and insisted she would stay and hear it. Morrissey flashed Lasry a look that said *I told you so.*

Frightful screams, hoarse babbling. Gambino chokes and shrieks: *Ambulance! Police! Three ks out of Winchelsea! I can't see a thing!* The operator's deep male voice: *Where are you? I'm sorry, I don't understand the problem. Where are you?* In the background Farquharson is jabbering at her: he blacked out, he woke up in water, he doesn't know where the car went in. And all the while, behind her in the dark, Moules's boy Zach is shrilly piping, his voice thin and sharp as a piccolo.

Farquharson's face, in the dock, was fat with horror. Gambino sat hunched with her hanky over her mouth, uttering a high, weak whimpering sound. When they helped her to the door at the end of the tape she staggered along, bowed over, clutching herself with both arms like someone who had been shot in the belly. Court rose.

Outside in the courtyard, with his father, Stephen Moules, the little boy Hezekiah was rolling on the ground with a dummy in his mouth, laughing and playing, bored, waiting for his mother, while she huddled in a side hall, surrounded by attendants, letting out long cries of pain.

...

By four o'clock Gambino's turnaround was on the news. I got myself to the bar where I had arranged to meet a magazine editor I worked for. He chattered away gaily, not noticing that I sat there mute. I longed to tell someone, anyone, about the 000 tape; but a line had been crossed in court that day. I had heard something obscene, something it would have been indecent to speak of: a grown man gabbling like a child who, in a fit of angry spite, has broken a thing precious beyond price and, panicking now, has led his mother to the wreckage to show her what he has done.

...

'For what purpose,' texted my gallant old barrister friend next morning, 'is Mr Morrissey so hard on Ms Gambino? Should not he be gentle with her? I cannot believe what I am reading.'

Gentle? Gambino was a woman so crazed with loss and pain that she was beyond caring. Cross-examination was trauma, said Morrissey to the judge next morning, but it was the only weapon his client had—and Morrissey was fed up, he said, with being constantly reminded that he was dealing with a grieving mother. Yet Morrissey was no sadist. Behind the lachrymose tabloid drama queen he sensed—and, I thought, respected—not only his client's nemesis but a wild and worthy adversary who was spoiling for a fight. He gave her both barrels. She crawled away wounded, came back head high and faced him again. He goaded her and she bit.

It was under pressure that she had changed her position, was it not? Pressure from the police? And her family? And her psychiatrist? People who kept telling her she would never recover from her grief until she admitted she was 'in denial'?

'I have a mind of my own,' she ground out. 'I am a very intelligent person. I can make up my own mind.'

Hadn't she and Farquharson, after the accident, worn twin lockets containing the children's pictures?

He bought them. She no longer wore hers because she no longer believed in him.

Morrissey depicted Farquharson on the dark bank of the dam as an isolated, forlorn and rejected figure, bereft of consolation. Had she offered him a single word of kindness, or a blanket for his shoulders? Invited him to sit in the car with her? Did he not approach Gambino to offer comfort? Did she not push him away?

'Why wouldn't I?' she snapped. 'He'd just drowned my kids.'

And how come *she* didn't jump into the water? Did anyone attack *her* on the night? Tick her off for not jumping in? Tell her she was weak for not diving down after her kids? Rob was attacked for having left the accident and gone straight to her—but who was the first person *she* called? Her new partner, Stephen Moules! And Moules' parents!

He ranged more widely. Was she not the boss of the marriage?

'The boss? Huh. If I didn't do a lot of what I did in our relationship there wouldn't be much done. Controlling the bills, controlling the groceries, controlling the children.'

Who got their way?

'I did.'

When she said Farquharson had left the disciplining of the kids to her, why didn't she say what *her* techniques of discipline were? Didn't *she* ever go over the top? Did she not hit them with

---

the wooden spoon? Did she ever slap any of the boys to the head?

'My children had respect for me,' she said sharply. 'I would count to three, and if I got to three then consequences would happen. I would be lucky to get to two.' In a couple of vivid sentences that made me look at her with fresh regard, she described a clash with a rebellious and destructive Jai, and demonstrated the three-fingered slap to the cheek she had given him to jolt him out of his insolence.

Morrissey wheeled in the heavy artillery. What did she have to say about her role, if any, in the chiselling of Farquharson's name off the children's granite headstone?

She exploded in a passion of sobs: 'You disgust me. My children's resting place! I paid for that headstone! He owes me money for that headstone! How dare you!'

He showed her a press photo of herself and Farquharson at the church door, weeping in each other's arms as the pallbearers carried the three white coffins out to the hearse. She hissed like a snake, made as if to hurl the photo at Morrissey, then screwed it up and dashed it to the floor. He held it up to the judge, a trophy. When Lasry told her she must identify it, she refused to touch it. Later, in the absence of the jury, Morrissey insisted on tendering the crumpled page as an exhibit. Lasry ruled against him: it would only remind the jurors of her emotional outburst.

The battle swept this way and that. The court air thrummed with the trauma of it, as if people longed to shout, or even to barrack, but sat wincing, tight-lipped, swinging their heads in unison.

And in the end, exhausted, backed into a corner, Gambino flung at Morrissey the reason she had turned against Farquharson. It was because he had refused to let her visit him in prison. It was the 'pathetic letter' she had received in response to her pleas. It was the promise he made two years ago, to see her after Jai's fourteenth birthday—the promise he broke when, once again, he changed his mind.

'And *that*,' she said, her lips stiff with loathing, 'was when I decided I was no longer supporting him.'

It was exactly what Morrissey was after: a deeply 'feminine' shift, inspired not by reason but by wifely grievance and the bitter desire to settle a score. He stood and let it radiate its static. Then he thanked her for her patience, and sat down.

...

Out on Lonsdale Street I bumped into another barrister I had known in the Carlton pubs of our youth. I sketched the day's wild carnage. He let out a little moan of commiseration.

'That sounds disastrous. Disastrous. I hesitate to take on a woman. Especially one as wounded as she is. Three kids! Beyond comprehension. When a wounded man's in the box, he'll cower. But a woman'—he bared his teeth and clawed with one hand—'a woman'll come *back* at you.'

...

I texted my old barrister friend. 'Does it matter what Cindy feels towards Farquharson? In the end it doesn't prove anything, does it?'

'My very thought,' he replied, 'at first. But I see the wisdom in Mr Morrissey's approach. The strongest evidence that would put paid to the coughing fit theory would be that of MOTIVE. Gambino's new slant provides motive loosely defined, id est, reasons consistent with wanting to offend. Mr Morrissey has no option but to meet it head on.'

...

In the third week a new witness, a woman in her forties, entered the court, wearing very high heels and a chic black skirt-suit that showed discreet cleavage. In her hand she pressed a neatly folded pad of tissues. Her face was broad and pleasant, ready to smile. When she spoke she revealed a clear New Zealand accent. This was Dawn Waite, an accounts manager and dairy farmer from the Western District, down Warrnambool way. She had an important story to tell and some hard explaining to do about why she had only now, at the retrial, come forward to tell it.

She had spent the weekend of Father's Day 2005 in Melbourne, shopping with her teenage daughter and the daughter's friend. Soon after dark on the Sunday evening, carrying gifts for the girls' respective fathers, they were flying along the Princes Highway west of Geelong, sitting on a hundred, nearly halfway home. There was hardly any traffic on the road, and Waite had the lights of her Falcon on high beam.

Just before they approached the long run-up to the railway overpass, a few kilometres short of Winchelsea, Waite became aware of a car some distance ahead of her that was behaving oddly—moving slowly, its brake lights going on and off, and wandering from side to side in the left lane.

She came up behind the car, a light-coloured Commodore, and had to slow right down to about sixty. She disengaged her cruise control and for a few moments rolled along about a car's length behind the Commodore, trying to figure out what it was doing. She flicked her headlights a few times, to let the driver know she needed to pass. No response. She did not want to pull out—what if it swerved towards the centre again and pushed her across the white lines? Once more she flicked her lights. Still it crawled along at sixty, moving vaguely to left and right.

Now she was getting cranky. Next time the Commodore moved to the left she put her indicator on, pulled out, and drove alongside it for several seconds, looking into the car.

The driver was a man, dark-haired, clean-shaven. He was facing straight ahead, ignoring her, except that every now and then he would slightly turn his head and glance out to the right. She did not know this stretch of road well, or the landscape it crossed. She thought he must have been looking for a turn-off, or a gate. She could see several children in the back seat—three, she thought, and squashed in, since one of them, a fair-headed boy of seven or eight, was leaning right up against the driver's-side window, with his face against the glass.

She made an irritable gesture at the driver, the sort that means *What are you doing?* He paid her no attention, and gave her no eye contact. Finally she planted her foot and surged past him. She sailed up and over the long rise and down the Winchelsea side. Just as she reached the flat, having regained highway speed, she took a quick look in her rear-vision mirror and saw a set of headlights pop over the crest behind them. The lights headed down the slope, then suddenly veered across the road to the right, and were lost to her view.

'Well,' she said to the girls, 'I guess that guy found what he was looking for.'

The following evening, Monday, just after she had finished the milking, she came inside to cook the tea. The TV news was on. While she worked, she looked up briefly at the screen and saw a pale Commodore being pulled out of what looked like a lake. She called to her daughter, 'That's the car! That's the car!' Sleepless during the night that followed, she got up at 2 a.m. and made a few notes of what she remembered of the incident.

Astonishingly, Dawn Waite did not report to any authority her troubling encounter with the Commodore and its driver. She simply went about her business. For four years neither the prosecution nor the defence had any idea that someone had observed Farquharson on the road that night.

During Preliminary Argument, before the jury for the retrial was empanelled, Waite had been closely questioned before Justice Lasry about her long delay in approaching the police. She had tried earnestly to explain her failure to act. She knew that she should have come forward; she felt strongly that she ought to have. She had always been the sort of person who wanted to do the right thing. But she had a number of reasons.

She and her family had migrated to Australia only six months before the Father's Day crash. She was dealing every day with a three-hundred-strong dairy herd as well as holding down a job.

In New Zealand, she said, if you saw someone driving dangerously, it was the done thing to take down the offender's numberplate and give it to the police. She and her husband had done it plenty of times. Back in the nineties a young man ran a stoplight and cut them off. They reported him and charges were laid. But before they were called to give evidence in court, the poor lad killed himself. This deeply shocked the couple, for Waite's brother-in-law had also taken his own life. They had never got over the horrible sense of being partly responsible for the young driver's death.

For a good year before Father's Day 2005, Waite said, she had been mysteriously unwell, fatigued, lacking in energy. No doctor could find out what was wrong with her. It was not until 2008 that she was at last diagnosed with a lymphoma, well advanced, and had to undergo chemotherapy. During the nausea and weakness of her treatment a friend had come over to do some housework for her, and in clearing out her office she had inadvertently thrown away the note pad on which Waite had scribbled down her memories of the incident near the overpass.

The two years leading up to 2005 had been traumatic for the Waite family in other ways: in quick succession her father, her father-in-law, and her beloved mother-in-law had passed away. Here her voice weakened and she wept. The day after the third funeral they had tried to have a little birthday party for their daughter Jessica. The very next day, Jessica's close friend was killed in a car crash.

'We buried her, and then we moved countries. I just couldn't, I could not put my daughter through something like that again. I wasn't strong enough.'

'So,' she said in a trembling voice, 'forgive me for not coming forward at that time.'

But, on 17 December 2009, when the success of Farquharson's appeal was reported on the news, Waite's husband said to her, 'Really, now, you must go forward.' On 23 December 2009, Dawn Waite walked into the Warrnambool police station.

...

Morrissey came down like a wolf on the fold.

Waite was quite a newcomer to this case, wasn't she? She would hardly deny, would she, that by not coming forward for five years she had failed to help the accused man through his trial, his imprisonment, his appeal? And that, when she finally did come forward, it was with the aim not of helping the accused but of *assisting the police*? He insinuated that she was a prim-lipped, officious Kiwi who enjoyed jotting down numberplates and dobbing in other drivers. And wasn't she exaggerating her unwellness? She can't have been feeling all that bad if she could drive from Warrnambool to Melbourne to shop, go out to dinner, stay a night somewhere and then drive home, a three-hour drive each way, on top of working, so she said, seven days a week, twelve hours a day, on her farm, trying to make a quid? As a driver, even if she had had an unblemished licence since the age of fifteen, she did not set much of an example for her young daughter, did she? Didn't she pass that Commodore in a bad temper, at a very fast clip? Yelling at the driver? Calling him a lunatic and a dickhead and giving him two fingers as she went by? Putting her daughter and her daughter's friend in the lane with a weaving lunatic? Oh, so she went past slowly? It took two seconds? She drove beside him for two whole seconds with her left-hand wheels crammed into the lunatic's lane? Wasn't that a ridiculously negligent and dangerous thing to do? And to pass with her lights on full beam—wouldn't that risk dazzling the other driver in his mirror? If there was a word of truth in what she was saying, wasn't that insanely dangerous driving? She was making all this up, wasn't she?

Waite fought to keep a clear head. At every mention of her bad temper at the wheel she would smile. Sometimes she deflected Morrissey's salvos with a soft, disarming laugh. When he pressed her for precise distances she would shrug and calmly stonewall him, taking the old-fashioned female prerogative. Women jurors registered with visible pleasure her firm replies. She did not strain to persuade. She acknowledged that, though she believed there had been three children in the back seat, she might have been mistaken. Perhaps there had been bags in the back and that was why the boy she had clearly seen with his face against the window had looked so tightly 'squished'. But Morrissey suggested that she had transposed on to her idea of the car's back seat the photo of the kids she had seen on the TV news: the famous shot of the three Farquharson boys lined up on a couch with the little one in the middle.

Waite was tiring. 'I just remember they looked squashed,' she kept repeating. 'They were squashy.'

So she was sticking by the blond child at the window behind the driver, correct? With its face pressed against glass? Eyes open or closed? Ears visible? Mouth open? Remember anything about the clothes? How did she know it wasn't a girl? Or was she sure she didn't just see a football?

Waite spat the dummy. 'Oh, don't be ridiculous. It was a child with fair hair. I have said a boy.'

Smiles flashed among the younger jurors. They liked to see a harried witness get bolshie with counsel. Waite had manners.

She drew on them for patience.

'I was there,' she said. 'I saw these things. I'm not making them up.'

But when it came to the angle of her headlights, to what she claimed to have seen *inside* the other car—three children crammed into the back seat, nobody in the passenger seat beside the driver—Morrissey got her in a full nelson. Even the judge weighed in once or twice on this point.

What exactly could she see, asked Morrissey, inside the Commodore into which she claimed to have had such a clear view? She really couldn't make out anything at all about the so-called dark-haired clean-shaven Caucasian driver, could she? Was his mouth open? Was he talking? Could she see his nose? His chin, did she see his chin? His ears? Were his eyes open? Were his hands gripping the steering wheel? Did she *see* his hands on the steering wheel? Oh! She merely presumed his hands were on the wheel, did she, because she didn't actually see them! Was he coughing? Hadn't she said earlier, on the voir dire, that she knew he wasn't coughing because he was not bending forward and his face was not red? What colour was his face? How could she be sure his face was not red? She had trouble distinguishing one colour from another, did she not? Hadn't she thought the Commodore was grey or pale blue? And anyway how could she see the driver's face at all? What was the source of the light by which she saw his face? She didn't have rabbit-spotting lights mounted on the side of her Falcon, did she? Where were her headlights pointing? If she was passing him, if she was driving parallel with his car, surely her lights would have been pointing straight ahead rather than into the other car? What? Was she saying she could see his face by the light coming off his *dashboard*? Did she notice that the Commodore's side and rear windows were significantly darkened? Surely she would agree that tinted windows considerably reduce visibility, especially on a country road at night? Were there any louvres on the rear window of the car? No? Look at this photo, please—its rear window had louvres! Which somehow she had managed not to notice! She had also failed to observe that the front seats had headrests, which would surely have blocked her view of the driver's head movements and of whoever was in the front passenger seat. The conditions that night for her to see anything at all in the other car were absolutely pitiful, were they not?

Strafing, blitzing, he got her to acknowledge that in the two-second look she shot into the car, she simply could not rule out that the driver was coughing at that very moment.

...

That evening a friend came to my house for dinner. She had seen the news report of Dawn Waite's evidence, and questioned me keenly. She must have been expecting me to dump on Waite, for when I described her as a very good witness, stable, intelligent and, at the core of her testimony, credible, she stood up and shouted at me.

'Are you telling me you believed her?'

'Yes, I did, and I bet you would have too, if you'd seen her.'

'But she didn't go to the police for five years! How could you not go to the police?'

'She gave reasons. I thought they were convincing.'

'Oh, bullshit. So she had cancer. If one of my *legs* had been amputated I would have crawled in to make a statement! And how could she have seen into his car, the way she claimed?'

I tried to describe how I thought cross-examination worked.

'The whole point of it is to make the witness's story look shaky, to pepper the jury with doubt. So you get a grip on her basic observations, and you chop away and chop away, and squeeze and shout and pull her here and push her there, you cast aspersions on her memory and her good faith and her intelligence till you make her hesitate or stumble. She starts to feel self-conscious, then she gets an urge to add things and buttress and emphasise and maybe embroider, because she knows what she saw and she wants to be believed; but she's not allowed to tell it her way. You're in charge. All she can do is answer your questions. And then you slide away from the central thing she's come forward with, and you try to catch her out on the peripheral stuff—"Did you see his chin?"—then she starts to get rattled, and you provoke her with a smart crack—"Are you sure it wasn't a football?" She tries to put her foot down—"Oh, don't be ridiculous"—and the judge gives her a dirty look and she sees she's gone too far, so she tries to recoup, she tries to get back to the place she started from, where she really does remember seeing something and knows what she saw—but that place of certainty no longer exists, because you've destroyed it. And now she's floating in the abyss with her legs dangling and everyone can see the lace on her knickers, and the next thing you put to her she'll agree to, just to stop the torture. And then you thank her politely and sit down, and she's dismissed, and she staggers out of the building and she can't stop howling, and the cameras shoot her with her hair in a mess and her jewellery hanging crooked, and then next day there she is on the front page looking like something the cat dragged in—like a liar who's been sprung, or a flake who makes things up just to get herself into the limelight. Is it any wonder people don't want to come forward?'

I was hot in the face, almost panting. My friend deflated somewhat and sat down.

'It doesn't matter what she looks like in the street, though, does it,' she said at last. 'All that matters is how she seems to the jury.'

A long, thoughtful silence.

'I read in *Who* magazine once,' I said, 'about a woman up in New South Wales. She lived in a flat that overlooked a big park with a bushy path running through it. One day she's having a cup of tea on her balcony when she sees a young girl walking along the path. A bloke in a tracksuit comes jogging after her. The woman on the balcony actually sees him knock the girl down, rape her and strangle her, drag her body into the bushes and run away. And even *she* didn't go to the police. She said she didn't want to get involved.'

We ate the fish and the potatoes. We drank some wine.

'I've never been on a jury,' said my friend. 'Have you?'

'No. Never been called. But I've heard stories and read books. And I've seen *Twelve Angry Men* about a hundred times.'

'How about you boil Waite's evidence right down,' she said. 'Just say you leave out all the iffy stuff about headlight angles and tinted windows. What do you get?'

'You get,' I said, 'that she saw his car behaving weirdly, well before it went up the overpass and got to where *he* says he started coughing. You get that his car was doing sixty, moving side to side in the left lane.'

'You get that he was distracted,' she said, 'in another

space—wouldn't look at her, probably didn't even notice she was there.'

'And you get that he wasn't coughing. That part I believe, tint or no tint. *He's* never said he started coughing before the overpass. Maybe he was just dawdling? Waiting for there to be no traffic on the road?'

'Or maybe you get that something was going on in his mind,' she said. 'Some sort of struggle. Two parts of him slugging it out.'

'Yes! And she saw him right on the cusp of it. The face in the back must have been Tyler, the middle boy. She was the last person to see him alive.'

My friend asked if I had Gambino's *60 Minutes* interview on tape. Grateful for company, I dug it out and we settled on the couch. The boys played in the bath, shyly smiling at the camera. Moules and Gambino sat on the grass beside a creek, declaring their love and talking about a 'summer wedding'. And there was Gambino competently handling Bailey, the heavy-headed newborn, tiny enough to be swaddled in a single nappy. I turned to tell my friend that, at the time the children drowned, Bailey was still being breastfed once a day, that the symbiotic bond between mother and infant had not yet been broken. But my guest's head had dropped towards her chest. Cradling a cushion in both arms, she was sound asleep.

Once I would have jostled her, shouted, 'Wake up! Pay attention!'—but I had been learning, during the second trial, that the desire for sleep does not betray only boredom or fatigue. In these weeks of long, slow trauma interspersed with bloody skirmishes, I had found that suddenly falling asleep was a way of defending oneself against the unbearable.

I turned down the volume and watched the rest of the interview on my own. My friend woke in time to see its final moments—Gambino in her crushed pink blouse, her cheeks glossy with tears, saying, 'I've got so many anniversaries throughout the year. It's always there. I'm never gonna be that person who used to have three children fed, bathed, showered, and bouncing out the door at 8.30 in the morning—I'm never gonna be that person again.'

'You've got to, darling,' murmured my friend, pressing the cushion against her belly. 'Somehow you've got to find a way.'

...

The mysterious child's face that Dawn Waite said she saw pressed to the side window, making her think that all three children had been riding in the back seat, caused a brief flurry. Justice Lasry sent the jury out, and Dr Michael Burke, the pathologist who had performed the autopsies, was recalled and asked to account for two small bruises that had been noticed on Jai's shoulders, at the point where the collarbone reached the shoulder joint. Was it possible that Jai had been sitting not in the front passenger seat but in the centre of the back seat? That, at impact, he had been vaulted forward between the two front seats, bruising his shoulder tips, before his head hit the dashboard and incurred the injuries to his forehead and left cheek? By the time Dr Burke came to give his evidence before the jury—when he spoke more frankly about the distressing surgical processes of post mortem than he had at the first trial—the only new suggestion that surfaced was that Jai might not have been restrained by a seatbelt at the moment of impact. Waite's observation that the children had all been squashed in the back could not be validated. But it left a residue of confusion, a little jet of fresh sorrow.

...

In the three years since the first trial, Shane Atkinson and Tony McClelland, the young men whom Farquharson flagged down on the road and persuaded to drive him to Gambino, had lost their wild beauty, and perhaps their youth. They looked haggard: paler, thinner, more lined. McClelland had got his carpenter's ticket, and had done something to the colour of his hair. Atkinson, the mill-worker, was still, or again, unemployed; his baby, whose birth they had been on their way to celebrate that Father's Day, must be nearly old enough to start school. I could not tell if the two men were still friends, but surely the experience they had shared that night would link them for the rest of their lives, whether they wanted it to or not.

Mr Morrissey was gentle with Atkinson. 'I'm wrong and you're right,' he said at one point, and Atkinson replied patiently, 'Thank you.' But when pressed too hard, Atkinson's hackles went up. 'I think you were here last time,' he said to Morrissey, 'puttin' words in me mouth.' A soft laugh flew along the bar table and up to the bench. I heard it as affectionate, but the witness's face darkened and I saw the humiliated schoolboy behind the country battler he had become. He raised his eyes to the judge, and stretched his long back. Then, for a few minutes, I must have nodded off. When I came to, both he and McClelland had been dismissed, and I never saw them again.

...

Across the road near the coffee cart I came upon Bob and Bev Gambino sitting on a cold metal bench. They shuffled along to make room. Bob wanted to show me a photo he had taken of the defaced headstone on the children's grave. Morrissey's suggestion that it could have been their daughter's doing, or done at her behest, filled Bev with fury.

'Steve reckons it was a shotgun blast,' said Bob, 'but that can't be right. Too dangerous to the shooter. More likely done with a hammer and chisel.'

He held out his phone to me. On the tiny screen I saw a close-up of the name 'Farquharson'. Below it, where the dead children's parents were named, the surface of the shining granite was pitted by a splatter of matte white nicks: a rectangle of assault on the word 'Robert'.

...

While Mr Rapke in the original trial had been content to let the Crown case float between two alternative versions of murder—either a head of steam that suddenly exploded, or a carefully planned and coolly carried-out act of revenge—the Crown now plumped for the latter theory, and Mr Tinney drove it hard, to the point of suggesting that the sight of Gambino's face when Farquharson personally brought her the bad news would have been his 'delicious reward'.

My private doubts about this gothic detail were not shared by the young journalist who had sat beside me while the telephone intercepts were being played. When Gambino told Farquharson that all the children's seatbelts were found to be undone, when he burst into shocked sobs both on the tape and in the dock, the journalist glanced up from the game he was playing on his phone and scribbled in my notebook, 'Did you see his crocodile tears?'

One day, when court rose for lunch, I took my sandwich to the Flagstaff Gardens and lay on the grass under a tree. Why had Farquharson, during the first trial, flashed outraged grimaces and vehement head-shakings at his sisters whenever the word 'suicide' was mentioned? Was there a moral register on which suicide was more disgraceful than murder? Perhaps the most shaming thing of all, a failure of nerve that no 'Anglo-Saxon country bloke' could possibly admit to, would be to launch a murder-suicide and not complete the act. I recalled a famous Sydney story about a man who threw himself off the Gap and was caught before he hit the rocks by a huge and timely wave. The coastguard vessel picked him up unhurt. 'The minute your feet leave the ground,' the saved man said, 'you change your mind.' An American mother I read about drove her car full of children into a river; she drowned and so did all her kids except the eldest, a ten-year-old, who fought his way across her lap and out through a part-open window. He told police that as the car began to sink his mother had cried out, 'I made a mistake. I made a mistake.'

Was the core of the whole phenomenon a failure of imagination, an inability to see any further forward than the fantasy of one clean stroke that would put an end to humiliation and pain?

Cindy Gambino had observed that Farquharson had become a better father after their break-up. Perhaps a hard-working husband is screened from his children by the domestically powerful and emotionally competent presence of his wife. When the marriage ends and access visits begin, he has to deal with the kids on his own. He is shocked at first, finds his new duties exhausting and difficult and often tedious; but gradually, by virtue of this unmediated contact, the children's reality penetrates his armour and flows into his nerves, his blood. Now that he knows them, and knows their love, his exile from their daily life causes him a sharper suffering. To a man who is emotionally immature, bereft of intellectual equipment and concepts, lacking in sustaining friendships outside his family, his children may appear to be not only the locus of his pain, but also the source and cause of it. If only he could put an end to it—amputate or obliterate this wounded part of him that will not stop aching! As the judge in the first trial put it in his sentencing, he forms a dark contemplation...

I watched the thought, to see what it would do. It firmed up, like a jelly setting. And there it sat, quivering, filling all the available space.

...

As the retrial established its own momentum, as Justice Lasry bent over backwards and tied himself in knots to make it fair, efficient and appeal-proof, my respect for Mr Morrissey grew. He was on the ropes, but he fought gamely on. Again and again he had to be pulled up by the judge for referring to his client as 'Rob' instead of 'Mr Farquharson'. It embarrassed him but he could not seem to help it.

The new jury looked as sceptical of his submissions as the first one had, but its style was different. Among the ranks of the serious, the mature and the anxious sat a scattering of student-like young people whose demeanour was relaxed to the point of irreverence.

One would lower his chin to the desk in front of him, stretch out a bare arm along his cheek, and blatantly doodle on his notebook or let his yellow biro dangle from his lips. He and another languid youth became inseparable. They entered and left the court together, exchanging whispered comments and muffling their amusement. It was a bromance. Much later, when the journalists were herded into their dismal office so the deliberating jurors could take the air, these two romped together in the sunny yard like puppies.

But among their fellow members I sensed a growing anguish. A third of the way through the trial there occurred an unexplained change of foreperson: the tough-looking older man who relinquished the job moved along one seat and was replaced by an imposing woman of forty or so, swathed in an elegant ruby shawl, who had previously struck me as reticent and rather solitary. A visiting barrister sitting beside me whispered, 'Maybe a personality clash? There's a few mothers up there.' The new forewoman took the seat in the front corner of the box, nearest the judge, pale but determined.

...

It was winter, and in this courtroom coughing was what one did. Every morning when Justice Lasry entered, exactly halfway between the door and the bench he would clear his throat in a spasm that caused his long cheeks to puff out. At any given moment half a dozen people would be trying to stifle their coughs in scarves or handfuls of tissues. But Farquharson's was the worst. Whenever it took hold of him and a guard had to bring him water, the jurors would slide their eyes in his direction. What if he had an attack of cough syncope here, right in front of everyone? Would it end the trial at once? Could we all go home? One day his hacking got so bad that a lowly member of the defence team had to take him out at lunchtime to get a throat spray from a chemist. He reappeared at two o'clock wearing a huge charcoal suit jacket over his usual shirt-sleeves and tie. It must have belonged to Morrissey: its shoulders were too wide, its sleeves too long. Child-like pathos was Farquharson's default mode.

…

From the day Farquharson's imminent second trial was reported in the media, poignant scraps and echoes had come to light from here and there to expand and illuminate the story or simply add to it a dab of colour. Men from Winchelsea and its environs surprised their mates by bursting into tears in back sheds and relating incidents they had not previously thought worthy of mention. Some of these fragments made it into the retrial. Others were scotched in Preliminary Argument as hearsay or fantasy.

But two of them that did surface in court, sad and ironic, stuck to my mind like burrs.

At four o'clock on Father's Day, before he hit the road to Geelong with his boys, Farquharson stopped off at the house of Michael Hart. Hart had made no appearance in the first trial. He was a carpenter who had done some work on the Farquharsons' unfinished house in Daintree Drive. He was also a single father involved in the boys' football club. Farquharson invited him and his son to come along on the drive, but Hart was not in a mood to go anywhere, and said no. To Morrissey, intent upon demolishing the Crown's scenario of a planned crime, Farquharson's invitation showed that he could not possibly have been intending to drive into the dam on the way home that night. To anyone interested in psychological states, however, it added one more rock to the burden of loneliness that Farquharson was dragging.

The role of the reluctant friend in this brief incident echoed a bigger knockback that Farquharson had had to swallow the year before. His friend Darren Bushell, the shearer nicknamed DB, broke up with his wife a few months before Gambino gave Farquharson his marching orders. Newly cut loose, Farquharson went round to DB's place and said he was looking for somewhere to live. 'He was hinting to move in with me and share,' said DB to the police in his statement. 'But I had just gone through all that myself and I didn't want it again. So I never offered.'

...

The experience of repetition was very disagreeable for some of the people who took the stand. One uniformed officer who had been among the first at the dam seemed to be in a bad way. He clasped his hands and relaxed his shoulders into the stance of endurance that police are trained in; but his distress was manifest, his voice muffled, his cheeks hollow and dark. The older members of Major Collision, lined and limping, gave their evidence again with the low, guarded burn of men who have had a gutful.

Cindy Gambino's change of heart must have rolled like a tide through the Surf Coast region; other returning witnesses took a less cooperative tone, no matter how Morrissey tried to jolly them along.

More often, though, they seemed less hostile than simply weary, their testimony a trek across a distant plain—for by now almost five years had passed since the night at the dam, and in the onward rush of life outside the Farquharson and Gambino families, the reality of Jai, Tyler and Bailey, as with all people who have died, had grown threadbare and dim.

But Morrissey declared that his cross-examination of Senior Constable Glen Urquhart, the tall young civil engineer and reconstructionist from Major Collision, would turn 'a giant witness' into a much lesser one.

Morrissey worked his way with slashing skill through the errors and equipment failures and self-corrections of the police investigation. The famous police mistakes he hung round Urquhart's neck like an albatross. He derided the competence of several less experienced officers who had helped him at the dam. He took him apart for having changed his opinion about which of Sergeant Exton's yellow paint marks was supposed to pinpoint which wheel of Farquharson's car. He rubbed Urquhart's nose in the awkward fact that the Commodore he had used in his video road tests turned out not to have had the preparatory wheel alignment that Urquhart believed it had.

To us listeners, without access to the photo booklets that the jury was studying, the argument was only a flood of talk, but I saw how Urquhart suffered on the stand. His jaw was clenched with mortification, and he kept raising his chin and stretching his neck as if his collar were too tight. It ran counter to one's sense of fairness that he was not allowed to explain in his own words (or what Morrissey called 'make excuses for') how things in his testimony had come to be as they were. The repeated order 'Just answer the question' came to sound insultingly tyrannical, like a gag or a bridle. How crude, how primitive were the words 'yes' and 'no' in the face of questions on which so much hung! Yet although his brow was sometimes beaded with sweat and his mouth flattened with suppressed anger, somehow Urquhart continued to answer neutrally, readily, politely. He would not make a statement on the matter of exactly where Farquharson's car had started its rightward drift out of the left lane. It cost him something to acknowledge that he could not say, but there was no evidence for it, and on this he held his ground.

And the jury liked him. They felt for him. He was one of the witnesses they instinctively trusted. When he was pulled up by Morrissey for illustrating a point with hand gestures, and said good-humouredly, 'Sorry! I'll put my hands in my pockets', two of the women jurors in the front row sent him open smiles of sympathy. There was something earnest and endearing in his demeanour that withstood Morrissey's most ferociously detailed attacks. When Amanda Forrester rose, I saw again the miracle of redemption that an air-clearing re-examination can bring about.

As the American writer Janet Malcolm says in her magisterial work *The Journalist and the Murderer*, 'Jurors sit there presumably weighing evidence but in actuality they are studying character.'

...

When Greg King was about to be called, to betray his mate for the third time, I would have been grateful to save myself by falling asleep.

But at that moment a bright-eyed, black-browed teenage

boy strode boldly into the court and took the seat beside me. The laminated card on his lanyard gave his name as 'Eggleston'. He was in year ten, he told me, at a certain eastern suburbs private school, and was doing work experience 'in a lower court'. Taken by an urge to see 'a manslaughter trial', he had crossed Lonsdale Street and wandered into the Supreme Court. He had many resounding opinions on the law and the conduct of the courts, and outlined them for me with the airy aplomb of the school debater, but when Greg King sidled in, wearing jeans and a short-sleeved shirt, the boy's bumptious monologue died on his lips.

Tinney wound up his witness and set him in motion like a mechanical toy. King threw himself at his story, pouring it out by heart in one unpunctuated trembling stream, gasping, sniffing, raking his forearms and sometimes his shins with his fingernails.

Could he explain, asked Tinney, why he had not put the full version of the fish-and-chip-shop conversation to Farquharson, on the two secret tapes? The version that included 'hate', and 'kill'?

'I didn't have the heart to,' said King. 'I've known the Farquharson family, the Gambino family most of my life. I've worked with her parents. I've got to come between them and put in my best mate. I mean, I've got my own kids. It's a small town. What are they going to think of me? I was fearing for my family and everyone.' The tipstaff handed him a bunch of tissues and he bent forward, wiping his eyes.

The judge allowed the jury a short break and left the bench while King went outside to compose himself. I turned to Eggleston. 'What do you make of this witness?'

'He's lying,' he said at once.

'How can you tell?'

'Easy,' he said. 'While he was having the alleged conversation with Mr Farquharson outside the fish-and-chip shop, where were his children?'

'Oh, they were inside the shop, waiting for the chips.'

'Why did he leave them on their own?' cried the boy in a triumphant tone. 'He should have stayed there with them.'

An old court watcher doing a cryptic crossword behind us laughed under his breath and muttered, 'What about somebody who leaves his kids in a dam?'

'In my view,' said the oblivious Eggleston, 'he just read about the case in the newspapers and decided to make sure Farquharson's found guilty.'

'Why on earth would he do that?'

'Any parent would. And,' he went on smoothly, 'I can tell that Farquharson hasn't slept for six or seven nights. His eyes are all swollen.'

'Hey,' I said. 'You should be a detective.'

He bridled. 'Oh no. I've definitely decided to study law.'

Greg King, red-eyed, skulked back to the stand. He tried to reassert his manliness by giving cheek and striking cocky poses. He addressed Morrissey by his first name, and had to be put in his place. When Morrissey described Farquharson as 'a peaceful, non-violent person'—*not like King*, who had shown himself to be a violent bully, had he not, in the Winchelsea pub brawl that the police delayed charging him for?—King squared his shoulders and put his hand on his hip with a defiant little swagger. Morrissey worked him over, hauling him through the transcript of his evidence in the first trial, setting traps for him big and small, but King was so literal-minded, so lacking in emotional vocabulary, that Morrissey's ironic strokes were wasted on him, and we heard only the heavy whizzing of the sword. Flummoxed in the dreary acres of transcript, King spread his hands at last and said, 'I'm lost.'

In a stage whisper Eggleston pointed out to me the admirable way in which Morrissey 'made the witness think hard about his answer, in case he contradicted something he'd said before'. But the jurors' mouths were set in firm lines. They did not like the clever barrister for running rings around this broken-hearted boofhead. And even the censorious grammar-school boy turned pale and silent when King choked up and said, in a flood of helpless tears, that he blamed himself for the children's deaths because he had not taken seriously what Farquharson said to him outside the fish-and-chip shop.

There was no getting past this. It was the cross King had to bear, and his clumsy carrying of it endowed him, in the end, with a dignity that withstood the worst that the defence could throw at him.

...

I was not brave enough to face the police submergence videos again, but I watched the jury sit through them, with their hands over their mouths. The erstwhile foreman strained his chin so high that the lump in his throat moved visibly. In my memory of the first trial the videos were silent, but this time, at the point where the diver struggled to open the passenger-side door, I became aware of a series of muffled thumps, the sounds of adult effort, and then a horrible low gurgling and rushing. I risked a glance upwards at the yellow boiling of the water, its violent force and huge bubbles, and for the first time I allowed myself to accept the possibility that Jai never did open his door, as Farquharson had endlessly related. What about the reddish abrasions the pathologist found on Jai where his face hit the windscreen—one to the forehead, and a palm-sized one to his left cheek? Wouldn't a child have been stunned by such a blow? Perhaps it was Tyler in the back, uninjured, who unbuckled his own belt and tried to get Bailey out of his harness? Could the whole thing have happened as the second video test suggested? The car crashes into the water and floats a moment, tilting. Farquharson scrambles out while the force of the water against his door is still weak enough to be overcome. As he swims away, the weight of the water clips his door shut behind him. The dark car fills fast while Jai—or Tyler—fights to unbuckle his brothers' seatbelts. The rear doors are locked, the offside door handle broken. Jai goes for the driver's door but the huge pressure from outside defeats him. Tyler's and Bailey's lungs are already full by the time the pressure equalises and Jai gets the door open. But he too has run out of air, and when the police diver gropes blindly up the side of the car, hours later, Jai is lying across the front seats with his head protruding through the wide-open driver's door.

...

Farquharson's silence about what had happened that night, his inability or his refusal to say how the car went into the dam, was throwing everyone around him into a state of agitation that was hard to bear. Even Justice Lasry, in the absence of the jury, made a slip as telling as the one that Morrissey claimed had put me in contempt: 'Did the accused drive the vehicle deliberately, or, if he was unconscious, did he fall forward in a way that affected the steering wheel? *No one knows except him.*'

We, his fellow citizens, could not live in such a cloud of unknowing. The central fact of the matter would not let us rest. It tore at our hearts that inside the plunging car, while their father fled, three little boys had fought with their restraints, breathed filthy water, choked, thrashed and died.

There was something frantic about the way we danced attendance on the silent man, this 'horrendous snorer', this 'sook', this 'good mate' and 'loving dad' and 'good provider'; this stump of a man with his low brow and puffy eyes, his slumped spine and man-boobs, his silent-movie grimaces and spasms of tears, his big clean ironed handkerchief.

Every accused person has the right to remain silent. Juries are clearly instructed that they must not draw any adverse inference if the accused decides to exercise that right. An eminent barrister once told me he never put his clients in the witness box unless they insisted. It was too risky, he said. Lay people have no experience of what a skilful advocate can do and are not equipped to stand up to it; if you try to prepare them they lose all flexibility.

The first witness Morrissey called for the defence was his client, Robert Farquharson.

His family and his supporters had been watching the trial from the upper gallery; but one of their cohort, a strikingly pretty, well-dressed and motherly-looking woman of sixty or so, was allowed by the judge to come down into the body of the court as a person of comfort while he gave evidence. I knew that her son was engaged to a niece of Farquharson's, and that she and her clergyman husband were paying the rent on the serviced apartment in which Farquharson lodged for the duration of the trial. She herself was staying there with him during the court weeks, to console and support him. She was given a seat in a direct eye-line from the high witness box. She sat with her hands clasped in her lap and shone her attention straight into Farquharson's face.

It was awful to see him out of the dock and exposed up there, in his tight collar and big stripy tie: such a pathetic figure to be carrying our terrible projections. Morrissey smiled at him, and took it slow. At first Farquharson spoke clearly, drawing the odd quivering sigh: yes, he used to be a window cleaner, but he had been unemployed since his release on appeal. When Morrissey began to talk about the boys' football club, and then asked him about the presents his sons had brought to his house on the afternoon of Father's Day, Farquharson's voice splintered. Yeah, a really nice photo of the boys, he got. Some pots and pans from Cindy—and there were some other presents that he was supposed to get but didn't until after they died. And what were these gifts? Farquharson covered his face with one hand and blew out air between his lips. He could hardly form the words.

'Jai got me a back-scratcher,' he faltered, 'and Tyler—Tyler—a block o' chocolate.'

Shocked by the tears that rushed into my eyes, I glanced along the jury. I was not the only one. At that moment I would have given anything to be convinced that he was innocent—and not because I 'believed in him', whatever that meant, but because, in spite of everything I had heard and observed and thought in this court, in spite of everything I knew about the ways of the world, it was completely unendurable to me that a man would murder his own children.

Within minutes Morrissey had squandered his advantage.

'And so,' he said gently, 'what was the conversation in the car, driving home?'

'Jai said,' droned Farquharson, '"I have got you a back-scratcher", and Tyler said he had a block of chocolate there for me.'

The journalists rolled their eyes and laid down their pens. A third time Morrissey pressed Farquharson to name the humble gifts. His hapless client trotted them out, and the tender moment, milked of its pathos, shrivelled and died.

And yet, as Morrissey took Farquharson by the hand and drew him into the bombed-out rubble of the story, aiming a hose at every smoking point of doubt, my heart softened again towards the awkward, unhappy figure on the stand. He still spoke of his dead boys in the present tense. He talked about Cindy, how she was 'a terrific mother' who, after their separation, never did anything bad or mean. The subtext was obvious—nothing bad or mean enough to make him want to murder their children in revenge. But then, needing to have it both ways, Morrissey coaxed from him the story of the day the shit car was in again for repairs, when Farquharson asked Gambino to let him take the boys to football in the good car, the one she got at the break-up, that he had seen Moules driving round the town. She knocked him back: 'You're not drivin' that.'

Once, said Farquharson, he took Tyler back to Cindy's place and found her absent and the other two boys in the house on their own. It turned out that she had gone to the local hospital to get a migraine injection, leaving Jai in charge of Bailey. After this and several other incidents that troubled Farquharson's sisters, there was vague talk that he might go for custody. It never came to anything, though, because he worked full-time.

Greg King had spoken guiltily of Farquharson as his mate, and had copped scalding rebukes on the stand for having betrayed such a close old friend. But Farquharson now told the court that by 2005 King was someone he rarely saw, and in whom he never confided. If he had been in a confiding relationship with anyone, he said, it would have been with Darren Bushell or Michael Hart.

Oh, how bleak and windswept it seems to women, the landscape of what some men call friendship. Hart was the one who couldn't bring himself to drive to Geelong with his gloomy, half-sick mate and his boys on Father's Day; and Bushell, a year earlier, had not wanted to offer house room to the dumped and drifting Farquharson—'He was hinting…but I never offered'. Still, when Bushell chanced to drive past the rescue scene at the dam and heard what had happened, he and a woman he knew turned back to Geelong and went looking for Farquharson at the hospital. This was surely the spontaneous act of friends. They got to Emergency just after the two Major Collision interviewers had been surprised by Farquharson's emotionless state and lack of interest in the fate of his boys. 'We went in,' DB told the police, 'and I didn't know what to say to him. Rob was saying "I've killed my kids." He was shaking. I didn't know what to say to him so I didn't push it.'

Morrissey asked Farquharson to explain why he had refused to let Cindy Gambino visit him in jail. Farquharson sighed. 'It was a very tough time,' he said. 'You only get an hour a visit, so you're not going to have a full conversation in an hour about what she obviously wanted to talk about, and the emotional state of me going back to my cell with no one to talk to, nothing—it's just too hard. Too hard.' He flapped one hand past his ear. 'No counsellors, no nothing. You're in prison.'

And finally he described two witnessed attacks of cough syncope that he had recently suffered. The first happened when he was in custody. Another inmate cracked a joke at the worktable. Everyone burst out laughing, and Farquharson turned his chair away to cough. He came to on the ground with medics and prison officers leaning over him, and a fractured leg. The second attack occurred in his sister Carmen's lounge room, just after he was released on appeal. He started coughing and the next minute he was on the carpet.

The emotional weight of this evidence-in-chief was such that, by the time Morrissey sat down, Farquharson had taken on the lineaments of a tragic figure, a bereaved victim of fate outrageously burdened by the state's accusations.

...

Then the prosecutor, Mr Tinney, got to his feet. He tore into Farquharson in a fast, rough style that made people sit up with a jolt.

'Bailey was two years old at the time he died, correct? And he was quite incapable of undoing his car seat, wasn't he? On your oath you never knew him to be able to undo his own car seat? Can't you remember the last trip you had in a motorcar with your children? Don't you have a good memory of the last minutes your children lived? Haven't you tried to think about every single thing that happened in these last minutes and hours of their lives?'

The jurors' faces froze. I heard Morrissey's instructing solicitor utter a sharp gasp of protest.

Where Rapke in the first trial had been lightning on his feet, a fencer slicing the air with invisible steel, Tinney, after his initial onslaught, slowed his pace and settled into a slogging demolition job, phlegmatic, at times plodding, but always meticulous. He folded the story into tight pleats, then ripped it into jagged holes that soon began to emit a lurid glow. The familiar tale started to look bedraggled, misbegotten, full of contradictions and mysterious blurs. His juxtapositions of Farquharson's differing accounts were so intricately detailed that the gaps between them, spotlit, made me feel like cowering in my seat with a coat pulled over my head.

For the first time I was obliged to register the complete absence of sensory detail in Farquharson's account of being in the dam. For the physical reality of his experience we had only what our imaginations could supply. The sole bodily sensation he could come up with was the word 'pressure' and, in the way he used it, it was more of an exculpatory concept than a sensation—an idea, suggested to him in Emergency by Leona Daniel, the kindly grief counsellor, that he had remembered and clung to. Each time Tinney drew him to a specific point and leaned, leaned, leaned on him, Farquharson would slide off sideways into a vague generalisation, or a drab cliché: 'It was a very confusing time.' 'It all happened so quick.' 'Like I said, I was going through a lot of shock, a lot of grief.' 'To be honest, it was a very painful time.' 'Like I said, in a state of confusion and everything else, I—'

'Of course,' said Tinney, 'you could have reached back from where you were if you'd wanted to, couldn't you?'

'What—you mean lean over?'

'You're sinking in a dam—you could have leaned over and undone the seatbelt on Bailey?'

'I probably could have. I don't know. Like I said, everything happened so quick.'

Now and then the judge would underline or clarify Tinney's point: 'But did you not think—that's the question—did you not think it was important to do whatever you could to save your children?'

'Like I said,' repeated Farquharson doggedly, 'I probably had no thought process.'

He had never told anyone before today, had he, said Tinney, that, when he got out of the dam and headed for the road, he had scrambled through a fence and hurt himself?

'With everything I've been through,' said Farquharson on a derisive out-breath, 'I've got to try and think of every little detail? Going through grief, trauma—?'

He said he had 'seen' Jai open the passenger door—but how could he have seen it? Didn't he say it was completely black? That the lights were off and he couldn't see anything at all?

'I may have saw it,' said Farquharson, 'or I may have thought it. I can't recall.'

He had plainly been coached to stand up to the assault, but he came across as a strange, bristling automaton that pumped out repetitive answers and sometimes forced a smile, as if the flesh from nostrils to chin had hardened, drawn inwards and turned grey. Questioned on discrepancies between what he had told different people, he fell back on little mantras. Scores of times he said, 'If that's what was said, that's what was said.' 'If that's what I did, that's what I did.' In his first day on the stand he used the phrase 'like I said' twenty-nine times. Occasionally he would use an oddly dated expression. 'The car was stopped when I was awoken.' When the GP came to the house he was 'bed-bound. Bed-ridden.'

The matter of whether or not he had manipulated Dr Steinfort, the Geelong thoracic physician, gave rise to serious dismay. Had he given Steinfort exaggerated accounts of his earlier coughing fits, saying he had blacked out? As Farquharson fumbled to answer, I saw one woman juror tighten her lips: her face, usually shining with good humour, darkened and turned sombre. The woman beside her sat with one hand over her mouth, but a sceptical smile leaked out on either side.

Challenged on what he had told police in the Homicide interviews about whether or not he had dived down after the car, he became huffy and put-upon: 'Like I said, two days after me accident and you want me to be clear-headed?'

'But in the interviews at Homicide, in the car, and at the hospital,' Tinney pointed out, 'you showed yourself to be very clear-headed.'

'Who knows,' said Farquharson in one of his rhetorical flourishes, 'what was racing through me mind?'

If he knew all along that the cause of the crash was a coughing fit, why did he talk to the first people he met beside the dam, the young men who picked him up on the roadside, about a wheel bearing?

Farquharson said he had no memory of the two men. He did not recall what he said to them. He did not even know what a wheel bearing was. 'I'm not a mechanic,' he said with his grey smile.

Why did he mention it, then?

He had no answer; but it gave me a pang that at such a moment there should rise to his lips the words 'I musta done a wheel bearing'—the sort of cool, blokey throwaway line he must have heard from other men, perhaps his father, or his workmates on the shire.

Had he ever looked up a book, or the internet, about coughing fits? 'No. That's why I go to the doctor for.' Did he ever do a Google search in his whole life? No. He would look at cars sometimes, but his sisters had to set it up for him.

How come he made no mention of coughing to the first police officer he spoke to at the dam, but told him he had had a chest pain? And how was it that he had told his friend Darren Bushell that he blacked out in his car at the Winchelsea service station, days before the crash, yet never mentioned this to the police?

'It's just something I forgot about. I mean, like I said, two days after me accident, losing my children, you want me to remember every detail?'

Whenever Farquharson made one of these petulant replies, Tinney would look down and riffle through his documents. Had he really lost his place, or was he leaving a pause for the weirdness of the answer to settle in the jurors' minds? His cross-examination would have seemed slack-textured had it not been for these dreadful silences, thick with Farquharson's resistance and the listeners' growing suspicion. After each pause, the prosecutor would look up slowly as if a new idea had just occurred to him.

Wasn't it strange that Farquharson had never asked anyone about how his children were found in the salvaged car? Their seatbelts? Where they were in the vehicle?

Farquharson appeared genuinely baffled. 'Who was I supposed to talk to?'

He did not know how the headlights and the ignition of the Commodore had come to be turned off. He told the police he had no memory of doing it. But in the bugged phone conversations with

Gambino, said Tinney, he told her he had turned the motor off in case there was a fire. Farquharson had no explanation for this discrepancy.

'Why did the ignition of the car get turned off at all?'

'I don't know. I can't answer that.'

'Is there any other person who could have turned it off other than you?'

'I can't answer that.'

'Oh, witness,' said Tinney reproachfully. 'Is there any person in the car who could possibly have turned off the ignition, other than you?'

'Well,' said Farquharson, 'Jai could have, easily.'

The journalists turned to each other, their mouths ajar. Farquharson wiped his palms on his trousers. The jurors' brows were knitted, their faces full of trouble.

'Are you seriously suggesting that one of your children, in the moments before they died, would have had any reason to turn off the ignition of that car?'

'I'm trying to answer it the best way I can.'

'Why did you turn off the headlights?'

'They could have been bumped or anything, I don't know.'

'Bumped? Bumped? Did you have some reason for wanting it to be dark out there?'

'No, I did not.'

Tinney pressed him hard on why he had wanted so desperately to be taken from the dam straight to Cindy Gambino—wasn't it his negative feelings towards her that made him want to tell her straightaway that her children were dead?

'No.'

'What was she going to be able to do, to help?'

'All I know is that I had to see her. That's all I know.'

'To do what?'

'I just had to see her.'

'To do *what*?'

'I don't *know*.'

'What were you intending to do when you saw her?'

'Tell her that I'd had an accident.'

'Tell her you'd killed the kids?'

'No. That I'd had an accident.'

'And what was she going to be able to do about it?'

'I don't know, but I had to see her. Like I said, she's the mother of my children.'

'So you left the dam? And, when you left, your children were in a motorcar somewhere submerged in the dam? There was no one else there at the dam, and you just went off in a car and left them there?'

'Well, that's what happened, yes, but not in the terms you're trying to put it.'

'And you were a loving father, were you?'

'I'm a *very* loving father, *thank* you.'

When Tinney pointed out to him the surprising haste with which he had assumed his children were dead, Farquharson uttered an aggrieved, angry laugh, thrust out both hands palms up, and protested, 'I'd just lost me children in front of me eyes!'

He would not acknowledge that he had been angry about the whole set-up after Gambino ended the marriage. 'Upset' or 'annoyed' was as far as he would go. Tinney prised open this denial with a needling little manoeuvre that I wished young Eggleston had still been there to see.

'Of course,' he said, 'Mr Moules would have had a perfect right to drive your wife's car if he wanted to, wouldn't he?'

Five years had not healed this wound. Farquharson flared up. 'Well, why? Drive our car? It was *our* car still, at the time.'

'It wasn't your car, was it, once you were separated?' said Tinney. 'It was your wife's car, your ex-wife's car.'

Farquharson flushed with old anger. 'It was still *both* our car.'

But by then there had been no more 'our'. Everything that had been 'ours' was wiped and gone.

Except the children.

…

Years later, a man I knew who had been in the upstairs gallery that day said to me with a groan, 'It was like watching some poor animal dying. You wanted to call out, "For God's sake, shoot him!"'

Yet all the while, Farquharson's person of comfort, the pretty, motherly woman with her hands folded in her lap or pressed as in prayer under her chin, seemed immune to the awful effect of his demeanour. She gazed up at him from her seat with a wonderfully tender-hearted expression of approval and encouragement. She tilted her head, she nodded it slowly, thoughtfully, as if pondering the incontrovertible truth of everything he was saying. Once or twice she gave a tiny wink. While the wretched man blundered his way across the scorched earth of his story, she poured out upon him great streams of love from some inexhaustible Christian store.

That Sunday evening I went to the Evelyn Hotel in Fitzroy to hear my sister sing in the Melbourne Mass Gospel Choir. I hardly expected a big crowd for gospel in that hip part of town, but the bar was packed shoulder to shoulder. The first song was about the water of salvation reaching the feet, rising up the body…In shock I looked behind me, half expecting to see Morrissey and Tinney and Farquharson and his sisters rocking alongside the pierced and tattooed locals on the swell of the brilliant harmonies. Atheists and believers swayed in unison, surprised by joy. By the time the sixty-strong choir burst into 'Jesus Dropped the Charges', I had air-lifted the whole mighty throng of them plus the band and the audience and the entire dramatis personae of the court out through the roof, away from the city and along the Princes Highway to the banks of the nameless dam, where we threw down our swords and sang and shouted and testified together, while the three children in pure white robes were raised gasping and dripping from the depths and restored all perfect to their mother's arms.

Next morning, sobered, I ran the gauntlet of the defence team's hostile faces and took my seat in Court Eleven, where the Old Testament spirit of retribution still reigned. But when the tipstaff called us to our feet and ceremonially opened proceedings—'All persons having business before this honourable court are commanded to give their attendance, and they shall be heard'—I had to bite my lip to keep from shouting 'Amen!'

Farquharson endured three days on the stand. The defence case never recovered. The edifice that Morrissey would go on to erect with such labour and concentration and loving devotion was weak at its foundations, for, toil as he might, he could not make the jury like or trust his client. From then on, the final fortnight of evidence was like watching, in ghastly slow motion, a man slither down the face of a cliff. Sometimes his shirt would snag on a protruding branch, or his fall would be arrested by a tiny ledge, a fragile outcrop; but the fabric would stretch and snap, the narrow shelf would crumble, and down he would go again, feet first, eyes wide open, arms outstretched into the void.

A clinical psychologist from Box Hill named Dr Rob Gordon seemed likely to offer a landing place. He had white hair and the quiet, rather bureaucratic manner of someone accustomed to spending long hours being patiently coherent in meetings. His expertise lay in the diagnosis and treatment of trauma-related disorders. Unlike Farquharson's loyal grief counsellor, Gregory Roberts, on whose authority as an expert witness Justice Cummins had cast stern shade,

Gordon had decades of respect-worthy experience in his field.

Morrissey led Dr Gordon through the whole story: Farquharson on the roadside, in the car to Gambino's, and back at the dam where the would-be rescuers were infuriated by his affectless manner and his failure to take part. At first (as with many a psychological expert witness) I was tensed in expectation of insulting dot-point diagrams of the mental processes that life had taught me were complex and mysterious; but instead Dr Gordon delivered an extended, fascinating lecture, quite beautiful in its clarity, about the mechanisms of trauma, its physiological effects on the brain, and what it can do to human behaviour. His eloquent discourse—the kicking in of the reptile brain, dissociation, numbing, detachment—reframed Farquharson's experience on the night in a deeply sympathetic and convincing way. Farquharson in his fall had come to rest, trembling, on a stable ledge.

Without a struggle, Tinney got Dr Gordon to acknowledge that many of Farquharson's actions on the night were 'at the unusual end of the spectrum for a person in a traumatic situation'—for example: that within minutes of the crash he had accepted and resigned himself to the deaths of his children; that he had left his children in the dam and departed the scene; that he had refused offers of help or the use of a telephone; that he took no interest in the rescue attempts and gave no help to the rescuers regarding the likely whereabouts of his car in the water; and that at Emergency, without making even cursory inquiries about the fate of his children, he pressed police for information about what would happen to him.

But when Tinney took the next step, and began to ask Dr Gordon to give his opinion on such odd behaviours if they had been seen in a person who had not had an accident, but who had deliberately driven into the dam with intent to kill, Justice Lasry pulled him up short, and sent the jury out with the tipstaff. In their absence, Tinney dug in. Lasry challenged him. Morrissey fought him. In the end Lasry, in a thoughtful (and, I sensed, reluctant) *ex tempore* ruling, decided against Tinney: he was not to pursue this line of questioning.

Dr Gordon was flying to the Middle East that very afternoon and had to be at the airport by two; it was getting on for one o'clock and he was still waiting outside in the hall. But before he could be dismissed, the tipstaff re-entered the court and formally handed up to the judge a scrap of translucent paper. It was a message from the exiled jury. Lasry scanned it. He could not suppress a smile. He read it out. It contained the very questions that he had just denied Tinney permission to put to the psychologist. The jurors had sensed the drift of the argument and were determined not to be shut out.

'Your Honour,' said Mr Tinney drily, 'I can only say that they are the two best jury questions I've ever heard.'

There was not much humour in this retrial, but for once the whole court burst out laughing.

Dr Gordon was called back. Justice Lasry put the questions to him: '1. Can trauma exist regardless of whether an event is intentional or unintentional? 2. If yes to question one, is there any distinct behavioural difference between someone who has had an accident as opposed to someone who has planned the event?'

'It would be hard,' said Dr Gordon, 'to predict exactly what behavioural differences there would be. But the structure of the trauma will be different. In the first case—an accident—the trauma is the tragedy that's happened. In the second case—intentional—the trauma will be, "This is what I've done.'"

And while a large chunk of cliff with a man on it peeled off behind him, away went the psychologist, in his dark-green suit, to catch a plane to Israel.

...

I found it easy to believe that Farquharson had no clear memory of the two men who found him on the roadside, of the police interview in Emergency, of many of the things that happened or that he did after he crawled out of the dam. But listening to Dr Gordon's clear explanation of the brain under terrible stress, I recalled from the first trial a discussion, in the absence of the jury, when Farquharson's Colac psychologist, Peter Popko, was about to take the stand. Judge and counsel had to work out a way to introduce certain material that had sprung from intercepted phone calls between Popko and Farquharson, after the crash. Farquharson had expressed to the psychologist a strong fear that the police investigation might 'push him into a nervous breakdown'. The particular focus of his fear was the looming lie-detector test that he had volunteered to take, despite the fact that these tests are not admissible in Australian courts. His insistence on subjecting himself to a test seemed a sign of his transparency. But if he knew that he was innocent, I had thought then, why would he be racked with such terror? Now it hit me. It was not that he feared being found out in a lie. What he dreaded, what drove him half-demented with fear, was that the polygraph machine, with its nasty electrodes and its computer power immune to all human appeal, might reveal to *him* the truth of what he had done that night on the road, the facts that he had blotted out, or convinced himself he did not know, or genuinely did not remember. And he was right to fear the test, for he failed it.

...

The Crown produced again, and lavishly garlanded, its expert witness from the first trial, Professor Matthew Naughton from the Alfred Hospital. Naughton had never seen with his own eyes an attack of cough syncope. He attested to its extreme rarity with a high-level physiological expertise that seemed, the longer he spoke, to become more and more remote from coarse, solid, grassroots experience.

To counter this professor in what the defence made out to be his ivory tower, Morrissey called again the physician Dr Christopher Steinfort, Farquharson's treating doctor and the keeper of a database of cough syncope sufferers. It seemed that Steinfort was building himself a cough syncope empire down in Geelong. People from the community, hearing of Farquharson's successful appeal against his first conviction, had approached Legal Aid with stories of their own coughing fits and blackouts, and had been referred to Dr Steinfort. One of these, an intelligent and articulate middle-aged man, took the stand and gave an account of the frequent fits of hard coughing that rendered him briefly unconscious. His wife described the blackouts as she had witnessed them. Their testimony was unnervingly convincing. The authority of this personal testimony arrested Farquharson's downward slide for several breathless minutes. But then Morrissey delved further into the witness's medical history—no doubt to keep Tinney away from it—and revealed that, when doctors investigated a stroke the man had suffered, it was found that he had a hole in his heart, thought to have been undiagnosed since childhood. How on earth could a jury be expected to evaluate a medical case so complex?

Another citizen who had come forward when he read about Farquharson's troubles, and had been sent to Dr Steinfort in Geelong, was a sixty-one-year-old security guard with a red face, popping eyes and a blustery manner—formerly a heavy smoker, who had suffered from asthma and had also been diagnosed with emphysema and high blood pressure. He reported, over several years, up to a dozen blackouts after coughing. His first witnessed fit of cough syncope had been brought on at home by his laughter at a Billy Connolly DVD. His next attack, unwitnessed, was not so funny. Driving home one morning from a night shift at the Melbourne Stock Exchange, he blacked out on the Western Ring Road, veered across the carriageway, and was collected by a semi-trailer. At first he and the attending police thought he must have fallen asleep at the wheel. A charge of dangerous driving was dismissed when he remembered he had been coughing before he passed out.

But Morrissey really shot himself in the foot by screening, twice, a grotesque little video of an elderly gentleman, wheelchair-bound with lung disease, his head sprouting electrodes, who demonstrated that he was able to cough himself unconscious at will. At a signal he gave three determined croaks and went limp. His false teeth flew out and were deftly caught in one hand by a plump, exuberant nurse. In a few moments he came to. He uttered word-like sounds, replaced his teeth, and was given a cup of tea.

Thus, for all the eminence and the conflicting hands-on experience of the medical experts, for all Tinney's long, battering cross-examination of Dr Steinfort—under which that excellent witness lost his temper and got defensive and poured out torrents of technical explanation that made the jurors' eyes go dull and their heads droop left and right—the cough syncope evidence hung once more in a balance that neither side could weight to its advantage.

Later, in his charge to the jury, the judge would lay down their duty very clearly: 'If you can't resolve the conflict between expert witnesses, the benefit of the doubt *must* go to the accused.' I wondered what chance there was that this would happen.

. . .

Leona Daniel was the social worker and grief counsellor whose name Farquharson had mentioned many times—the person who first suggested to him the word 'pressure'. Now she took the stand. She was a woman of mature years, with a dry, warm, deeply appealing manner and a face that opened when she smiled. At ten o'clock on the night of the crash, she had walked into the Geelong Emergency ward and found Farquharson thrashing about in his bed. He was tremendously flushed, she said, sweating, at one point coughing, rolling his head from side to side, and very dishevelled: 'the bedclothes were everywhere'. He was 'clearly in great anguish about his children'. Her role was not to challenge or question him about what had happened. She simply accepted what he said at face value. She placed her hands on his forearms and spoke to him gently. He was not Superman, she told him. He would not have been able to open the doors because the water pressure would have been so great. The car would have sunk quickly. There was nothing more he could have done. She even told him that his children might be 'up in heaven with his mum'. But nothing could comfort him. He kept saying that he shouldn't be there. He wanted to go home. He wanted to go for a long walk. Everyone would blame him, he said, and he blamed himself. He said, 'I should have done something. I should have done more. I should be with them.'

Several times, without interpreting them, Leona Daniel quoted his words. 'I shouldn't be here. I should be with them. I shouldn't be here.'

...

A bunch of eager young men and women, friends of the fiancé of Farquharson's niece, had recently gone to the overpass and shot amateur videos of each other driving four ordinary sedans down the slope. 'Drive-by, rough-and-ready experiments', as Morrissey called this volunteer contribution, would clearly show that the crossfall of the road, unmeasured by Major Collision in its lapse of attention, did cause vehicles to drift to the right, instead of moving to the left or maintaining a straight line as Senior Constable Urquhart's own video tests had demonstrated. Justice Lasry seemed to be humouring Morrissey when he allowed these new videos to be shown, with their faint, giggling soundtracks and rain-spattered windscreens. But it was true: the cars did appear to diverge slightly to the right. The crossfall did have meaning. The police were shown to have been remiss in not measuring it.

Farquharson watched all this with his head tilted back, his little eyes glaring. Once he glanced at the jury with his chin out, as if to say, *'See that?'*

The defence expert witness on this matter was David Axup, the former member of Victoria Police who now ran his own private traffic consultancy. In the original trial, Mr Rapke had skilfully backed the gravel-voiced, Kiplingesque oldtimer into a corner: he was obliged to acknowledge that in order to have left the rolling prints between the gravel and the dam's edge, the car's trajectory must have included three 'steering inputs'—a term that Morrissey had gradually beaten back to the more neutral 'changes of direction'. But Axup's concession had drastically weakened the possibility that Farquharson could have been unconscious at the wheel.

In the retrial Mr Morrissey concentrated on what Axup's cross-fall diagrams showed about terrain. Just about everything Axup had measured at the scene showed, he said, that a car rolling down that slope without a conscious driver would have had a tendency to bear right. The middle section of the rolling prints in the grass, as Axup saw them, lay in a curve, not a straight line as Urquhart had claimed. And this time Axup asserted that there had been not merely three changes of direction or steering inputs, but an unknown number of much lesser ones, due to something called 'bump steer': small changes of angle when the front wheels of the car had encountered objects on the rough terrain—tussocks, the fence, invisible grooves perhaps left in the dirt by tractors or livestock and disguised by grass.

When Axup was asked to use the Smart Board, I slipped out of my side seat and into the centre row. From there, seen full face instead of in profile, he looked markedly older and more fragile than he had seemed three years ago. Often now he had to ask counsel to repeat a question. Sometimes, under cross-examination by Amanda Forrester, his whole person radiated alarm: his head would rear back, and he would show white all round his irises like a startled horse. Later I noticed with a sharp pang the hearing aid on the arm of his spectacles.

Forrester took him on with a leisurely, teasing confidence. She was completely at ease in the territory of arcs, radii, percentages and degrees. Axup addressed her as 'Ma'am', but it must have been galling to be roughed up by a woman young enough to be his daughter. Each time he threw in a technical correction or a piece of jargon, she would pause to let him think he had got the upper hand, then tilt her head and, with a twinkling smile that showed her white teeth and swelled her rosy cheeks, scoop up his point and enlist it into her larger argument. At every coup, the faces of the younger women in the jury would flicker with what I read as relief—or perhaps it was a version of the general exhilaration outside the court in those same weeks of June 2010, when the country's first female prime minister took office: the heartening spectacle of a woman who was not afraid, who was out there in her natural sphere where she would proceed to kick arse as she pleased.

In Forrester's hands the confusing mists of the defence case dissipated and left a prospect of clean, dry lines. If the car was not being steered, then it would follow the lie of the land. Thus, the car could not have gone down the slope as Axup had measured it and still have followed the arc of the rolling prints through the grass to the dam unless some leftward pressure had been exerted against the rightward drop of the terrain.

Was this, at last, the nub of the matter?

· · ·

In a slow cascade of pathos, the defence case narrowed down to a handful of witnesses with personal knowledge of Robert Farquharson at work and at home.

One of these was Wendy Kennedy from Birregurra, a housewife and part-time receptionist in her thirties with a clear brow and dark curly hair. On her way past the dock she flashed Farquharson a warm smile. She had been friends with him and Gambino when they were a couple. Her son was close to Tyler, and she had spent a lot of time at their house. She had delivered the eulogy at the boys' funeral.

Rob was angry about the separation, yes. Upset, yes. But like other defence witnesses Kennedy seemed to sidestep the word 'angry'. When pressed on this point, she let fall a nervous silence, as if she had been told to downplay it. Frustrated, she said at last. Gutted, maybe. Like, venting. Frustrated and hurt. This was as far as she wanted to go. She had to be urged to tell the court the word she had heard Farquharson use about Moules: 'Should I say it here?'

'You can speak,' said counsel. 'Whatever it is, you can say it in court.'

She whispered it, with a girlish laugh and a rising intonation: 'Dickhead?'

Still, when people criticised Cindy, Rob would always stick up for her: 'She's a good mum. It's just a patch she's going through. She'll settle down.' And he certainly did not want to go for custody. Rob worried, though, about the effect on his kids of the comparative looseness of Gambino's domestic life with Moules. When Rob and Cindy were together the kids had routine. They went to bed at a regular time. But in their new household things ran…differently. For Rob 'it wasn't good enough'.

What was Farquharson's daily routine, asked Morrissey, when he and Gambino were still a couple? What contribution did he make to the running of the household?

Kennedy outlined the extra hard work that Farquharson faithfully did, full-time and part-time, both before and after the separation, and his determination to put aside money for Jai to go to university. Then she sketched in an artless way what she called a routine person: 'That's Rob. He just does the same thing, really. Get up in the morning, go down the hallway, shut the sliding door. Get ready for work, go to work, come home from work. As soon as he walked in, he would put his lunchbox down and unpack everything. He used to take his own bowl and cup and spoon even though there was a kitchen at work—it's just Rob. Then he would usually take the kids to kick the footy, come back in, feed the cats. Cindy would cook the tea, Rob would do the dishes. One of them would run the bath, one of them would bath the kids, the other one would dry the kids. Then put the kids to bed and then after the kids were in bed you would see Robert come out, and if you were sitting on the corner of the couch you would have to move across because he laid his work clothes, like the trousers and the jumper, over the corner of the couch. And then he would sit down.'

Farquharson listened to this with his brows high, keeping his eyes on her face and blinking fast. Morrissey had wanted a picture of an industrious, well-organised husband and father, and it pleased Kennedy to provide one, but inadvertently she had played right into the classic paradigm of a man whose sense of domestic order and personal control is wrested from him when his wife breaks up their marriage.

...

Soon after the boys' funeral, when the miserable Greg King visited Farquharson with a voice recorder down the front of his pants, Farquharson told him a garbled tale about a secret business plan he had been discussing with his mate Mark in Lorne: a yogurt-distributing outfit worth $300,000 a year. I had thought of 'Mark' as a figment, a name Farquharson had pulled out of the air in a moment of panic. But now this phantom walked into court and took the stand: a big, shy, agreeable-looking fellow of forty or so in a short-sleeved blue shirt. Mark Barrett was a self-employed window cleaner from Aireys Inlet who used to work with Farquharson at the Cumberland Resort and knew how he adored his kids. Barrett liked working there, but the money was so bad that he had to leave. As for the yogurt, it was the Greek sort, called Evia, made in a big factory in Sydney by Mark's brother-in-law's brother-in-law, and it was selling so well that they couldn't keep up with the demand. They were looking for a distributor along the Surf Coast. Barrett didn't want to take it on himself so he told Farquharson about it, because he knew Farquharson 'wanted to start new roots'. But, as far as Barrett knew, Farquharson had never made any moves towards investigating the opportunity. It was never, he said, anything more than talk.

Gary Davis, a houseman at the Cumberland, was a thin, stooped, haunted-looking man with long arms and big hands. He had always been surprised that Farquharson took every second Sunday off work. 'Sunday is where you make your money, you know. That's where the money is. It's a low-paid job.' He mimicked his own amazement when he found out that Farquharson had been taking his boys to play football at Auskick and working the Monday instead, for much less pay. About a fortnight before the children died, Davis was wheeling a trolley back to Housekeeping at the Cumberland when he came across Farquharson hunched over the steel grate of a stormwater drain. 'He had his hands on top of his kneecaps, and his whole face was just like a tomato, cheeks blown out—he was coughing violently non-stop into the grate. You could see like spit spray coming out. I thought it was a virus and I didn't want to go near him so I went round him and waited for it to end.'

. . .

On my way home I went to the shopping strip near the station. The greengrocer who had told me about his own blackout on the freeway said he could not get past the evidence of the car's path into the dam. I asked whether he thought Farquharson might have wanted to kill himself as well. The greengrocer would not wear this. 'If he'd tried that, he'd be more of a mess now. He looked really healthy in the photo I saw. He didn't look like a man whose three children were dead.'

But what is a man supposed to look like when all his children are dead?

. . .

On the last day of the defence case, Farquharson's sister, Carmen Ross, in a soft grey cardigan with pearl buttons, gave a vivid and convincing description of the blackout her brother had suffered at her house halfway through the retrial. When he started coughing, she was in the kitchen cooking the tea and he was in the lounge room with his back to her. He made a sound like 'shhhhh', and 'dropped like a sack of spuds'. By the time she had turned off the hotplates and got to him, he was sitting half upright on the floor, wedged between the chair and the drinks cabinet. His eyes were open and he was staring at her, but without recognition or response. She could not feel a pulse. He was clammy and pale. She shook him and called his name. His hands began to twitch and his head to move from side to side. Then his eyes blinked. She helped him up on to his hands and knees, and into a chair. He mumbled, but was not aware of his surroundings until he had sat still for a good minute.

As I listened to this pleasant-faced woman, I thought that many a murderer must have plausible, decent siblings. What did it mean, that I believed her account and yet still thought that her brother had been conscious when he drove into the dam? It struck me for the first time that the two propositions were not mutually exclusive. And once again I was overwhelmed by a sense that vast quantities of the evidence in this case were beside the point. Mighty barrages of fanatical detail had gone rushing and chattering past like a river after heavy rain. Battered by the apparatus of so-called reason I would feel my dark sense of Farquharson's guilt tremble and falter. But as soon as a momentary quiet fell, the same little worm would wriggle to the surface: *None of this proves anything either way about what happened on the night.*

What was the point? What was the truth? Whatever it was, it seemed to reside in some far-off, shadowy realm of anguish, beyond the reach of words and resistant to the striving of the intellect.

The two closing addresses, gruelling in their detail, took up exactly a week.

On the Thursday afternoon, stunned by mental exertion, I thought I heard a faint scratch or bump near the ceiling. I glanced up. High in the court's western wall, a narrow stick about the size of a ruler swept back and forth across the outer surface of a windowpane. It was a squeegee. If Farquharson had looked up, he would have seen his own ghost, already at work.

When Justice Lasry began his charge to the jury, he announced, in a tone that could have been either reassuring or apologetic, 'I won't imitate the flourish and invective of counsel.' At first he stuck to his declaration. He droned dutifully through Mr Tinney's closing address for three and a half mortal days. He read out hunks of it with samely intonation. He commando-crawled, he scrub-bashed his way through it. The jury fought their boredom. Faithfully they kept their faces turned to the judge, faithfully they took notes. Every time I glanced at Farquharson sitting in the dock, ugly and white with tension, his knotted brow straining up into his hairline, I pitied him simply for the fact that he had to sit there and endure it all again. Sometimes he blew out air through loosened lips, or flapped the sides of his shirt as if to let his sweat evaporate. Every now and then he drew a great, tearing sigh.

But when it came to his one-hour account of Morrissey's closing, Justice Lasry's demeanour underwent a startling transformation. No doubt the fact that the last word in a murder trial goes to the defence is testament to the tremendous power of the state; but I was shocked by the gusts of vitality that swept through his discourse. His tone brightened. He freely varied his emphasis and tempo. It was true that Morrissey's address had been much warmer than Tinney's, slangier, more direct and spontaneous. Delivering his précis of it, Lasry could not resist imitating the rhythms of forceful speech. Surely he could not have been conscious that his voice was suddenly full of expressive vigour? Despite his disclaimer, he *was* using barrister's flourishes. He invested Morrissey's arguments with the life they had had in their original delivery. He made them sound more persuasive than they were when Morrissey himself uttered them. He even cracked one of Morrissey's jokes. His intonation was so tuneful that he sounded as if he were giving voice to his own thoughts. He allowed himself the odd hand gesture. He shook his head for emphasis; the double queue of his wig bounced in the air behind his neck. He kept looking up from his text and engaging the jurors' eyes. Were they registering this extraordinary change of tone? I could hardly believe what I was witnessing. Suddenly I felt sure that Farquharson would be acquitted.

At last Justice Lasry sent the jury out to deliberate. He stood the court down, bowed, and swept grandly through the heavy timber door behind the bench, holding a pink foolscap exercise book against his chest with both arms, as if to comfort himself.

...

I left the court with the media people.

'What do you reckon?' I said to one of the young women.

She gave me a bleak look. 'I think there's a good chance he'll get off. I think he did it, but I don't think they've proved it.'

That evening I turned on the radio and heard a Sydney criminal barrister being interviewed on Radio National's *Background Briefing* about a high-profile case he had just won.

'Can you say with certainty,' asked the journalist, 'that your client is innocent?'

'It's none of my business,' said the barrister in a harsh, grating voice. 'I am a lawyer conducting his case. Whether he's guilty or not is none of my concern, and I've never conducted a case in which the result has been of any concern to me.'

At such a jarring moment I could not help recalling a remark I had once seen quoted from a speech by Lord Bingham, a former Lord Chief Justice of England and Wales. He was robustly in favour of the appointment of lay magistrates, he said, because they were free of 'the habits of thought, speech and bearing which characterise professional lawyers and which most people find to a greater or lesser extent repellent'.

Years later, though, in the *Age* death notices one morning, I read column after column of tributes to a member of the Victorian criminal bar who had died in his forties of an aggressive cancer.

He was held by countless people in the highest and most tender regard. In lofty phrases or stumbling clichés they tried to express their sorrow. One simple message moved me more than all the rest: *I am free today because of you*.

···

The jury was out. I hung around the yard with the journalists, or wandered off by myself into the building's distant corners. A weird, glassy spell hung over the corridors. Once I fancied I heard faint piano chords issuing from the depths of an empty hallway.

The defence team when they passed looked remarkably merry. Several of them greeted me with cheerful smiles, as if their three-month snub had occurred only in my imagination. One afternoon, through the lace curtains of the empty, fluoro-lit pressroom, I watched the jury file into the yard, fan out into its bluestone spaces, and begin to pace around it, exactly like prisoners. Someone had heard raised voices from their room.

'Hung jury, or they'll acquit,' said an ABC reporter.

Three days passed.

Wandering the streets at lunchtime on day four, I ran into Bev Gambino outside a kitchenware shop near Southern Cross station.

'It's Tyler's birthday,' she said, with her sad smile. 'He would have been twelve today.'

'What sort of a boy was he, Bev? I hear about the others, but not about Tyler.'

'Oh,' she said, 'a very loving boy. Quiet. Lots of hugs.'

We stood together on the footpath. It was a coldish day, with a misty drizzle. I would have liked to take her arm.

'I just drift around,' she said. 'I see things, but they don't sink in.'

. . .

At a quarter to five that day the jury came back. In the thick silence, even the judge's breathing was audible.

Three times guilty.

They say it is a terrible thing to see a man go down, but I had never seen a face as stark, staring white as that of Peter Morrissey.

Farquharson's sisters and his person of comfort sat in a row with their hands covering their eyes like visors. Only their mouths were visible, quivering with shock and pain. Later, on the radio, I would hear that Farquharson 'trembled, looked astonished and annoyed, and mouthed the word "What?"' But all I saw was the back of him when they took him to the cells, a guard on either side: his slumped shoulders, his short neck with its recent, harsh haircut that left a band of pale skin above his collar.

And Cindy Gambino neither wailed nor wept. Instead, she drew her swooning mother's head into the curve of her neck and kissed her on the temple. It was a moment of such intimacy, such unexpected grace, that I had to turn away.

. . .

Towards the end of Farquharson's plea hearing on 16 September 2010, Mr Morrissey burst the bonds of his case. He was going against his client's instructions, he said—his instructions were absolutely otherwise—but he urged, he pressed the judge to see Farquharson's act for what it really was: 'a suicidal driving off the road, taking the kids with him'. It was a wild, last-ditch claim for mercy. Justice Lasry's face remained impassive, but Farquharson's flushed, and twisted into a knot of anger.

. . .

The sentencing was scheduled for one month later, 15 October 2010. A crowd gathered early outside the locked door of Court Eleven. At 10.15 the tipstaff emerged. He went from group to group announcing in a whisper that the hearing was postponed for an hour. He gave no reason. People wandered off. I went into the Supreme Court Library and tried to read a newspaper. I returned at 11.15 and found the court doors open and everyone already inside, packed in their rows. I managed to grab a spot in the centre behind a line of five large Major Collision members. Silence. At 11.30 came the tipstaff's loud formal knock. Justice Lasry in wig and red robes swept in.

Mr Tinney rose. For unexplained reasons, he said, Ms Gambino and Mr Moules had left Winchelsea a bit late. They were now delayed by heavy traffic on the Westgate Bridge. Would His Honour consider holding proceedings a further ten minutes, until they could get there?

Lasry rocked back in his throne. He remained speechless for several seconds, with the expression that greets a manifestation of unusual gall. Ten minutes from the Westgate Bridge, he said, was not a realistic estimate. The sentencing was likely to take about half an hour. They would probably get there for the end of it. Morrissey said he did not object to the wait. The judge agreed to leave the bench for a short period, to give them a chance to make it.

Farquharson's family sat massed in the side seats from which I had observed the majority of the trial. A hum of talk arose in the room. A journalist told me that Gambino and Moules had married five days ago, on the auspicious date 10/10/2010. While we waited, my eye accidentally caught that of Kerri Huntington. We held each other's gaze for a second, without acknowledgment or expression, then looked away. I dashed a glance at Farquharson in the dock behind me. His hair was longer, his face puffier and older, his skin a creamy grey. Ten, twenty, thirty minutes passed. Then I heard a woman's voice, low, with an edge on it: 'Roll out the red carpet. *The red carpet.*' Along the row of policemen's backs I saw Gambino and Moules slide into the room. As they took their seats behind the bar table, Gambino whipped out a yellow comb and ran it through her purple hair from scalp to shoulders. I glanced at Huntington. Again our eyes met. Motionless under the springy perm, her face radiated hostility and disbelief.

Justice Lasry strode back to the bench. He read out his remarks in a vigorous, expressive tone. He deplored the crime, but said he did not accept the 'extreme version' of Greg King's evidence and was not sentencing Farquharson on the basis of it. He said that Farquharson was not a risk to the public, and that before the murders of the children he had been of good character. He gave him three life sentences, with a minimum term of thirty-three years.

Before the crying could start I grabbed my things and bolted. Outside, the heavens had opened. I ran into a sandwich shop and gulped down a hot pie. Back in Lonsdale Street, I encountered Bob and Bev Gambino charging away from the TV cameras under a big umbrella, hurrying towards shelter. They saw me and waved. Their faces looked more open and free than I had ever seen them. We called goodbye and kept going in opposite directions. I stumped home, my umbrella blown inside out, my trousers soaked to the knee.

...

Nobody knew, that day, how much longer this story would drag on.

A year and a half later, in May 2012, still represented by Mr Morrissey, Farquharson appealed again in the Victorian Supreme Court, and was rejected.

On 16 August 2013 he made application, in Melbourne, for special leave to take his case to the High Court in Canberra. This would be his last chance. Louise, my long-gone gap-year girl, turned up at the hearing without warning and slid into the seat beside me. She was a young woman now. It was six years since she had seen any of the story's people. She was shocked by how much older and wearier they looked.

Before a trio of august High Court judges from the nation's capital—a woman and two men—Morrissey was permitted twenty minutes on his feet. When he rose, his black robe flapped loose on a torso that had lost an alarming amount of its bulk. Justice Lasry, he argued, had failed to tell the jury that they could find Farquharson guilty of manslaughter rather than murder: Farquharson had known he suffered from a respiratory condition that could make him black out at short notice, thus he was a negligent driver who knowingly imperilled other road users, and risked the lives of his own children.

The judges listened and questioned, cool, dry, polite. The twenty-minute limit was rigorously enforced: 'Sunset time, Mr Morrissey,' said the judge in the middle, with a regretful smile. The three of them got up and left the bench. In their absence three solemn young officials, like figures in a fairytale, stood motionless behind their empty chairs, holding the backs of them with formally placed hands. No one dared to speak. Four minutes later the judges surged back in and took their seats.

The answer was no. The High Court would not hear Robert Farquharson's appeal.

On the TV news that evening Cindy Gambino and Stephen Moules faced the cameras outside the court.

'This has taken nearly a decade of my life,' she said quietly. 'My boys are at peace.'

The couple turned to walk away. From the back they looked forlorn, diminished somehow, as they stepped out of the limelight and down into the bluestone gutter to cross the road.

If there is any doubt that Robert Farquharson drove into the dam on purpose, it is a doubt no more substantial than a cigarette paper shivering in the wind, no more reasonable than the unanswered prayer that shot through my mind when I first saw the photo of the car being dragged from the black water.

I come back and back to the old Commodore in the Kmart car park. When Farquharson pulls in, he finds that the youngest child, Bailey, has nodded off in his baby seat. Farquharson has forgotten to bring the stroller, so, to pass the time until the toddler wakes, he turns on the radio. The sad father sits with his boys in the shit car, listening to the football. This clapped-out bubble of steel and glass is the only home he has to offer them.

I was born and brought up in Geelong. I remember winter Sunday afternoons in that part of the country, their heavy melancholy. The Barwon flows between its neat banks. Cars glide in silence through the colourless streets. Along the bottoms of fences dank weeds sprout. The air is still and chilly. The steely cloud-cover will never break. Time stalls. There is no future. One's own desolation is manifest in the worn-down volcanic landscape. The life force burns low in its secret cage.

By nightfall the shit car would become a weapon, and then a coffin.

When I let myself think of Jai, Tyler and Bailey lying in their quiet cemetery, watched over by the golden emblems of Bob the Builder and the Bombers, I imagine the possessive rage of their families: 'You never knew them. You never even saw them. How dare you talk about your "grief"?'

But no other word will do. Every stranger grieves for them. Every stranger's heart is broken. The children's fate is our legitimate concern. They are ours to mourn. They belong to all of us now.